Beverley Ellison Warner

English History in Shakespeare's Plays

Beverley Ellison Warner

English History in Shakespeare's Plays

ISBN/EAN: 9783743399709

Manufactured in Europe, USA, Canada, Australia, Japa

Cover: Foto ©Thomas Meinert / pixelio.de

Manufactured and distributed by brebook publishing software (www.brebook.com)

Beverley Ellison Warner

English History in Shakespeare's Plays

ENGLISH HISTORY

IN

SHAKESPEARE'S PLAYS

BY

BEVERLEY E. WARNER, M.A.

" We can say
He shows a history couched in a play.
A history of noble mention, known
Famous and true : most noble, 'cause our own ;
Not forged from Italy, from France, from Spain,
But chronicled at home."
—*Ford's Prologue to Perkin Warbeck.*

NEW YORK

LONGMANS, GREEN, AND CO.

LONDON AND BOMBAY

1899

To

WILLIAM PRESTON JOHNSTON, LL. D.

PRESIDENT OF THE TULANE UNIVERSITY OF LOUISIANA

IN APPRECIATION OF A VALUED FRIENDSHIP

PREFACE.

This volume had its origin in a course of lectures on the study of history as illustrated in the plays of Shakespeare. It is never safe to assume that what has been listened to with attention will be read with interest. The lectures, however, have been recast, pruned, and amplified, and much machinery has been added in the way of tables of contents, bibliography, chronological tables, and index. With such helps it is hoped that these pages may effect a working partnership between the Chronicle of the formal historian and the Epic of the dramatic poet. They are addressed especially to those readers and students of English History who may not have discovered what an aid to the understanding of certain important phases of England's national development lies in these historical plays, which cover a period of three hundred years —from King John and Magna Charta to Henry VIII. and the Reformation.

New Orleans, October, 1894.

CONTENTS.

CHAPTER VIII.

CHAPTER IX.

APPENDIX I.

APPENDIX II.

APPENDIX III.

APPENDIX IV.

ENGLISH HISTORY
IN SHAKESPEARE'S PLAYS.

CHAPTER I.

AN INTRODUCTION TO THE ENGLISH HISTORICAL PLAYS.

Thoroughness of Shakespearean criticism.—His merits as an historical
teacher passed over.—Knight's comment.—Purpose of this work.—
The use of the historical plays.—Anachronisms and omissions.—
Shakespeare's purpose in writing.—The student warned against expecting too much.—The Elizabethan environment.—Cranmer's prophecy.—The English Zeit-geist.—The unity of the historical plays.—
The theme is the decline and fall of the house of Plantagenet.—
Epitome of each play.—Character contrasts.—Shakespeare's illuminat-
ing pen.—His patriotic bias.—Conclusion.

THERE is little enough in the works of Shakespeare
that has escaped the critic's eye and pen. Every line
has been measured, every word scrutinized, every punc-
tuation mark solemnly adjusted, every printer's error
in the First Folio has its " significance " pointed out,
and emendations are a weariness to the flesh.

One field of Shakespearean lore, however, has not
received the attention it deserves. The art of the
poet, the skill of the dramatist, the wit of the humorist,
the wisdom of the philosopher, the genius of the man,
all these have been turned to account and to good
account. But the use and value of Shakespeare's contribution to English History has been passed over, or
too lightly touched upon, and Coleridge's declaration,

that the people took their history from Shakespeare
and their theology from Milton, could not, in the case
of the former at least, be truthfully quoted of this
generation. Some critics have pointed out the obvious
fact—which others have yet denied—that a unity of
purpose runs through the poet's treatment of English
history in the ten chronicle plays from King John to
Henry VIII. Thomas Peregrine Courtnay has taken
the trouble to set forth, in his valuable commentaries,
the discrepancies in events and persons, between the
poet and history. But there has been almost no
attempt to illustrate the people and life of England,
by the light thrown on them in these great historical
dramas. One notable exception is the little volume,
"English History," now out of print, by the late Professor
Henry Reed, of the University of Pennsylvania. This
has a quaint and fascinating interest; but the lectures
as studies are not always accurate, and if Professor
Reed had access to the original sources of the chronicle plays he does not seem to have often used them.

The following chapters seek to interest students of
history in Shakespeare, and readers of Shakespeare in
English history. Some of the plays rise to the dignity
of history in its most engaging form. The broad sweep
of events is neither swamped in the child-like annals
of painful chronicles, nor smothered in the profundity
of the modern school historian. "History strictly so
called," says Charles Knight, both historian and critic,
"the history derived from rolls and statutes, must
'pale its ineffectual fire' in the sunlight of the poet."

It is not claimed, to be sure, that the plays could
take the place of formal history. We do not read

Shakespeare for annals, or diaries, or even accurate succession of events; but for the illumination he throws upon these—their interpretation, as subtly indicated in the process of dramatic evolution—for vividness of detail and richness of local color.

Lord Bacon exactly defines, in this spirit, the value of the historical drama, and hence the function of Shakespeare as a teacher of history: "Dramatic poetry is like history made visible, and is an image of actions past as though they were present."

Heine, whose criticism is not always sound or based upon any canon beyond the author's own prejudices, does yet fairly estimate and sum up the historical value of these plays. "The great Briton is not only a poet but an historian: he wields not only the dagger of Melpomene, but the still sharper stylus of Clio. In this respect he is like the earliest writers of history, who also knew no difference between poetry and history, and so gave us not merely a nomenclature of things done, or a dusty herbarium of events, but who enlightened truth with song, and in whose song was heard only the voice of truth."

So writing, Shakespeare taught history as it has never been taught since—not in tables, nor dates, nor statistics—not in records of revolts or details of battle-fields; but history in its highest and purest form—the uncovering of those springs of action in which great national movements take their rise.

The dramatist was bound by fidelity to his main purpose, to subordinate the details of history; and according to the preponderance of the dramatic or the historic, we have a tragedy like Macbeth or a chronicle

like Richard III. We are neither misled nor deceived
therefore, when we find in these historical plays what
would have no place in formal history. The very anachronisms of the poet are often most valuable in the
interpretation of events described, just as a discord in
music heralds the resolving chords which introduce
new harmonies. "They are perfect," these plays, in
their way, "because there is no care about centuries
in them."

The England of Shakespeare's day was a potent environment for both poet and people. Before Shakespeare left Stratford for London, began "the dawn of
that noble literature, the most enduring and the most
splendid of the many glories of England." It was the
threshold of a new world. It was the golden age of
Elizabeth, whose long and glorious reign left an after-
glow during the first years of her pedantic successor,
James. In that splendor Shakespeare lived and did
most of his work; in that after-glow he completed his
task and died. "That epoch," as Motley finely says,
"was full of light and life. The constellations which
have for centuries been shining in the English firma-
ment were then human creatures, walking English
earth." All England was thrilling with the sense of a
finer national life, a higher ideal of religion and patriotism, an ever clearer conviction that the Anglo-Saxon
was the race of destiny.

The great captains—Raleigh, Hawkins, Gilbert,
Thomas Cavendish, and Sir Francis Drake—were pushing their bold prows into all seas, planting colonies in
all new lands, and extending the dominions of the Virgin Queen with a mighty hand and a stretched-out arm.

Shakespeare was impregnated with the Zeit-geist. In almost the final passage of the last chronicle play (" Henry VIII.") Archbishop Cranmer utters a prophetic strain upon the theme of Elizabeth and James, which well denotes for what state of national feeling the poet wrote and in what mood of the national mind he found reception for his work.

After describing the glory and honor of Elizabeth's reign at home, the times of James I. and the settlement of the New World are thus referred to :

> Nor shall this peace sleep with her; but as when
> The bird of wonder dies, the maiden phœnix,
> Her ashes new create another heir,
> As great in admiration as herself,
> So shall she leave her blessedness to one
> (When heaven shall call her from this cloud of darkness)
> Who, from the sacred ashes of her honor,
> Shall star-like rise, as great in fame as she was,
> And so stand fixed. Peace, plenty, love, truth, terror,
> That were the servant to this chosen infant,
> Shall then be his, and like a vine grow to him :
> Wherever the bright sun of heaven shall shine,
> His honour and the greatness of his name
> Shall be, and make new nations ; he shall flourish,
> And, like a mountain cedar, reach his branches
> To all the plains about him ; our children's children
> Shall see this and bless heaven.[1]

Such resounding periods voiced the sentiment of all England, of which London was then, even more than now, the mouthpiece. In those times, before the newspaper press had begun to mirror each day's record with

---

[1] Henry VIII., Act V., Scene. 4.

photographic minuteness, the pulpit and the stage were the enunciators and moulders of public opinion. But while there is a great deal of valuable current history to be extracted from pulpit utterances of the Reformation period, the stage was best adapted to reflect the. tastes and exhibit the humors of the day. In this England and with these inspirations, all sorts and conditions of men and women thronged the playhouses, where they would hear the story of their ancestors told in swelling words and their glory sung in martial strains: "Wherein," says Thomas Nash, "our forefathers' valiant acts, that have been long buried in rusty brass and worm-eaten books, are revived, and they themselves raised from the grave of oblivion, and brought to plead their aged honors in open presence."

The intellectual soil of that Elizabethan England, was thus a veritable hot-house, fertilized by a spirit of nationalism which was broadened, deepened, and continually nourished, by that colonization of new lands which had become a passion with every rank and class.

Shakespeare was stimulated to the production of historical dramas, and the people were stimulated by their presentation. This reciprocal relation of stage and pit is one of the curious phases of the social life of the day.

It is evident that Shakespeare, as a wise and prudent playwright, knew his audience, and wrote for it. It is also evident that the demand upon him fired his imagination to its loftiest heights, and plumbed his philosophical insight to its lowest depths.

We have a sustained and sometimes, it must be admitted, a strained note of eulogy upon all things English, which the thoughtful reader will mark as not only an ebullition of the Zeit-geist, but an example of that insular contempt for all things un-English which has not been entirely lost to succeeding generations. This was to supply the demand of the "groundlings." But we have, too, what no other poet of that day offered, in either such kind or degree, the moral of England's history, set forth as an interpretation of the past and a guide for the future; all the more valuable because not put forth as a theory, and so obtruded upon our view.

This moral will sufficiently appear in the course of the following pages and is summed up in the final chapter.

Before taking up the thread of the story, an epitome of its contents will be found helpful and suggestive.

There are ten of the English historical plays in all, not written in chronological order, although so arranged for convenience in all modern editions.

Schlegel remarks of them, "The dramas derived from the English history are ten in number: one of the most valuable works in Shakespeare, and partly the fruit of his natural age. I say advisedly one of his works, for the poet has evidently intended them as parts of a great whole."

The unity of the series thus noted by the German critic is an important consideration in their study.

An exact title might be accurately stated as "The Decline and Fall of the House of Plantagenet, with a prologue on King John and an epilogue on Henry VIII." The body of the series deals with the house of

Plantagenet from Richard II. to Richard III. It is a family struggle for the English throne, varied by dreams and actualities of foreign conquest. The " seven phials of the sacred blood " of Edward III. are nearly all drained in the internecine contest. The bloody flux is stayed only by a political marriage, the Earl of Richmond with Elizabeth of York, which seats a Tudor where Plantagenets had reigned for generations.

As a prologue to this story the play of King John gives us a glimpse at the conditions which had in them the germ not only of division, but of reunion. John's England was an example of the futility of attempting to hold transmarine heritages or conquests in common bonds of interest with the throne of the "sceptred isle " of England. The Plantagenet family would not learn this lesson, and the Shakespearean epic describes the external trials and humiliations which were a consequence.

John's England gave utterance to the voice of the people also, speaking, with no uncertain sound, through the Magna Charta of the Barons, who were, as nearly as could be, the representatives of the people in that day ; and with faithful pen the poet historian has written down the internal misery which followed upon the ever-recurring deafness of royal and noble ears to the mandates of that voice. So King John, although separated by six generations from the first overt event in the downfall of the Plantagenets, is a noteworthy and necessary preface to that dramatic tale. It may be likened to the last warning cry of the prophet, who then wraps himself in silence and waits for his Word to crystallize into Fact.

The poet maintains this silence during the reigns of Henry III. and the three Edwards. The leaven is working however. In Richard II. decay begins. The king, with his " incurable leakiness of mind," is a product of the times. We pity but hardly condemn him. He is the child of those external and internal conditions of which we have spoken. We realize that the usurpation of Bolingbroke is an historical necessity, and it is almost with a sense of relief that we throw up our caps for Henry IV. And yet Bolingbroke has no hereditary right to that title, and in his usurpation of the claims of an elder brother's son lies the germ of the fratricidal Wars of the Roses. The melancholy end of Richard II. is revenged in the gloomy, remorseful reign of his cousin Henry IV. But now a ray of sunlight emerges, from this internal gloom of the Plantagenet family, as Henry V. succeeds his father and brings the house of Lancaster to its highest pinnacle of glory. And yet the seeds of dissolution are shooting up through this too fertile soil. For, biding its time, the feeble but legitimate house of York is lifting its head above the surface of events. To secure internal peace Henry V. picks a foreign quarrel and embarks upon that career of transmarine conquest, the glory of which is fallacious because unnatural. Henry VI. inherits two kingdoms, and after a reign accented by the deeds of a Warwick and upheld by the fiery brilliancy of a Margaret of Anjou, dies in the possession of six feet of grudging earth.

Henry VI. is a fruitful study. As in the career of King John, Shakespeare shows that positive evil done by kings reaps its reward of failure in spite of auda-

cious boldness and criminal sagacity, so in Henry VI.
he makes it equally clear that goodness and saintliness
do not preserve a king from defeat, if he be negatively
evil. The appeal to God to preserve his kingdom, because he himself is a godly man and tells his beads,
is of no avail unless Henry VI. be a man and plays a
kingly part. John was weak because he was unkingly
in his evil. Henry was weak because he was unkingly
in his virtue. Each earned his defeat, though in a
different way.

The poet historian passes over with brief notice the
reign of Edward IV. and the pathetic episode of Edward V., using them as a framework for the last scene
in the fall of the house of Plantagenet, that of which
Richard III. is the central figure.

There are still " historic doubts " as to the justice of
assigning Richard to the disgraceful niche he occupies
in the corridor of English royalty. Shakespeare has
done more to fix the orthodox impression of the hunchback's character than any writer of formal history.
And yet he took the foundation and superstructure of
that characterization from contemporary historians.
He has simply illuminated and immortalized what he
found at hand. He may have exaggerated, but he did
not invent the infernal Duke of Gloster. As an historical study this Richard III. is a portrait worthy of
more than a superficial glance.

Bolingbroke did accomplish something for England
as well as for himself in his usurpation. Warwick carried kings at his girdle, pulling them down and setting them up, not by intrigue, but by the sword and
his good right arm. There were confusion and blood

and strife in the reign of Henry VI. and during the whole Lancastrian occupation. But there was a noble quality in it all. There were problems of large calibre involved.

In Richard III., while we see the same things accomplished, it is in ignoble ways. The court and the council-room smell of chicanery, demagogism, cant. Over all, the demon of unholy selfishness broods in sullen, snarling possession. The noblest moment of Gloster's career is that of his death. He had put all to the hazard of battle, and Bosworth Field has its heroic side, apart from the victorious Richmond.

The story that ends with the fall of the last Plantagenet must have its epilogue, or Shakespeare were no true patriot. With an unsparing hand he has uncovered England's weaknesses and recorded her defeats. But all for a purpose—a purpose which we can now see, whether or not it was a conscious purpose of the poet historian.

He gives England time to settle down after her exhausting civil wars, her fallacious foreign essays in conquest, and when he lifts the curtain again it is upon that transformed England suggested in the final event of the last historical drama in chronological sequence, the baptism of Elizabeth, daughter of Henry VIII. The murmur of that baby at the font was the first note of a splendid roll of harmony which was to thrill and inspire the English people as never before. Shall we not say as never since? With that last wave of his magic baton, the master singer paused. It was enough. The England of Elizabeth was worth all the blood and bigotry, the pain and wretchedness, the shock of foreign wars and the miseries of civil arms, with which her people had been afflicted for three hundred years.

This is the story of the English plays. They are fibres of England's life.

To object that the historical student finds them full of anachronisms is nothing to the purpose. That the poet is biassed by his own consuming patriotism is still less so.

We know that in his " King John " no record is made of the Great Charter of English liberties, yet throughout the play breathes the very spirit of which Magna Charta was but an outward sign.

Henry VIII. barely mentions the English Reformation, yet it is the very story of the Reformation with every alternating shade of progress and retrogression set down ; every broad and narrow motive indicated ; every occasion, political, social, and religious, subtly woven throughout its scenes. "Henry VI." is as confused in its dramatic conceptions as the actual historic events were in fact, yet the Wars of the Roses are therein better understood as to their causes and in the way they sorrowfully touched the great suffering body of the English people, than in any severe record of the rolls and statutes.

It is here that the historian and poet becomes the illuminator, the prophet, the accurate teacher of realities. We people those former centuries with shadows, which become more and more attenuated in the hands of the dry chronicler. Shakespeare shows these shadows to have been men and women who lived, loved, hated, fought, and died. "Behold therefore, the England of the year 1200 was no chimerical vacuity or dreamland, peopled with vaporous Fantasms, Rymer's

Fœdora, and Doctrines of the Constitution; but a green solid place that grew corn and several other things. The sun shone on it, the vicissitudes of seasons and human fortunes. Cloth was woven and worn, ditches were dug, furrow fields ploughed, and houses built. Day by day all men and cattle rose to labor, and night by night returned home to their several lairs. In wondrous Dualism, then as now, lived nations of breathing men, alternating in all ways between life and death, between joy and sorrow, between rest and toil, between hope, hope reaching high as heaven, and fear deep as very hell."[1]

What Carlyle thus says of the year 1200 is still true of the centuries that followed. Shakespeare makes us realize this. No periods of English history are so well known to the average reader as those illuminated by his pen. Henry VII., with many points of extraordinary dramatic interest, is comparatively unknown; while Henry VI., one of the most unspeakably dreary of reigns, with little or nothing in its confused and bloody revolutions to attract the reader, is a well-articulated bit of the known historical framework of England, because the poet philosopher has supplied us with "the inner life of the people in all things."

As to the poet's patriotic bias, the critic must admit it to be a blemish upon his work. Under their proper headings instances of this are noted in the following pages. It is sufficient here to point out the fact, as, for example, in the anti-papal spirit of "King John," the partisan unfairness of "Henry V.," and the brutal mis-

---

[1] Carlyle's Past and Present, Book II., The Ancient Monk, Chap. L

conception of the character of Joan of Arc in "Henry
VI." These are blots, indeed; yet, as compared with
contemporary writers, Shakespeare was very far in
advance of his age. While he allowed himself to be
swayed by the applause of the "groundlings," he was
in truth a veritable reformer of the stage along these
very lines. There is nothing mean or bitter in his
bias, while there is much that was evidently the over-
flowing of a heart devoted to England as to a mother,
and concerned as deeply for her majesty and honor.
The speech of dying John of Gaunt in the play of Richard II. is imbued with this spirit of nationalism which
characterized Shakespeare's whole treatment of English
history. If he vaunted her glory, he wept for her shame;
if he boasted of her victories, he chronicled her defeats.

> This royal throne of kings, this sceptred isle,
> This earth of majesty, this seat of Mars,
> This other Eden, demi-paradise,
> This fortress built by Nature for herself
> Against infection and the hand of war,
> This happy breed of men, this little world,
> This precious stone set in the silver sea,
> Which serves it in the office of a wall,
> Or as a moat defensive in a house,
> Against the envy of less happier lands;
> This blessed plot, this earth, this realm, this England,
> This nurse, this teeming womb of royal kings,
> Feared for their breed and famous for their birth,
> Renowned for their deeds as far from home
> (For Christian service and true chivalry)
> As is the sepulchre in stubborn Jewry
> Of the world's ransom, blessed Mary's son.[1]

[1] Rich. II., Act II., Scene 1.

Shakespeare loved his England and so sounded her praises. The imagination of the poet seized upon the skeleton of the chroniclers and clothed them with flesh and blood.

From King John to Henry VIII., from Magna Charta to the Reformation, whether conscious or not of the splendid scope of his achievement, the poet historian has sung an immortal epic of the English nation, having for its dominant note the passing of feudalism and the rise of the common people.

The germ of this development has never died out of the souls of that hardy race whose forefathers crept across the gray waste of the German ocean in their frail boats of wood and hide, to grapple with unknown foes upon unknown shores, and to lay the corner-stone of that great and free nation, of whose best life Shakespeare was the poet, chronicler, and seer.

KING JOHN.

The foundation of Shakespeare's play is an anonymous work in two parts, entitled "The Troublesome Raigne of John, King of England, with the discourie of King Richard Cordelions Base Sonne (vulgarly named the Bastard Fauconbridge). Also the Death of King John at Swinsted Abbey. As it was (sundry times) publikely acted by the Queenes Maisties Players, in the honourable Citie of London. Imprinted at London for Sampson Clarke, and are to be solde at his shop, on the back side of the Royall Exchange. 1591. 4°."

This play was reprinted in 1611, with the initials W. Sh. upon its title page ; but it is conceded on all hands that this was a publisher's trick, and not an acknowledgment of the poet's authorship.

Shakespeare's play was published about 1596, in quarto ; was mentioned by Francis Meres, in his "Wit's Treasury" (1598), and was included in the first Folio of 1623, among the "Histories."

1199. John crowned at Westminster, May 27. Arthur Plantagenet (lineal heir), Duke of Bretagne, asks assistance of Philip of France to maintain his rights over the French provinces. John enters France with an army to enforce the English claim.

1200. By agreement between John and Philip, Lewis the Dauphin and Blanche of Castile (John's niece) are married, and a satisfactory division of the provinces in dispute is made, Arthur retaining Brittany.

1202. Philip breaks this treaty. War resumed. Arthur taken prisoner by John.

1203. Arthur dies under suspicious circumstances at Rouen.

1204. All Normandy lost to John and united with the crown of France.

1205-7. In the election of an Archbishop of Canterbury, Pope Innocent insisted upon his right to nominate Stephen Langton. John defies the Pope, maintaining his own supreme right of nomination, and refuses to allow Langton at Canterbury.

1208-9. Interdict and excommunication of John by Innocent III.

1212. Innocent deposes John, and commands Philip of France to invade England and carry the sentence into effect.

1213-14. John, frightened at the result of his opposition to the Pope, basely submits and does homage to Rome for his crown. English nobles, led by Stephen Langton, confederate to resent this betrayal of the kingdom and their liberties.

1215. Magna Charta signed, but almost immediately violated by John. The English nobles appeal to France and promise to choose the Dauphin Lewis as their king, if he will help them with an army against John.

1216. The French army comes over. Before battle John dies —(Oct. 16). His son is crowned as Henry III., and Lewis forced to return to France.

2

CHAPTER II.

KING JOHN.—THE TRANSITION PERIOD.

Introduction.—Successive waves of conquest that swept over Britain and their blending in one strain.—Continental complications.—John's incompetency causes loss of foreign territory, and completes the solidarity of the English people.—Shakespeare's play covers this transition period.—Three historic centres of dramatic action.—(I.) The disputed title of King John (a dramatic fiction.)—(II.) The quarrel of John with Pope Innocent.—(III.) Magna Charta and revolt of the Barons.—The minor events violate historical accuracy and anachronisms abound.—The reason found in the poet's adherence to an old play.—Philip of France espouses the cause of Arthur Plantagenet.—Chatillon's demands.—Negotiations ensue.—Arthur's claims abandoned.—The disputed territory in France given mainly as a dower to Blanche (John's niece) on her marriage with Lewis (Philip's son).—Arthur is kept alive by poetic license for dramatic purposes.—John's refusal to accept the Pope's nomination to the see of Canterbury.—The curse of Rome.—Philip of France commissioned to carry it into effect.—Peter of Pomfret's prophecy.—John receives his crown as a fief of Rome.—Omission of any mention of Magna Charta.—Revolt of the Barons and alliance with Prince Lewis of France, who lands with a force in England.—Skirmishing between the King's faction and the Barons.—The Barons, discovering treasonable intentions on the part of Lewis, begin to treat with their King —In the middle of negotiations John dies.—Lewis dismissed and John's son (as Henry III.) comes to the throne.

WHETHER designedly or not, Shakespeare fastened upon a period for the first, in order of time, of his English chronicle plays, which may be accurately distinguished as the great turning point of English historical development. For it was in the reign of that most sordid and despicable monarch John Lackland, that the nation was severed from Continental embar-

rassments by the loss of Normandy and other transmarine provinces, and the English constitution began
to take deeper root in and flourish out of the religion
and patriotism of the English people.

Allusion has been made, in the introduction, to the
broad stage upon which these historical dramas were
acted, as having had an influence upon their spirit and
scope. The date of "King John's" appearance, especially, may account to a certain extent for the fervid
nationalism which pervades every scene and inspires
the utterance of its *dramatis personæ*. It was produced in the year 1596, but eight years after the destruction of the Spanish Armada. All Englishmen
were still thrilling with a hatred of the foreigner, and
were bound to their Virgin Queen and to each other
by ties of a sort of religious patriotism like that which
moulded the life of the Hebrew people in the first
days of the conquest under Joshua.

The interest of this play, however, to modern students, lies not so much in its illustration of the England of Elizabeth as in its interpretation of the England of John. To approach the story of the play with
a proper appreciation of its historical accuracy, we
must note in brief the steps that led up to the first
scene, where the phrase "borrowed majesty" is flung
at the occupant of the English throne by the French
ambassador.

John came officially to the throne in 1199, the successor of Richard Cœur de Lion.

Four generations before this, in 1066, on the field of
Hastings, died Harold, last of the Saxon kings, and
William Duke of Normandy came by right of con-

quest to the English throne. Before this conquest by the Norman, there is little enough to tell of connected English history. From the early occupation by the Romans under Julius Cæsar, A.D. 24, until Harold expired, there had been a long course of successive upheavals and settlements. There were wars on a large and small scale; peoples divided against each other, fighting for the love of war, and not for peace; hordes of savage invaders overcoming aboriginal tribes, and driving them in torn remnants to the caves of Cornwall and the mountain fastnesses of Wales.

Wave after wave of conquest swept the island of Britain: Danes, Jutes, Angles and Saxons, the two latter on the whole predominating. The language of these raiders dominated the land as Anglo-Saxon, and the name of one tribe, doubtless the bravest and hardiest, became the name of the whole miscellaneous immigration of pirate settlers, whence from Angleland we have the modern England.

The final wave of conquest was that upon whose crest William Duke of Normandy swept into power. With William came prelates, nobles, and men-at-arms, and Saxon veins began to run with Norman blood. Here was that mingling of races, out of which, as the elements finally settled, emerged the English people.

How did it happen that "this sceptred isle" became Angle-land instead of Norman-land?

First of all, the Norman conqueror was too wise to carry his victory to the point of extermination. He did not seek to blot out or drive out the Saxons. The common people, serfs and freemen, were of too much use as hewers of wood, to be got rid of without grave

cause. Even the Saxon thanes were permitted, here
and there, not only to occupy their castles and lands,
but to mingle on nearly equal terms with their con-
querors.

The chief reason, however, why the Anglo-Saxon
rather than the Norman became the parent of civiliza-
tion in Britain, lay deeper in events than William or
his nobles could reach. In casting in their lot with
the Anglo-Saxon people to the extent of adopting
manners, customs, and finally language, the Normans
were but going back home. For Angle, Saxon, and
Norman had a common ancestry in the heart of the
German forests, and along the slopes of the Scan-
dinavian hills. Their differences at the time of the
Conquest were the result of environment. While the
Angle and Saxon were still lying in their native lairs,
or embarking on predatory excursions to the low-
lying, sedgy shores of Britain, their brethren in the
north, called Northmen, of common race and almost
common tongue, had descended upon the northwest
coast of France, where by force of arms they wrested
a fine province from the French kings, and set up for
themselves as Dukes of Normandy. They were in
course of time Gallicised, and in Duke William's time
were French in everything but blood and name. But
even then to scratch a Norman was to find a Northman,
elder brother to Angle, Jute, and Saxon, and kin to the
people with whom he was placed in intimate domestic
relations by the Conquest. Hence Saxon and Norman
blended in one not unnatural strain ; and a new people,

Feared for their breed and famous by their birth,

came into existence—having, in time, the vigor and brawn of the ancient sea-kings and marauders, united with the wit, polish, and *finesse* of the Norman knight.

This did not happen easily or all at once. There were continuous battles, feuds, race troubles, and rivalries; but when John came to the throne, four fruitful generations after the battle of Hastings, these internal broils had ceased. The names Saxon and Norman were forgotten, and only Englishmen remained.

One important element in the development of the English as a homogeneous people remained to be added. Her kings were still half foreigners. The Norman provinces were appanages of the royal family. The political life of the growing English people was thus bound up in an unnatural manner with what was practically a province of France. It remained therefore, in the curious irony of historical evolution, for the reign of one of the least patriotic of English kings to witness the beginnings of a larger and more splendid life for the English people. For, through John's shuffling, time-serving, and criminal incapacity, Normandy was cut off from allegiance to the royal house of England. Thereafter, with no foreign interests to clash, and perhaps take precedence of those at home—with no alien quarrels for which they were bound to become responsible—the English people grew together more closely and with a greater identity of aim.

Shakespeare's play of "King John" is a dramatic picture of this transition stage of English history.

Observing carefully the action of the play, it is found to revolve about three distinct historical events, which are, however, more or less confused with each other for dramatic purposes :

I. The disputed title of John, and the political intrigues of Philip of France resulting therefrom, including the use of Arthur, John's nephew, as a movable pawn by all parties.

II. The quarrel of King John with Pope Innocent III. concerning the filling of the vacant see of Canterbury, which ended in John's disgraceful reconciliation, at the price of holding the crown of England as a fief of the Pope.

III. The revolt of the Barons, which the poet attributes to discontent over the violent death of Arthur, but which historically was caused by the king's attempted nullification of Magna Charta.

This is the framework of Shakespeare's play. In the essential facts he preserves the spirit and history of the times, but in some glaring instances is far astray. The reader who knows history and reads this play for the first time, and superficially, is tempted to make the criticism that either the poet was not acquainted with the reign he describes, or that he ruthlessly sacrificed historical accuracy on the altar of dramatic necessity. In both judgments there is a measure of truth. Shakespeare was never troubled by anachronisms when they served his purpose, and in this play, contrary to his usual custom, he did not consult the chroniclers who were his faithful allies for all the others of the series. There is not an allusion in the whole play, *exempli gratia*, to the greatest event not only of John's reign but, in one aspect certainly, of all English history, the granting of Magna Charta. Many

of the events leading up to and evoking it are touched
upon, and the especial event which occurred because
of its attempted nullification is minutely detailed,
namely, the calling over of Prince Lewis, of France,
to lead Englishmen against their king; but this event
is linked with the alleged death of Arthur at John's
command, and the Great Charter is not so much as
mentioned.

The explanation is simple enough, however. Shakespeare did not look into the chronicles here as when
he dealt with other periods; but, finding an old play
by another hand, remodelled it for his own need. The
real source, the general framework, and many of
the passages, barely disguised, of the play of " King
John" are to be found in a piece in two parts, by an
anonymous author (some attribute it to Samuel
Rowley), entitled " The Troublesome Raigne of King
John." This was written or at least published some
twenty years before Shakespeare's performance, and
was plainly a tractate against Rome, one of the swarm
that sprang into life in the first years of the Reformation. It was rabid, ill-tempered, and frequently unfair, and Shakespeare wisely, both for his fame and
his art, did not decant its spirit into his performance.
An occasional quotation of parallel passages will give
the student opportunity to note how the great dramatist, while sometimes copying slavishly from material
at hand, almost always transmuted the base metal of
others into the fine gold which was all his own.

To resume the thread of history where the play of
" King John " takes it up, it begins with a claim made
upon John of England, by Philip of France, for the

crown of England and all its territories, together with
the Norman provinces, in the name of Arthur Plantagenet, John's nephew.

Chatillon, the French ambassador, speaks :

> Philip of France, in right and true behalf
> Of thy deceased brother Geoffrey's son,
> Arthur Plantagenet, lays most lawful claim
> To this fair island and the territories,
> To Ireland, Poictiers, Anjou, Touraine, Maine;
> Desiring thee to lay aside the sword
> Which sways usurpingly these several titles,
> And put the same into young Arthur's hand,
> Thy nephew and right royal sovereign.[1]

The "Troublesome Raigne" has it :

"Philip, by the grace of God most Christian king
of France, having taken into his guardian and protection Arthur, Duke of Britaine, sonne and heir to
Jeffrey thine elder brother, requireth in the behalf of
said Arthur, the kingdom of England, with the lord-
ships of Ireland, Poitiers, Aniow, Torain, Main; and
I attend thine annswere."

Before this formal claim is made, Chatillon sets the
key of the whole play as follows :

> Thus, after greeting, speaks the king of France,
> In my behavior, to the majesty,
> The borrow'd majesty of England here.[2]

That phrase the "borrowed majesty" is a reflection
upon the title by which John reigned in England as
well as over the French provinces which were an in-

---

[1] Act I., Scene 1.   [2] Ibid.

heritance of the Angevins. Shakespeare, following the old play, assumes that John was an usurper, and that the English people were at heart devoted to the claims of young Arthur Plantagenet. The French provinces and Arthur's rights over them will be touched upon presently. Just now it must be made clear to the reader who "takes his history from Shakespeare and his theology from Milton," that this alleged usurpation of the English crown was a mere assumption of the poet, of which he makes vivid dramatic use in the sorrows of young Arthur. King John of England had, for those days, a particularly strong title. He was the oldest living brother of Richard I., whom he succeeded, and had acquired reputation and influence, as a sort of deputy, during the Lion Heart's crusades against the Saracens. When Richard died, it is true that, according to strict laws of primogeniture, the heir of the throne was Arthur Plantagenet, son of John's dead elder brother Geoffrey. But primogeniture had not by any means been accepted as the only law of succession to the English throne. Nor indeed have the English people ever been so wedded to the law of primogeniture but that for good and sufficient reason they could break it. The names of Henry IV., Oliver Cromwell, and William of Orange, testify to the existence of this inherent independence of the people, who have ever been the king-makers themselves, in one form or another, and never surrendered their rights.

King John succeeded legitimately to the throne by virtue of three claims: (a) Nearness of kin to the late monarch. (b) A revised will of Richard, quoted by contemporary chroniclers, setting aside a former bestowal of the crown upon Arthur, because of his youth and weakness, and bestowing it upon John. (c) And most important and conclusive of all, a free election of the Barons, representing the whole realm, among whom he was crowned at Westminster. For those days this constituted a good title. Shakespeare, however, has so fastened the idea of usurpation upon the English mind, that John has had added to his other crimes that of being, what he certainly was not, an unconstitutional ruler. There was never any question among Englishmen as to his right to reign over them, until toward the end of his career, when the Barons were exasperated into the attempt of dethroning him as a liar, a slanderer, a breaker of promises, and a bawd of the nation's honor.

It must also be noted in the interest of historic truth (although it is no part of the author's purpose or intention to go into the details of these events), that the French king did not make the claim, as in the play, for the crown of England, but in behalf of Arthur solely for the transmarine provinces. Arthur's claims to these provinces were partly in virtue of his lineal right to the throne of England, and partly through other sources. The conflicting and overlapping claims of John and his nephew are thus clearly stated by Mr. Henry Hudson in his introduction to this play:

" Anjou, Touraine, and Maine were the proper patrimony of the Plantagenets, and therefore devolved to Arthur as the acknowledged representative of that house, the rule of lineal succession being there fully established. To the ducal chair of Bretagne, Arthur was the proper heir in right of his mother (Constance) who was then Duchess regnant of that province. John claimed the dukedom of Normandy as the proper inheritance from his ancestor, William the Conqueror, and his claim was there admitted. Poitou, Guienne, and five other French provinces were the inheritance of Eleanor his mother ; but she made over her title to him, and there also his claim was recognized. The English crown he claimed in virtue of his brother's will, but took care to strengthen that claim by a parliamentary election. In the strict order of inheritance all these possessions, be it observed, were due to Arthur; but that order it appears was not then fully established, save in the provinces belonging to the house of Anjou. As Duke of Bretagne, Arthur was a vassal of France, and therefore bound to homage as a condition of his title."

In this complex condition of affairs Philip Augustus of France saw an opportunity of striking a final blow at the power of the Plantagenet family and dissolving the connection which had existed, since the Norman conquest, between the English monarchy and French provinces. He lent himself therefore the more readily to the interests of Arthur Plantagenet.

The first two acts of the play are occupied with negotiations between France and England, ostensibly over Arthur's rights, actually with diplomatic fencing for political advantage. These tilts end, after many complications of intrigue and policy, in the completion of a truce between Philip and John, in which the cause of Arthur is entirely set aside as of slight importance in the larger affairs of kings. John retains a portion of the disputed territory, and another portion is set aside as a marriage dower for the Lady Blanche, of Castile, John's niece, on her union with Prince Lewis, Philip's son and heir. Arthur was confirmed in his dukedom of Brittany.

During the course of these two acts, while very few of the recorded incidents are historically accurate, the spirit of the times is admirably preserved, and the relations of personages and events are set forth with faithfulness. If we should attempt to trace every poetic statement to its historical source, we should find ourselves in a preposterous entanglement. But having concern only with the broad movements of English life, Shakespeare is a vivid and lucid interpreter.

John maintained his authority in the transmarine provinces, with now and then a rebellion on the part of the French nobles, until he was mortally crippled by the refusal of his English knights to aid him in quelling these revolts, which sometimes assumed serious shape. During these conflicts, John took Arthur prisoner, who afterward died mysteriously, some say by the hand of John himself. All historians attribute truth to the public fame that the unnatural king was directly or indirectly responsible for his nephew's death. Shakespeare, following the scheme of the "Troublesome Raigne," shows that, while John made his plot with Hubert de Burg for Arthur's sudden taking off, he was so frightened at the public storm the report of violence created, that he repented and bitterly reproached his Chamberlain for taking him too literally at his word. Arthur, in both plays, is spared by Hubert, and is accidentally killed in an attempt to escape from prison.

Shakespeare keeps Arthur alive, after the fashion of the old play, for some years after the real date of his death, and uses him as a dramatic puppet in events which had no relation whatever with him or his claims upon the English throne. Indeed this use of Arthur Plantagenet is the great puzzle in any effort to discriminate between what is historical in the play and what is purely dramatic license. The reader of the play must infer that this twelve-year old boy was the central figure of human and political interest in the England of that day. He was nothing of the kind. He was of very small importance in the actual shuffling of the cards. But he offered dramatic material of considerable value, and Shakespeare used him, as the older dramatist did, without reference to the chronicles and with no attempt at preserving the real perspective of history.

Thus the assumed position of Arthur, as an abused and oppressed rightful claimant to the throne, is connected, on no legitimate grounds whatever, with the quarrel between the Pope and King John; and also with the revolts of the Barons. All the critics note the importance attributed by the play to Arthur's movements, but not all of them point out the gross anachronism thus involved.

To illustrate the tortuous politics of those times— which, with many a misdate, overdate, and prolepsis, Shakespeare still preserves in their essential spirit, presenting withal a tolerable estimate of how life in camps and courts was carried on—the speech of Falconbridge at the end of the second act may be quoted. It is a summing up of what had been accomplished as

well as attempted in the royal quarrels over Arthur,
and a most just estimate of the reliance to be placed
upon the sworn faith of king and noble in the twelfth
and thirteenth centuries.

> Mad world, mad kings, mad composition.
> John, to stop Arthur's title to the whole,
> Hath willingly departed with a part ;
> And France (whose armor conscience buckled on,
> Whom zeal and charity brought to the field
> As God's own soldier), rounded in the ear
> With that same purpose-changer, that sly devil,
> That broker that still breaks the pate of faith,
> That daily break-vow, he that wins of all,
>
> .   .   .   .
>
> That smooth-faced gentleman, tickling commodity—
> Commodity, the bias of the world ;
>
> .   .   .   .
>
> And this same bias, this commodity,
> This bawd, this broker, this all-changing word,
> Clapp'd on the outward eye of fickle France,
> Hath drawn him from his own determined aid,
> From a resolved and honorable war,
> To a most base and vile concluded peace.
>
> .   .   .   .
>
> Since kings break faith upon commodity,
> Gain, be my lord, for I will worship thee.[1]

In such a passage as this we are able to weigh and
estimate the value of Shakespeare's contribution to the
philosophy of history. We are often bewildered in
his pages by a confusion of dates and events, but history rightly studied is something more than mere annals or chronicles. These are the raw materials which

---

[1] Act II., Scene 1 : 561.

the historian must explain and interpret or he be no true historian.

There are two most significant lines in the earlier portion of the play which illustrate the poet's method of transmuting whole reams of fact and poetry into a single paragraph of description. The lines are :

> Our abbeys and our priories shall pay
> This expedition's charge.[1]

In the "Troublesome Raigne" the corresponding passage is :

> And toward the maine charges of my warres,
> Ile ceaze the lasie Abbey lubbers' lands
> Into my hand to pay my men of warre.
> The Pope and Popelings shall not grease themselves
> With gold and groates that are the soldiers' due.

The anonymous play has also an exciting and suggestive scene in which Philip Falconbridge makes a raid upon the abbeys for moneys, which is omitted in the play of King John. But the two lines just quoted tell the whole story, and for dramatic purposes tell it better than the old writer's pages of bold and coarse attack upon the lives of the monks and nuns. Rulers in those times might be ever so faithful sons of Holy Church ; but when there was need of the "charges of warre," they did not hesitate long between their piety and their necessities.

The next centre of action of Shakespeare's play, after the disputed title of John and the political in-

----

[1] Act I., Scene 1.

trigues that were involved, is the quarrel between Pope Innocent and John of England.

It must be said of John that he was a stubborn man if not a truly courageous one, to brave the power of the Pope of Rome, with the memory still fresh of his father Henry creeping to the tomb of Becket in old Canterbury, a shivering penitent.

Henry II. was a far braver and better man than John, and had quite as good a cause. Moreover, he was a born ruler of men, and John was, in moral stamina, the most fickle and nerveless of leaders.

The beginning of the third act is an historical remnant left over from the second. It is the wail of Constance, mother of Arthur, for the shameful way in which his claim had been forgotten, in the selfish arrangement of the two kings and the marriage of Blanche and Lewis.

Constance. Gone to be married. Gone to swear a peace.
    False blood to false blood joined. Gone to be friends.
    Shall Lewis have Blanche? and Blanche those provinces?
    It is not so. Thou hast misspoke, misheard;
    . . . .
    Believe me, I do not believe thee, man;
    I have a king's oath to the contrary.[1]

And when the poor mother is assured beyond doubt that the compromise is made:

    O! if thou teach me to believe this sorrow,
    Teach thou this sorrow how to make me die;
    . . . .
    Lewis marry Blanche. O boy, then where art thou?
    France friend with England, what becomes of me?[2]

[1] Act III., Scene 1.   [2] Ibid.

3

The grief of Constance is broken in upon by the entrance of the two kings, the newly married pair, and
others, in the full flush of their recent joy. Her re-
proaches of them are interrupted by an influx of new
characters, and the beginning of the great quarrel
between John and the Pope.

It has been already said that the history is here
thrown to the winds, for purposes of the drama. Arthur had been dead for some years before the ecclesiastical censures of the Church were visited upon his
uncle. But Shakespeare, following the old play, vio-
lates the fact, in the introduction of Constance and
Arthur as though contemporary with Pandulph. To
the parties of the historic drama, grouped upon the
stage, comes Pandulph, announced by Philip :

"Here comes the holy legate of the Pope."

To connect this with the story, we must recall one or
two historic facts. At a vacancy in the see of Canterbury the Pope rejected the choice of an archbishop who
had the sanction of King John, and nominated his
own candidate, Stephen Langton, whom John refused
to receive. It might have been obstinacy, or as he
thought good policy, on the part of the English king
to resent the constant intrusion of the Pope in the
ecclesiastical affairs of England. Doubtless he was
really actuated by the spirit which has ever lain, now
dormant, now active, in the heart of the English
Church and which culminated and expressed itself in
the Reformation of the sixteenth century. England
had always protested, sometimes with success, some-

times in vain, against the idea of a universal bishop as accented in the see of Rome. The autonomy of the English church and the autonomy of the English people were ideas not always consciously, but always actually held in the intelligence of the nation as it grew to maturity.

So John, in resenting the imposition of an Archbishop of Canterbury against his will, was, from whatever motive, acting in harmony with the development of English thought and the evolution of the English ideal.

The Pope sent over his legate, as in the play, to argue with John, and transmitted through the same messenger a valuable present of four golden rings, set with precious stones, as a sort of political retaining fee. Either the bribe was too small or John's conscience was aroused, for the legate was authorized to "launch the curse of Rome" reserved for extreme cases. This scene, first of the third act, after the entrance of Pandulph, is wholly accurate as to the spirit of the event, and presents one of those fine outbursts of patriotic pride and national independence, for which the age in which Shakespeare wrote, just after the destruction of the Spanish Armada, was especially ripe, and was indeed the very offspring of the times themselves.

> *Pandulph.* I, Pandulph, of fair Milan cardinal
> And from Pope Innocent the legate here,
> Do in his name religiously demand
> Why thou against the Church, our holy mother,
> So wilfully dost spurn; and force perforce
> Keep Stephen Langton, chosen Archbishop

Of Canterbury, from that holy see?
This, in our foresaid holy father's name,
Pope Innocent, I do demand of thee.

K. John. What earthly name to interrogatories
Can task the free breath of a sacred king?
Thou canst not, cardinal, devise a name
So slight, unworthy, and ridiculous,
To charge me to an answer, as the Pope.
Tell him this tale; and from the mouth of England
Add thus much more; that no Italian priest
Shall tithe or toll in our dominions;
But, as we under heaven are supreme head,
So under him that great supremacy,
Where we do reign, we will alone uphold
Without the assistance of a mortal hand;
So tell the Pope; all reverence set apart
To him and his usurped authority.[1]

These words were like sweet honey to the Virgin
Queen, Elizabeth, to whom undoubtedly Shakespeare
paid his court in writing them. For she had been
through exactly such a papal struggle as was now to
follow in the case of John. She felt the "supreme
headship" of the Church as keenly as any who preceded or followed her. Largely through her personality, which was a sort of concretion of the English
thought and English feeling of the day, England was
an armed camp of religious and patriotic soldiers. It
was an intense age and the ideal England of Elizabeth,
of her nobles, of her commoners, was just that exploited in Shakespeare's line,

> That no Italian priest
> Shall tithe or toll in our dominions.

[1] Act III., Scene 1.

We find the basis of this fine speech in the "Trouble-some Raigne," and if we bear in mind the splendid periods, just quoted, of Shakespeare, and compare with them these words from the older play, we will have a fair example of the way in which Shakespeare was wont to use the material of others and make it peculiarly his own.

> *K. John.* And what hast thou, or the Pope, thy maister, to doo, to demand of me, how I employ mine own? Know, Sir Priest, as I know the Church and holy churchmen, so I scorn to be subject to the greatest prelate in the world. Tell thy maister so from me, and say John of England said it, that never an Italian priest of them all shall ever have tythe, tole or polling penie out of England; but as I am King, so will I raigne next under God, supreme head both over spiritual and temrall; and hee that contradicts me in this, Ile make him hoppe headless.

To resume the theme of the play. Pandulph proceeds to extreme measures.

> *Pandulph.* Then, by the lawful power that I have,
> Thou shalt stand cursed and excommunicate;
> And blessed shalt he be that doth revolt
> From his allegiance to an heretic;
> And meritorious shall that hand be called,
> Canonized, and worshipped as a saint,
> That takes away by any secret course
> Thy hateful life.[1]

This curse of the poet, set down in a few lines and as though pronounced at one breath, really involved four separate acts of the Pope against John and covered some years of time. First was the interdict, by

[1] Act III., Scene i.

which all bishops and clergy were forbidden to say the religious offices of the Church throughout the kingdom.[1]

This, failing of its intended effect, was followed by excommunication, which was to shut out John from all personal intercourse with his people. This, in turn, was succeded by a decree absolving John's subjects from their allegiance; and finally was pronounced a sentence of deposition from the throne of England. The great quarrel began in 1207, and John did not make his submission until 1213. Meanwhile the Pope must needs find force of arms to bring John to terms, and Philip of France, having previously won from John all practical foothold in Normandy, is found ready at the Pope's appeal to try for the crown of England. War is therefore declared between the two powers, and it is declared a holy war for the honor of the Cross, all privileges granted to crusaders being promised by the Pope to Philip and his knights.

Shakespeare tacks together the formerly made truce between Philip and John, cemented by the marriage of Blanche and Lewis, and this new outbreak. Although not historically accurate, therefore, the events depicted in this first scene of the third act are relatively so. We have a fresh-made compact broken for selfish reasons; we have the pathetic and touching by-play of the newly married happiness of the young people threatened and rudely brushed aside as of no importance compared with the affairs of kingdoms.

---

[1] Hume's description of the effect of the interdict is probably one of the finest passages in his history, and should be read by all who wish to realize the awful nature of the event.—Hume's England, Vol. I., Chap. 11.

"What," cries poor tortured Blanche;

> "Shall our feast be kept with slaughtered men?
> Shall braying trumpets and loud churlish drums,
> Clamours of hell, be measures to our pomp?
> O husband, hear me. Ah, alack! how new
> Is husband in my mouth; even for that name,
> Which till this time my tongue did ne'er pronounce,
> Upon my knee I beg, go not to arms
> Against mine uncle."

And again:

> Which is the side that I must go withal?
> I am with both; each army hath a hand;
> And in their rage, I having hold of both,
> They whirl asunder and dismember me.
> .   .   .   .
> Whoever wins, on that side shall I lose.[1]

But the love sorrows of a young couple, wedded out of policy, can never stand in the way of policy, and all private ties become as nothing before the necessities of state.

The rest of the act is taken up with the contest between the two kings, in which the seizing of Arthur by John plays a part, although historically Arthur has been dead three or four years. Toward the last of the act the historical facts are tangled together in absolute confusion. This struggle of the kings glides poetically into a plot arranged between the Pope's legate and the young French prince, Lewis, for the latter to enter England with an army and seize the throne on behalf

[1] Act III., Scene 1.

of Blanche, his wife, the niece of John. This is based in the play upon the disturbed relations between John and his English barons on account of the imprisonment of Arthur.

The situation was really this : At the request of the Pope, and to enforce his nomination of Langton, Philip had prepared an immense army for the invasion of England. The English barons were discontented with John's arbitrary, vacillating, and selfish policy. The English clergy almost to a man were arrayed against John because of his stubborn fight over the See of Canterbury, and the mass of the people were restless and frightened because of the withdrawal of religious functions and, in that superstitious age, were looking for trouble and disaster, finding strange omens and auguries in earth, sea, and sky. Agitators, taking advantage of this unsettled state of affairs, pushed their own disaffections industriously, and John was looked upon by all classes as the cause of their woes.

The papal legate is represented by Shakespeare as translating these signs of the times to Lewis, while urging him to take advantage of them to lay his claim through Blanche to the English throne. The passage is well worth remembering as indicative of the worldly-wise policy of the Roman See of that day in dealing with its enemies :

Pandulph. You, in the right of Lady Blanche, your wife,
　May then make all the claim that Arthur did.
Lewis. And lose it, life and all, as Arthur did.
Pandulph. How green you are, and fresh in this old world;
　John lays you plots ; the times conspire with you ;
　　.　　　　.　　　.　　　.　　　.　　　.

This act so evilly borne shall cool the hearts
Of all his people and freeze up their zeal
That none so small advantage shall step forth
To check his reign, but they will cherish it;
No natural exhalation in the sky,
No scope of nature, no distempered day,
No common wind, no customed event,
But they will pluck away his natural cause, .
And call them meteors, prodigies and signs,
Abortives, presages and tongues of heaven, .
Plainly denouncing vengeance upon John.[1]

And, again, when Falconbridge, ever faithful to the king, comes to him with reports of how affairs are progressing in the matter of despoiling the abbeys for war charges, he says :

Bastard. How I have sped among the clergymen
The sums I have collected shall express.
But as I travelled hither through the land,
I find the people strangely fantasied,
Possessed with rumors, full of idle dreams,
Not knowing what they fear, but full of fear.
And here's a prophet that I brought with me
From forth the streets of Pomfret, whom I found
With many hundreds treading on his heels;
To whom he sung, in rude harsh-sounding rhymes,
That e'er the next Ascension day at noon
Your highness should deliver up your crown.[2]

Unquestionably John's superstitious nature was so wrought upon by this alleged prophecy—for Shakespeare's Peter of Pomfret was really a vagrant fanatic who uttered the prophecy as recorded—that his fears brought about what neither threats of Pope nor armies

[1] Act III , Scene 4.   [2] Act IV., Scene 2.

of king had moved him to do. He succumbed before the lunatic chatter of a wandering mountebank, who had stood unshaken under the excommunication of Innocent III., and had not quailed in the presence of the greatest soldier of his times.

On that very Ascension day, John submitted to the Pope; agreed to all his terms; received Stephen Langton as Archbishop; and, most shameful of all, yielded up his crown to the Pope's legate, and after waiting five days received it back again as a gift from the Pope, promising to hold his kingdom in submission to Rome as feudal lord, and to pay a certain sum of money annually as token of the tributary relations of England to the " Italian priest," he had formerly so bravely scouted.

The submission being made, Philip was commanded by the Pope to make a truce with John. The rage of the French king was fierce, but fruitless. The fleet he had prepared for the conquest of England was destroyed, and he gave up English affairs in disgust. He then turned his attention to a war with Otto, Emperor of Germany, and finally established his power, as the arbiter of European Continental politics.

Shakespeare, following the older play, identifies the turning back of Philip from his attack upon England with the turning back of Lewis, who was summoned some years later by the English nobles to their aid. As a matter of history, all of those scenes which in the play have to do with the papal interference against Prince Lewis, on behalf of John, were actually true as toward King Philip, after the submission of John.

To get at the true history again, we must leave the

point where Pandulph is inciting the French prince to claim England in behalf of his wife, and go back to summarize the events which led up to the calling over of Lewis by the English nobility, which this passage suggests.

After his reconciliation with the Pope, John's troubles were by no means ended. Released from the distress of the excommunication he found himself at odds with barons and people. He hanged Peter of Pomfret on the historic Ascension Day, but the people knew that Peter had turned out a true prophet. John himself is made to acknowledge it at Shakespeare's mouth :

> *K. John.* Is this Ascension day? Did not prophet
> Say that before Ascension day at noon
> My crown I should give off? Even so I have;
> I did suppose it should be on constraint;
> But, heaven be thanked, it is but voluntary.[1]

This national humiliation entered like iron into the souls of England's proud nobility. It had a powerful effect in the disaffection, rebellion, and revolt, which finally culminated in the wresting from John of the Magna Charta, the great Charter of English liberties, one of the great and crucial turning points of English history, and immeasurably the event of greatest importance in John's reign. The Charter was given by John finally, and a council of the barons chosen to see that it should be faithfully carried out. But John was shifty and vacillating as ever. After

[1] Act V., Scene 1.

granting the Charter, he sought to evade it in all possible ways ; withdrew himself from all intercourse with
his barons, and finally collected about him a large
army composed of many of his own subjects, "lewd
fellows of the baser sort," who saw nothing to lose and
much to gain in the overthrow of the nobility—soldiers
of fortune, and mercenary troops from Normandy and
other places on the Continent. The mass of the
English people in deadly terror of civil war, and
taught by long ages of use, to bow meekly to the
strong hand and oppressive laws of the powers that
be, failed to support the barons, who in desperation
finally turned their eyes to France, and elected Lewis,
the son of Philip, in the right of his wife, Blanche,
niece of John, their king and leader.

The patriotic Englishmen who may question the
policy of this desperate course, because it turned out
badly, will remember, however, that under similar circumstances William of Orange was chosen and en-
throned King of England, by the lords and commons,
nearly five hundred years later. The revolution of
1688 succeeded, and that of 1216 failed, both for good
and sufficient reasons. But according to this measure
of worldly success or failure, the one is called a "glorious revolution," and the other a dismal rebellion ; the
one is counted a shining page in English history, the
other a dismal record to be blotted out of the memory
of England's sons.

Again, however, we must disentangle our minds
from the inaccuracies of Shakespeare's historical record. He assumes, again copying the "Troublesome
Raigne," all throughout those portions of the play

which deal with the sullen humors of the people and
the rising discontent of the barons, that these unhappy
circumstances are due to reports of the imprisonment
of Arthur. The Earl of Pembroke, answering the
king, who asks:

> What you would have reformed that is not well;
> And well shall you perceive how willingly
> I will both hear and grant you your requests,

says :

> *Pembroke.* Then I, as one that am the tongue of these
>   To sound the purposes of all their hearts,
>   Both for myself and them, but chief of all
>   Your safety (for the which myself and them
>   Bend their best studies), heartily request
>   The enfranchisement of Arthur ; whose restraint
>   Doth move the murmuring lips of discontent
>   To break into this dangerous argument.[1]

But, as already noted, Arthur had been dead for ten
years before the revolt of the barons which ended in
the giving of Magna Charta, and twelve years before
Lewis was chosen to lead the barons against John.
Moreover, there is no contemporary history to bolster
the deduction that Arthur's affairs ever had much sympathy, as for his claims against their own king,
among the English people. Shakespeare has so dominated the true history, by his wondrous picture of a
fair sweet boy deprived of his rights by a brutal tyrant, who was hated by the people for such a black
crime, that the average reader of history is insensibly

---

[1] Act IV. Scene 2.

led to adopt it as true. The reason for idealizing a boy of ten or twelve years, with presumably all the rough edges of that period of a lad's life, may be two-fold. First, it was necessary to the making of an acting play that the pathetic element should not only be included, but carefully exploited, as is the case in the drama of our own day ; and second, as Richard Grant White suggests in one of his studies in Shakespeare, the poet's " only son Hamnet died at the age of eleven years in 1596, and that ' King John ' was written in that year. It would seem as if the lovely character of Arthur (which is altogether inconsistent with the facts of history) was portrayed, and the touching lament of Constance for his loss written by Shakespeare, with the shadow of this bereavement upon his soul."

The true reason for the calling over of Lewis was, as has already been pointed out, the nullification of Magna Charta by John. Note now how in the whirli-gig of time the parties to this human drama had shifted ground. Stephen Langton, who had been forced by the Pope upon John, was the head and front of the barons' cause in securing the great Charter. The Pope, upon the complaint of John, was incensed against Langton and the barons, for getting the Char-ter without his consent as feudal lord of England. Lewis, the French prince, formerly the ally of the Pope against the king and barons, was now the ally of the barons against the Pope and king.

The play brings the army of Lewis to halt, after some large successes, by the submission of John to the Roman see. As we know, however, this interfer-ence of the Pope had been against the army of Philip.

While the events of the last scenes of the play therefore are very fairly accurate, they are so turned out of
their order in time, as well as twisted as to the relations of the prime actors, that there is not room for
the smallest pretence to suppose that Shakespeare ever
consulted history at all in the construction of this play.

The barons began to grow tired of their bargain
with Lewis. Rumors came to their ears that he was
only waiting to be seated fairly on the throne, to cast
them off and probably kill the most distinguished of
them, in order to replace them in the affairs of state
with Frenchmen from among his own nobles. It began
to look indeed like another conquest of the islanders,
by another French invasion. The English barons
weakened in their allegiance to the prince they had
sworn the most solemn oaths to support. John was
still holding out, but messengers were passing between
him and the fickle barons. Suddenly John, retreating
after some repulse, was overtaken with mortal sickness
at Swinstead Abbey. It was reported that he was
poisoned by the monks. At all events he died suddenly, and the rebellion of the barons came to an un-
timely end. Lewis, albeit somewhat indignant, was
persuaded to go back to France, not as in the play by
threats of the Pope's legate, but by force of circumstances, the falling away of the leaders by whom alone
he could be maintained on English soil for a day.

The young son of John (Henry III.) was crowned
king, and the Earl of Pembroke appointed regent.
Against such odds Lewis could not reasonably contend,
and he disappeared forever as a factor in English
politics.

So John died and his "troublesome raigne" came to an end. The implication of Shakespeare that the king was poisoned is based upon the old play, which has a long scene with conversations between the Swinstead monks upon the appearance of John in their midst, and an outlining of the way in which the poison was administered.

A quotation from this scene, being the soliloquy of Manet the monk, in Swinstead Abbey, may not be uninteresting, especially as Shakespeare in the play does not touch the details in his reference to the event.

> *Monk.* Is this the king that never loved a friar?
> Is this the man that doth contemn the Pope?
> Is this the man that robbed the holy Church?
> And yet will fly into a Friory.
> Is this the king that aims at Abbey's lands?
> Is this the man whom all the world abhors?
> And yet will fly into a Priorie.
> Accursed be Swinsted Abbey, Abbot, Friars,
> Monks, nuns, and Clarks, and all that dwells therein,
> If wicked John escapes alive away.
> .   .   .   .
> Ile free my country and the church from foes
> And merit heaven by killing of a king.

Shakespeare's method at times of crystallizing whole scenes into a single line or two, yet vividly in those few words presenting a picture spread over pages by his inferiors, is seen in the way he treats this incident:

> *P. Henry.* How fares your majesty?
> *K. John.* Poisoned, ill fare, dead, forsook, cast off.[1]

[1] Act V., Scene 7.

And yet the poisoning is pronounced apocryphal, and modern historians attribute John's death to either the fatigue of his dangerous passage of the river, aided by his anxiety and crushing weight of trouble; or to a surfeit of peaches and new cider; or to a distemper which had preyed upon his system for some months. But whatever its cause, the death of John was the salvation of England, as his miserable life had been, in the strange chemistry of Providence, her redemption from a Continental province to the state of a proud and compact nation.

We may not close our study of King John's "troublesome raigne" without noting again how the old play, to a greater extent than Shakespeare's, was infected with the violence of the anti-papal spirit of those days in which it was written, and how Shakespeare softened this down so that Roman and Anglican could witness its presentation side by side. One quotation may be made of a play, written it must be remembered in that transition period while the memory of Henry VIII. was still fresh in the minds of middle-aged men. The passage evidently had in mind Henry and the circumstances of his revolt from the Roman obedience. The words are put by the author of the "Troublesome Raigne" in the mouth of John while writhing under the sentence of interdict and excommunication.

> *John.* (Solus.) Then, John, there is no way to keep thy crown
> But finely to dissemble with the Pope.
> That hand that gave the wound must give the salve
> To cure the hurt, else quite incurable.
> Thy sinnes are far too great to be the man

4

To abolish Pope and poperie from the Realme,
But in thy seat, if I may gesse at all,
A king shall raigne that shall suppress them all.

This seems, even though it was written as having been
uttered three hundred years before the English Reformation, to be accurate as representing the spirit of
those very times of Shakespeare.

It was such waves of feeling gathering for many
generations that, swelling to high tide in the sixteenth
century, swept the Bishop of Rome from his long-
assumed authority over the autonomous Church of
England.

But if the religious feeling of the England of Shakespeare's day finds expression in this play, the patriotism of the times is no less interpreted, not in mere
word pictures, although the play ends with a fine
apostrophe which is quoted at the conclusion of this
chapter, but in its delineation of English manhood.

The character of Philip Falconbridge, the natural
son of Richard the Lion Heart, is looked upon as an
ideal of the poet's brain, with no other foundation
than the fact of the existence of such a person who
was not at all conspicuous in history. But Falconbridge seems to have been more than an ideal. He
did really exist, not as a faithful servant of King John,
as in the play, but in hundreds and thousands of loyal
steadfast men, citizens of England. Not nobles, nor
barons, nor degraded serfs, but men. The forgotten
men of most historic records. The men who are
ploughing and sowing; buying and selling; marrying
and bringing up sons and daughters like themselves;
paying the taxes of despotism and suffering the incon-

veniences of oppression, while doing their duty in that state of life to which it had pleased God to call them. Men who faced the daily problems of life, and as God gave them strength sought to deal with them, not complaining over much. Even giving their bodies to be set up as targets at the king's will, because he was the king, and they were loyal to him as sons of the soil.

Philip Falconbridge is an interesting study. It would appear that Shakespeare intended to have him represent the sturdy heart of English manhood, which, while often misused, humiliated, and beaten back, finally conquered and rose to its proper place in the making of later and nobler England, as the commons ; not the legislature of that name narrowly, but the makers of legislatures. So while Philip Falconbridge was an imaginary character he was not an imaginary force.

Another set of characters in this play are of more than passing interest, the women. Of Blanche we have already spoken ; how her youth and innocence were played with as common pawns to advance the interests of worldly-wise bishops and designing kings. But of Constance, the mother of Arthur, and Elinor, the mother of John, and hence grandmother of Arthur, something remains to be said. In the actual history of the times they did not play so important a part as is attributed to them by the dramatist. But that they exerted some influence upon the politics of their day cannot be doubted. Women have, noticeably, always managed to influence for good or evil the affairs of kingdoms and the actions of kings.

The picture Shakespeare draws of Constance is touching in the extreme. Her grief over the death of Arthur is one of the finest outbursts of the poet's genius. But we must read it apart from the other scenes in which the fair lady appears, or our sympathies will receive a shock. There are passages-at-arms between Constance and Elinor which exceed, in not always refined Billingsgate, the choicest scoldings of literature. Space will not serve to quote. Their relations as rivals were such that Holinshed, quoted by Malone, and requoted by Courtenay in his " Commentaries " on the play, must give us an idea of the trouble that lay at the root of their contentions.

" Surely Queen Elinor, the king's mother, was sore against her nephew Arthur, rather moved thereto by envy conceived against his mother, than upon any just occasion given on behalf of the child. For that she saw, if he were king, how that his mother, Constance, would look to bear most rule within the realm of England till her son should come of lawful age to govern of himself. So hard it is to bring women to agree in one mind, their natures commonly being so contrary, their words so variable, and their deeds so indiscreet."

Throughout the plays we see, however, that the women were not without influence in the adjustment or maladjustment of the affairs of state. A fact which is true to history then as now, and another evidence that Shakespeare paid more attention to the underlying philosophy than the outward accuracy of his chronicle plays.

The moral of the play, if we may so regard it, is the

exaltation of England's place among the nations of the
world and the inspiring of England's sons to attain
this bright ideal. To illustrate this, and as one more
comparison of the paraphrasing of the words of others
to his own use—paraphrasing which under his genius
became original — compare the last lines of the
" Troublesome Raigne " and the parallel passage from
Shakespeare's play.

Falconbridge. (After the crowning of Prince Henry.)
    Thus England's peace begins in Heuryes raigne,
    And bloody wars are closed with happy league.
    Let England live but true within itself,
    And all the world can never wrong her state.

    .   .   .   .

    If England's Peers and people join in one
    Nor Pope, nor France, nor Spain can do them wrong.

Now Shakespeare :

    This England never did, nor never shall,
    Lie at the proud foot of a conqueror,
    But when it first did help to wound itself.
    Now these her princes are come home again,
    Come the three corners of the world in arms,
    And we shall shock them. Naught shall make us rue,
    If England to itself do rest but true.[1]

                    [1] Act V., Scene 7.

RICHARD II.

There is no evidence that Shakespeare had access to, or, at all events, used another play based on the events of this reign.

The history is found in Holinshed's "Chronicle" and other less known publications.

"Richard II." is mentioned by Meres, and its date is 1597.

1216–72. Henry III. (son of King John) reigned. First reg-
ular English Parliament summoned, January 20, 1265.

1272–1307. Edward I. (son of Henry III.) reigned. Conquest
of Wales, 1272. Final organization of the English Parliament, 1295. Conquest of Scotland, 1296.

1307–27. Edward II. (son of Edward I.) reigned. Battle of
Bannockburn, defeat of the English, January 24, 1314. Semi-
conquest of Ireland achieved, 1316. Truce with Scotland,
1323. Edward deposed by Parliament, 1327, and murdered
in the following September at Berkeley Castle.

1327–77. Edward III. (son of Edward II.) reigned. Independence of Scotland recognized, 1328.

1327–77. Edward claims crown of France, 1337–38. Battle
of Cressy, 1346. Calais captured and truce with France,
1347. Renewal of French war, 1355. Battle of Poitiers,
1356. Treaty of Bretigny, May, 1360. "By this treaty the
English King waived his claims in the crown of France and
on the Duchy of Normandy. But, on the other hand, his
Duchy of Aquitaine was not only restored, but freed from its
obligation as a French fief and granted in full sovereignty
with Ponthiar, as well as with Guisnes and his new conquest
of Calais."

1376. Death of Edward, Prince of Wales, the Black Prince.

1377. Richard comes to the throne. The government in the hands of a Council, named by the lords but influenced by the king's uncles, the Dukes of Gloucester, Lancaster, and York.

1381. Wat Tyler's rebellion.

1386. Richard's favorite, the Duke of Suffolk, impeached, and a regency dominated by Gloucester appointed.

1388–89. After various trials of strength between the king and the opposition, Richard shakes off all control and reigns independently.

1397. For alleged conspiracies against the throne Gloucester is at first imprisoned, and then dies in Calais under suspicious circumstances, the king being implicated by common report.

1398. Shakespeare's play begins. Quarrel of the Dukes of Hereford (Henry Bolingbroke, son of the Duke of Lancaster) and Norfolk. Richard prevents a duel and banishes both contestants.

1399. Richard interferes with the marriage between Bolingbroke and the daughter of the Duke de Berri. Lancaster dies, and Richard, contrary to his promise to Henry Bolingbroke, seizes the paternal estates for the crown. Richard goes to Ireland to complete its conquest. Bolingbroke lands at Ravenspur (July 4th), and both nobles and people flock to him. Richard returns to find himself deserted by his Uncle York, whom he had left as regent, and is betrayed into the hands of Bolingbroke. Richard is impeached at Westminster, resigns his crown, and is deposed. Henry Bolingbroke claims the throne, and is elected by the Parliament under the name of Henry IV.

CHAPTER III.

THERE is an historical gap of about one hundred and
eighty years between the last scene of "King John" and
the first of "Richard II." Meanwhile England had
been working out her destiny, which destiny was largely
influenced by what had taken place in the reign of him
whose inglorious career is indicated by his inglorious
sobriquet of "Lackland." There is an analogy between the careers of dynasties and men. A youth

spent in weakness and folly foreshadows a manhood of decay and impotency. This was the history and the fate of the house of Plantagenet. We may not say that the sins of John were visited upon the head of Richard III. But, in writing out that story which ended in the deserved dissolution of a dynasty that had lasted for more than three hundred years, the poet has set forth a perfect syllogism in political morals, with John as its premise and Richard III. its conclusion.

The play of "Richard II." introduces us to a state of affairs which can be fully understood only by a brief survey of the score of years which had passed since the young king's accession to the throne ; and to understand this in turn, the reader of English history will require a rapid sketch of the interval of nearly two centuries, unilluminated by the genius of Shakespeare, between the accession of Henry III. (after the death of his father King John) and the month of September 1398, in which the opening scenes of the present play are laid.

Henry III. was a babe when he came to the throne. This always, or almost always, involves trouble. Unscrupulous ministers and back-stair influence are apt to be rife. Henry was fated, as his father before him, to have the kingdom taken from him for a time and put in the hands of a commission. Meantime Magna Charta had strengthened the national life, and the first representative parliament was assembled. Edward I. succeeded Henry and by comparison reigned brilliantly. Wales was conquered and made an appanage of the royal family, the heir apparent taking the title of Prince of Wales. Edward II. on the surface lost much of his father's prestige, and was deposed and murdered after a reign of twenty years, during which Ireland was conquered, to become a rankling thorn in the English body politic forever, and Scotland secured her independence, to become in later centuries the strong right arm of English loyalty. Here was a victory and a defeat, "of which it has been strangely but truly said, that the victory should be lamented by England as a national judgment, and the defeat celebrated as a national festival."

The discrowned and murdered Edward was succeeded by his son, third of the name, whose reign has ever been looked upon as one of the most glorious in English annals. It is marred in the eyes of the modern philosophical patriot by an insatiable desire for foreign conquest. We cannot blame the crass and immature statesmanship of Edward III., however, for not seeing, as clearly as posterity, that Continental complications, of whatever nature, which interfered with the insular solidarity of England were injurious, however fruitful of famous victories. It was a Plantagenet characteristic to look upon France as a province of England, and it was not until the last of the Plantagenets found a bloody end on Bosworth Field that the idea was actually given up. The Black Prince, who would have succeeded his father of glorious memory, died before the throne was vacant, and at the age of eleven years his son Richard II. was crowned king.

Edward III. left as an heritage to his grandson not only such victories as Cressy and Poitiers, but a people who had risen to power in national affairs, and a throne with acknowledged limitations. Magna Charta

had acquired character and was presently to assert itself in the Wat Tyler rebellion, which, although in one
sense a failure, was the means of striking off the shac-
kles of English serfdom.

It was at this period also that the English language
began to be spoken and written as the national tongue.
French and Latin had had their day. Chaucer had
started the rushing fountain of English speech. Wyck-.
liffe had added the element of the Holy Bible in the
vernacular; and although for lack of the printing press
literature was kept back for a few decades, the seed was
in the soil, and its time of flower and fruitage came.

Shakespeare's play is founded on Holinshed's "Chronicle." There was no previous dramatic work of the kind
at hand; or if there were, the poet preferred to fly on
his own wing. The historic accuracy of the drama is
undoubted. The gravest anachronism is that of making Queen Isabel a woman of mature years. She was
in reality but eleven years old, and Richard's marriage
with her (1396) and the alliance with France so secured,
was one of the incidental reasons of popular dissatisfaction which came to a head in his deposition. Isabel is
the only female character of any importance in the play,
and if her age was advanced a few years, so that her
relations with the king should add a touch of pathos
to the story, it must be admitted, with Skottowe, that
the effort was a failure. The scenes in which Isabel
appears are the weakest in the tragedy. Shakespeare's
was yet a 'prentice hand in the delineation of female
character, and the genius which was to rise so high in
the portrayal of Katharine of Arragon "imped on a
drooping wing" with Isabella of France.

The scenes grouped about the deposition of the king and the enthroning of Bolingbroke are reversed in order of time; and Aumerle's mother who pleads for him with the usurper, in the last act, had been dead some years. But as usual with the poet, his use of wide license in such matters tended to the greater vividness of his dramatic pictures.

These anachronisms are so few and trifling, and so practically unimportant to the literal historic movement, that for purposes of illustration "Richard II." is one of the best of the chronicle plays.

To sketch in brief the main thread of Richard's reign up to the point where the play opens, we must in imagination see Richard crowned at the age of eleven years. A commission of nine powerful nobles held the reins of power, among whom were conspicuous the king's uncles, the Dukes of Gloucester, Lancaster, and York. His coronation as the legal heir of the Black Prince of idolized memory, with its accompaniments of homage, fulsome praises, and gross flatteries, was calculated to inflate his boyish ideas as to the difference between the blood of kings and of common people. What else could be expected of a child who found himself, for no conceivable reason apparent to himself, the centre of adulation and a bone of contention between princes. It was in these scenes of his impressionable years that he learned the lesson of the divine right of kings, and that

> Not all the water in the rough rude sea
> Can wash the balm from an anointed king.
> The breath of worldly men cannot depose
> The deputy elected by the Lord. [1]

[1] Act III., Scene 2.

So surrounded by scheming relations, particularly the
older uncles, Gloucester and Lancaster; restless
barons beginning to feel the pressure and restriction
of the commons on their actions; held in tutelage beyond the years of nonage; alternately flattered and deceived; Richard one day bluntly asked his uncles if
he were not old enough to govern for himself, and
without more ado assumed the prerogative. Richard
may be pardoned for throwing off the bands of com-
missions and regencies at the age of twenty-two; but
the effects of his political infancy were to bear bitter
fruit. His suspicions of his uncles (doubtless well
founded) end in the exile of Lancaster for a time, and
the death in prison of Gloucester, which death was
laid by common report at his nephew's door. It must
be remembered in connection with this episode that
the Mowbray of the play was in charge of Gloucester
when his death was reported.

Richard had been growing more and more despotic as a natural result of his forced tutelage. The
people, who had begun to taste the sweets of parliamentary government, were rudely set aside, and by an act
wrenched from a subservient legislature, in the year before the play begins, all practical power was placed in
the hands of the king and his council.

The Irish wars and his private expenses made huge
inroads on the public purse, and finally the combined
avarice and necessities of Richard led him to "farm
out" the realm.

> And, for our coffers with too great a court
> And liberal largess are grown somewhat light,
> We are enforced to farm our royal realm;

The revenue whereof shall furnish us
For our affairs in hand.[1]

Gaunt, in his dying speech, " a prophet new inspired "
laments :

> This blessed plot, this earth, this realm, this England,
> .   .   .   .
> This land of such dear souls, this dear, dear land,
> Dear for her reputation through the world,
> Is now leased out, I die pronouncing it,
> Like to a tenement or pelting farm ;[2]

and hurls at the recreant king,

> Landlord of England art thou, and not king.

The chronicler Fabyan says (quoted by Knight), " In
this twenty-second year of Richard, the common fame
ran that the king had letten to farm the realm unto Sir
William Scrope, Earl of Wiltshire, and then treasurer
of England, to Sir John Bushy, Sir John Bagot, and
Sir Henry Green, knights."

It is evident from this why " Bushy, Bagot here, and
Green," are selected by Shakespeare as types of the
favorites about Richard's person, who, according to
Bolingbroke's charge on their apprehension, " misled
a prince, a royal king."

It is at this period that the play opens. The lords
and nobles are disgusted with the unkingly actions of
their sovereign. The commons have been deprived of
the sweets of self-government. Plots were thickening
and conspiracies gathering strength from the twenty
years of a reign in some respects as weak as that of
John.

[1] Act I., Scene 4.   [2] Act II., Scene 1.

Shakespeare deals with three historic events of importance within the limits of the play, around which cluster and out of which grow the minor incidents. These are (I.) the banishment of Bolingbroke; (II.) his return and rebellion, as Duke of Lancaster; and (III.) the deposition and death of Richard II.

The banishment of Bolingbroke is a natural sequence of the events of the reign which preceded it. The quarrel between Bolingbroke and Mowbray, with which the play opens, culminating in the lists of Coventry and the common exile of the participants, is one of those historical secrets, the explanation of which is lost in the mazes and intricacies which characterized the political life of the thirteenth and fourteenth centuries. The two contestants had been leagued together formerly in the "treasons of these eighteen years," and both had guilty knowledge of conspiracies to hold the king in leading strings. Mowbray was, on the whole, more loyal to Richard than Bolingbroke, although the latter had been pardoned for his share in the late treasonable practices. It was now recalled that Mowbray was in charge of the Duke of Gloucester when he met his suspicious death.

The mutual recriminations of the two nobles in the first scene of Act I. do not throw much light upon their quarrel, save that Mowbray is accused of being a traitor on general principles, which on general principles he denies:

> That all the treasons for these eighteen years
> Complotted and contrived in this land
> Fetch from false Mowbray their first head and spring,
> .   .   .   .
> That he did plot the Duke of Gloucester's death.

Mowbray, in a very eloquent plea, puts in a defence:

> And interchangeably hurl down my gage
> Upon this overweening traitor's foot,
> To prove myself a loyal gentleman.[1]

As a matter of fact there was no noble of Richard's court but that had some hand in the treasons of those eighteen years; and a charge of malfeasance in office and misuse of public moneys is a customary move of political warfare not unknown to our own days.

The accusation of Gloucester's death was a more serious one. In reality it was an arraignment of Richard over Mowbray's shoulders, and all the parties concerned knew it. It was well known that if Gloucester had suffered a violent end it must have been the inspiration of Richard. Gaunt and Gloucester's widow voiced the common opinion when the latter appeals to the old Duke:

> To safeguard thine own life
> The best way is to venge my Gloucester's death.
> *Gaunt.* Heaven's is the quarrel; for heaven's substitute
> His deputy anointed in his sight
> Hath caused his death.[2]

It was a bold cast of Bolingbroke to hurl that malicious dart, and he won by it. The king could not defend Mowbray without incriminating himself. Mowbray could not, from loyalty or, indeed, with any safety, lay the death of Gloucester upon the king.

The trial by battle is appointed at Coventry, and at the moment of beginning the contest the king (with the advice of his council, not arbitrarily as the play

---

[1] Act I., Scene 1.   [2] Act I., Scene 2.

5

suggests) throws down his warder, declines to allow
the duel to proceed, and sentences Mowbray to life
exile, and Bolingbroke to banishment for ten, afterward reduced to six years.

This change of front was quite typical of the king.
While it seemed to lean to the side of mercy, it was an
exhibition of that despotic power which, even in small
affairs, delighted Richard. And it was a logical sequence of those earlier years of his reign, during which
he had the semblance, while deprived of the reality of
power. Moreover, if Bolingbroke won the duel, he
had given boastful public notice that he felt it incum-
bent upon him to avenge his uncle's death.

> Which blood, like sacrificing Abel's, cries,
> Even from the tongueless caverns of the earth,
> To me for justice and rough chastisement :
> And, by the glorious worth of my descent,
> This arm shall do it, or this life be spent.[1]

Richard had proved the loyalty of Mowbray, and
their common guilty knowledge of Gloucester's death
acted as a further bond between them. It would be as
easy to recall Mowbray, after a short time, as to banish
him for life, and the king felt that Mowbray's loyalty
would stand the test of the temporary discomfort of
exile for his sovereign's sake. On the other hand,
Bolingbroke's popularity with the Commons, whom
Richard had offended, his royal blood and powerful
political as well as family connections, all conspired to
make of him a foe to be feared. This appears to have
been the secret of the change of the king's mind in

---

[1] Act I., Scene 1.

regard to the duration of his cousin's exile. It seemed
a master-stroke of policy. As though to intimate to
the haughty noble that his punishment were merely
nominal after all. Of Mowbray we hear but once
again. Sacrificed (although perhaps but temporarily)
to the selfish interest of the master he had loyally
served, and who was soon to lose the power, even had
he the intention, to restore his friend, the gallant
"Duke of Norfolk, Thomas Mowbray," took service
under the banner of the Crusaders, and when Bolingbroke, as Henry IV., would have recalled his ancient
enemy, it was too late. Norfolk was dead.

> Many a time hath banished Norfolk fought
> For Jesus Christ, in glorious Christian field,
> Streaming the ensign of the Christian Cross
> Against black pagans, Turks and Saracens,
> And toiled with works of war, retired himself
> To Italy : and there at Venice, gave
> His body to that pleasant country's earth
> And his pure soul unto his captain, Christ,
> Under whose colors he had fought so long.[1]

But the king's compromise failed. He had put off
the evil day of reckoning, not delivered himself from
the necessity of it. It was nearer even than any of
the prominent actors in it dreamed. Richard's public
reason, why the sentence of banishment on both contestants was preferable to allowing them to settle their
quarrel by the duello, reads strangely with our later
knowledge :

> For that our kingdom's earth should not be soiled
> With that dear blood which it hath fostered,

[1] Act IV., Scene 1.

And for our eyes do hate the dire aspect
Of civil wounds plowed up with neighbor's swords.[1]

He would avoid civil wars, but the banishment of the two nobles was the opening skirmish of the severest and bloodiest fratricidal strife in England's history, the "Wars of the Roses." Bolingbroke's absence emboldened the king to confiscate the estates of his house upon the death of "John of Gaunt, time-honored Lancaster." This act gave the ambitious noble a pretext to return from exile, and to gather a force under his banner for the restoration of his lands and seignories. Rebellion and the deposition of Richard followed; Bolingbroke challenged the throne and secured it. "Plume-plucked Richard" died by force or otherwise, in prison. The Bishop of Carlisle needed no more than ordinary inspiration to prophesy :

The blood of English shall manure the ground.
.   .   .   .
O ! If you rear this house against this house
It will the woefullest division prove
That ever fell upon this cursed earth,
Prevent it, resist it, let it not be so,
Lest child, child's children, cry against you, woe.[2]

Old Gaunt's speech also, already quoted, made to Richard from his dying bed, not only analyzes the state of the realm but, seer-like, predicts the course affairs must take unless,

Though Richard my life's counsel would not hear,
My death's sad tale may yet undeaf his ear.[3]

[1] Act I., Scene 3.   [2] Act IV., Scene 1.
[3] Act II., Scene 1.

Some of the learned critics sagely remark that there is no historic authority for this speech. Doubtless not for the literalists. Even dukes when about to die did not send for chroniclers in order that their final message to the world might be set forth in due form. It is sufficient for historical purposes, and adapted to dramatic exigencies, that the situation of affairs be summed up so accurately as in the words of this dying man, than whom no living soul was better versed in the trend of national politics and the connection with them of Richard's weakness and rapacity. We have anticipated the story here to illustrate Richard's fatal facility of deafness and blindness, when to hear and to see were easier. The Irish wars attract him.

> Now for our Irish wars.
> We must supplant those rough rug-headed kerns,
>
> . . . .
>
> And for these great affairs do ask some charge,
> Toward our assistance, we do seize to us
> The plate, coin, revenues and movables,
> Whereof our Uncle Gaunt did stand possessed.[1]

The scene shifts and with the same personages a new turn is given to this drama of real life. Bolingbroke hears of the escheatment of his estates and the death of his father. His heart is hot against Richard on another count beside that of his banishment, for the king's influence had prevented his marriage with a daughter of the Duke de Berri (Mary de Bohun) while he was high in favor at the French court. Bolingbroke hears of the continued discontent of the Commons and

---

[1] Act II., Scene 1.

the sullen attitude of the great nobles. He hesitates
no longer. Having, with all his faults, the genius of
catching the flood tide in the affairs of men, possessed
of inordinate ambition, inspired by hatred, and nerved
by a courage that never swerved in "plucking the
flower of safety from the nettle danger," he landed in
England with a handful of attendants on July 4, 1399.

This brings to our notice the second point of historic
action illustrated by the poet in this play—the return
and rebellion of Bolingbroke.

In taking his departure for the Irish wars Richard
had made his surviving uncle, Duke of York, regent
during the period of his absence. Ordinarily it was a
safe and crafty arrangement, for York was the most
timid, irresolute, and unambitious of men. No danger
could be suspected from any ulterior designs of his,
upon either the affections of the people or the throne
of the realm. But these very qualities made him as
paper-pulp in the hands of the scheming and arbitrary
Bolingbroke. Upon hearing of the latter's landing
and the growth of an army under his banner, York becomes as supine and helpless as a child.

> If I know
> How or which way to order these affairs
> Thus thrust disorderly into my hands,
> Never believe me. Both are my kinsmen :
> The one is my sovereign, whom both my oath
> And duty bids defend ; the other again
> Is my kinsman, whom the king hath wronged.
>   All is uneven,
> And everything is left at six and seven.[1]

[1] Act II., Scene 2.

Forces gather about Bolingbroke, among whom especially welcomed were the powerful Percys : Northumberland, his brother Worcester, and gallant young Harry Hotspur, three thorns afterward to sting the hand within whose grasp they had placed the sceptre of power.

There are two possible views of Bolingbroke's rebellion against Richard. It is within the limits of probability that before his banishment he was in correspondence with the nobles who afterward joined him, and that the conspiracy, nipped in the bud by the king's interference in the personal quarrel at Coventry, blossomed anew, with the pretext of the exile's return to reclaim his unjustly seized estates. Northumberland's speech, when he hears of the landing of Bolingbroke, implies that rebellion against the crown and not the restoration of a brother noble's lands, was his leading motive.

> If then we shall shake off our slavish yoke,
> Imp out our drooping country's broken wing,
> Redeem from broken pawn the blemished crown,
> Wipe off the dust that hides our sceptre's gilt,
> And make high majesty look like itself,
> Away with me in post to Ravenspurg.[1]

In Mowbray's counter accusation there may be an implication of some such plot :

> No, Bolingbroke. If ever I were traitor,
> My name be blotted from the book of life,
> And I from heaven banished as from hence.
> But what thou art, heaven, thou, and I do know:
> And all too soon, I fear, the king shall rue.[2]

[1] Act II., Scene 1.   [2] Act I., Scene 3.

On the other hand Shakespeare is historically correct in making Bolingbroke's protest, first to his allies, and afterward to the king's own face, that he was impelled to return in seeming rebellion only to win back his hereditary estates, and that the nobles and Commons forced him, for the sake of England's better government and honor, to assume the crown.

When poor old York endeavors feebly to withstand the rush of Bolingbroke's popularity, and petulantly cries, "Tut, tut! grace me no grace, nor uncle me no uncle, I am no traitor's uncle," he is very quickly silenced by his nephew's special pleading, backed by the powerful Northumberland's indorsement, who says:

> The noble duke hath sworn his coming is
> But for his own ; and for the right of that
> We all have strongly sworn to give him aid,
> And let him ne'er see joy that breaks that oath.[1]

York's attitude is really pitiable. He is a type of character quite common in stirring times, who slide along safely, and even gracefully, over the surface of events, until deep currents disturb the ordinary flow of life. In the main such a one perceives the right thing to do, and if he had his preference would choose to do it. But he will not commit himself irretrievably to the right, if it be in a minority. He will warn others, but go no further by example. Here York cries:

> Well, well, I see the issue of these arms :
> I cannot mend it, I must needs confess,
> Because my power is weak and all ill left :
> But if I could, by him that gave me life,

[1] Act II., Scene 3.

I would attach you all and make you stoop
Unto the sovereign mercy of the king:
But since I cannot, be it known to you
I do remain as neuter.[1]

Bolingbroke was very well satisfied to have no sharper opposition from the regent and his army than "neutrality," especially as the declaration was followed by an invitation to become York's guest at his castle for the night.

  Meanwhile Richard was acting out the character he had been accreting for a score of troubled years. He first heard of the rebellion in Ireland. Knight[2] quotes the contemporary account of a Frenchman, in the suite of Richard, as to the way in which the news was received. "Good Lord," he cries, turning pale with anger, "this man designs to deprive me of my country." Salisbury was despatched to Wales to raise an army, but for some unknown reason Richard dallied for nearly three weeks in Dublin, and when at last he landed on the Welsh coast the army had disappeared. The last scene of Act II. of the play tells the story vividly. The Welsh, ever a superstitious people, are convinced by the king's delay that he is dead, and that the expedition is ill-starred. Salisbury argues in vain. The captain says:

'Tis thought the king is dead: we will not stay.
The bay-trees in our country are all withered
And meteors fright the fixed stars of heaven,
The pale-faced moon looks bloody on the earth,
And lean-looked prophets whisper fearful change.

. . . .

----

[1] Act II., Scene 3.   [2] History of England, Vol. I., Chap. 33.

These signs forerun the death or fall of kings;
Farewell: our countrymen are gone and fled
As well assured Richard their king is dead.[1]

Richard, not aware of this defection, lands in the spirit
of one assuming, without fear of contradiction, that

The breath of worldly men cannot depose
The deputy elected by the Lord.
For every man that Bolingbroke hath pressed
To lift shrewd steel against our golden crown
Heaven, for his Richard, hath in heavenly pay
A glorious angel.[2]

But this high tone does not last long. He wandered
from castle to castle without additions from either
earthly or heavenly sources. The first news that
greeted him was the melting away of the Welsh army
on which he had chiefly relied. Quickly followed the
intelligence that the common people threw up their
hats for Henry of Lancaster.

White-beards have armed their thin and hairless scalps
Against thy majesty : and boys, with women's voices,
Strive to speak big, and clap their female joints
In stiff unwieldly arms against thy crown :
Thy very beadsmen learn to bend their bows
Of double fatal yew against thy state :
Yea, distaff women manage rusty bills
Against thy seat : both young and old rebel,
And all goes worse than I have power to tell.[3]

At length the inevitable end comes. With only a
handful of supporters—the chief men who had remained loyal to him in the hands of the rebels—York,

---

[1] Act II., Scene 4.   [2] Act III., Scene 2.   [3] Act III., Scene 2.

the regent, feebly remonstrating against revolt, while entertaining Bolingbroke at his board—the whole country permeated with the subtly sprinkled poison that Henry of Lancaster was but righteously contending for that of which he had been unjustly deprived, and that his grievance was only the common grievance of all English subjects,—Richard weakly, pitiably, succumbs. But not all at once.

There were yet sparks of the nobility of soul that caused him, when but a boy half grown, to ride forth alone and put himself at the head of a hundred thousand malcontents in Wat Tyler's ranks, as their natural leader who would see their wrongs righted.

One moment he cries:

> This earth shall have a feeling and these stones
> Prove armed soldiers, ere her native king
> Shall falter under foul rebellion's arms.

The next he sobs:

> Have I not reason to look pale and dead?
> All souls that will be safe fly from my side;
> For time hath set a blot upon my pride.

Again, under spur of Aumerle:

> I had forgot myself. Am I not king?
> Awake, thou sluggard majesty, thou sleepest;
> Is not the king's name forty thousand names?

But again:

> Of comfort no man speak:
> Let's talk of graves, worms, and epitaphs,

Make dust our paper, and with raining eyes
Write sorrow on the bosom of the earth.[1]

Brought face to face with Bolingbroke at last, the
king's temper shifts and veers in the same uncertain
way. But although his moods thus express themselves, it is not now from sudden bravery or sheer
affright. The whole of scene third, act third, in which
the first interview takes place, and which ends with the
setting forth of the chief personages in company to
London, marks a notable transition in the character of
Richard.

It must be remembered that, although Shakespeare
makes no mention of the fact, Richard, in these preliminary interviews with Bolingbroke and his messengers, was probably intending treachery as well as
expecting it. If he had been suddenly transformed
into an angel of humility it would have been a mirac-
ulous event. His bringing up in undignified bondage
to his uncles, while yet wearing the splendid pomp of
a heaven-anointed sovereign, had seemed to confuse
his moral sense. His reliance was not so much upon
God as that he believed even God could not but espouse the cause of "his elected deputy."

Shakespeare gives the substance but not the form of
Richard's meeting with Bolingbroke. In reality he
was betrayed by Northumberland. The latter came as
an ambassador, apparently unattended, to Conway Castle where the king was, and "admitted to the castle he
proposed certain conditions to the king, which were
willingly agreed to, as they impaired not the royal au-

[1] Act III., Scene 2.

thority, and to the observance of these Northumberland swore. It was promised that Lancaster should come to Flint and, having asked pardon on his knees, should be restored to the estates and honors of his family." [1]

The king was on his way from Conway to Flint when he was made a prisoner by the treacherous Northumberland's forces, and from that moment there was no further hope of a meeting on equal terms between the two foes. This episode is passed over by Shakespeare, for unknown reasons. The chronicles record it. It would surely have afforded a dramatic scene, and have helped to illustrate that entire change in Richard's character which is manifestly the design of Shakespeare in these later scenes. For, from the moment he appears, before Bolingbroke, practically a prisoner, the king is no longer the Richard of the earlier portions of the play, and we are indebted to the dramatist, far more than to the chroniclers, for this vivid character drawing of the last days of the once arrogant and proud Plantagenet.

It is not desperation, nor sorrowful bombast, nor the whine of despair that brings the king to his knees before the subject he had banished from the realm.

> Fair cousin, you debase your princely knee
> To make the base earth proud with kissing it.
>
> .   .   .   .
>
> Up, cousin, up ; your heart is up I know,
> Thus high at least (*touching his own head*) although
>   your knee be low.
>
> .   .   .   .

[1] Knight's History of England, Vol. I., p. 584, quoted from a contemporary MS.

Cousin, I am too young to be your father,
Though you are old enough to be my heir.
What you will have, I'll give, and willing too;
For do we must what force will have us do.[1]

This is not the language of mere sordid weakness
and cowardice. It is the yielding to fate of one to
whom the further game is not worth the candle.

Richard would never have won a crown by force of
masterful assertion and his good right arm. Having
royalty as an heritage, he held it as a right not to be
disputed, rather than a trust to be administered.

His weakness in defence was moral not physical.
So long as he was surrounded by a brilliant court and
backed by a powerful army, the crown was the most
glorious possession in the world. But, to him, it was
not worth " the stress and storm." Shakespeare's pathetic speech put in the king's mouth seems the justest
estimate of his feeble yet not undignified (if the para-
dox may be allowed) character.

What must the king do now? Must he submit?
The king shall do it: Must he be deposed?
The king shall be contented: must he lose
The name of king? O' God's name, let it go:
I'll give my jewels for a set of beads,
My gorgeous palace for a hermitage,
My gay apparel for an almsman's gown,
My figured goblets for a dish of wood,
My sceptre for a palmer's walking staff,
My subjects for a pair of carved saints,
And my large kingdom for a little grave,
A little, little grave, an obscure grave:
Or I'll be buried on the king's highway,

[1] Act III., Scene 3.

Some way of common trade, where subjects' feet
May hourly trample on their sovereign's head;
For on my heart they tread now whilst I live—
And buried once, why not upon my head?[1]

Coleridge would have him weak and womanish throughout, " what he was at first he was at last, except so far as he yields to circumstances." It was exactly in this " yielding to circumstances" that marks the transition and denotes the essential change in Richard. If he had yielded earlier he would have been a stronger king; that he did so eventually made him a better man.

The third and last historic centre of action in this drama is the deposition and death of Richard, and incidentally the crowning of Henry Bolingbroke as Henry IV. It was inevitable of course. A discrowned and imprisoned king seldom escapes his earthly trials save through " the grave, and gate of death."

The play assumes, in entire consonance with the chronicles, that Richard's resignation of the crown was voluntary, and that he designated Bolingbroke as a fitting successor.

York   Great Duke of Lancaster, I come to thee
From plume-plucked Richard; who with willing soul
Adopts thee heir, and his high sceptre yields
To the possession of thy royal hand.
Ascend his throne, descending now from him;
And long live Henry, of that name the fourth.[2]

The poet, for no conceivable reason, dramatic or historic, that appears on the surface, places Bolingbroke's

In God's name I'll assume the regal throne[3]

[1] Act III., Scene 3.   [2] Act IV., Scene 1.   [3] Ibid.

before the formal resignation of Richard. This slight anachronism does not prevent the fourth act (of which there is but one scene) from being an admirable picture, down to the least detail, of the dethronement of the king and the usurpation of Henry of Lancaster.

For dethronement and usurpation are the proper designations of these acts concerning which York utters the euphemism:

> Which tired majesty did make thee offer,
> The resignation of thy state and crown,[1]

The Bishop of Carlisle, loyal to his king, protested against both deposition and encroachment upon the royal demesne.

> What subject can give sentence on his king?
> And who sits here that is not Richard's subject?[2]

There is a suggestion throughout the speech that the good Bishop is standing up for the divine right of kings, but on closer reading it will be perceived that his argument is based mainly on the fact that Richard is not being treated fairly by being deposed in his absence.

> Thieves are not judged but they are by to hear.[3]

The dramatic and historic unity of the play is maintained by the prophecy already quoted of civil war, which is sure to result if Bolingbroke is crowned.

The effort is made to commit Richard to his own deposition, and Northumberland addresses him:

---

[1] Act IV., Scene 1.   [2] Ibid.   [3] Ibid.

> Read
> These accusations and these grievous crimes
> Committed by your person and your followers,
> Against the state and profit of this land :
> That, by confessing them, the souls of men
> May deem that you are worthily deposed.[1]

Richard's pathetic protest might have moved even the cold sternness of the powerful nobles who thus played, cat-like, with his griefs.

> Must I do so?   And must I ravel out
> My weaved-up follies?   Gentle Northumberland,
> If thy offences were upon record,
> Would it not shame thee, in so fair a troop
> To read a lecture of them?[2]

The bill of particulars referred to here, and contained in the impeachment of Richard before the Commons, had thirty-three charges, the most important of which were those laying the death of Gloucester at his door, the seizure of Bolingbroke's estates, and general accusations of despotism, unfaithfulness, and inconstancy. That they were untrue no one would claim. That they offered sufficient grounds for a forced abdication of the throne, in that rude age, is open to argument. Henry VIII. was far more guilty after a lapse of more than two centuries, and died in his bed, shrieking out with his last earthly breath a despotic command that was all but carried out.

Guilty as Richard undoubtedly was, "so variable and dissembling in his words and writings, that no man living who knew his conditions could or would

[1] Act IV., Scene 1.   [2] Ibid.

6

confide in him," still he was the victim of a youth
which had been formed for him by others, and chiefly
by those who shouted Hail! to Henry of Lancaster, as
he ascended the throne from which he had plucked
his cousin. And the marvellous skill of the dramatist
in these scenes portrays the reality, under the show of
things, in such a way that the reader knows the truth,
and that it is not with Bolingbroke. The act (IV.)
which tells this story concludes significantly. The
new king announces a day for his coronation and leaves
the stage to a handful of those whose loyalty to " un-
kinged Richard " remained unshaken.

> *Abbot.* A woeful pageant have we here beheld.
> *Bishop of Carlisle.* The woe's to come: the children yet
> unborn
> Shall feel this day as sharp to them as thorn.
>
> .   .   .   .
>
> *Abbot.* I see your brows are full of discontent,
> Your hearts of sorrow, and your eyes of tears:
> Come home with me to supper: I will lay
> A plot shall show us all a merry day.[1]

Two points of interest remain ; the death of Richard,
and the abortive plot to rise in rebellion against his
successor. Over the whole of the last act in which
these events are dramatically set forth, there is
thrown a glamour of pity for the dethroned monarch.
The interview between Richard and his queen does
not rise to more than mediocrity, perhaps because it is
both historically inaccurate and psychologically impossible. The king and queen did not meet again at
all after their parting when Richard set out for Ire-

[1] Act IV., Scene 1.

land, and Queen Isabel was a child. In no other point does the play show its early composition so certainly as in the poet's handling of this character. That knowledge and appreciation of womanhood which is one of the noblest components of his later works, is lamentably deficient here.

York's interview with his duchess, interrupted by sobs and weepings on both their parts, and containing the pathetic picture, trite but ever thrilling, of the double entry of Bolingbroke and Richard to London, ends with the duke's pious resignation :

> But heaven hath a hand in these events,
> To whose high will we bow our calm contents ;
> To Bolingbroke are we sworn subjects now,
> Whose state and honor I for aye allow.[1]

The frantic efforts of York to impound his own son for treason, in order to prove his own loyalty and "calm content," has something revolting in it. Yet it is dramatically in harmony with all that precedes, to indicate the germs of rebellion already beginning to swell in the souls of Englishmen, before the usurper was well settled in his royal chair. And perhaps our lack of sympathy with York is gratified, at having the stalk of revolt push itself above the surface of "calm contents" in the unstable Duke's own family. Otherwise, next to the scenes in which Isabel is introduced, those concerning Aumerle's discovered treason add least to the play, whether it be viewed as poem or drama.

The close student of our great poet will be interested

---

[1] Act V., Scene 2.

in comparing the 4th and 6th scenes of the 5th Act of
this play, with scene 3d of Act III., and scene 2d of
Act IV. of King John. In both cases a king inspires
his follower to murder. In both he repudiates the
murder once accomplished. King Henry and Exton are
cut from the same pattern as King John and Hubert.

It is disputed by historians whether Richard died
by violence or at the command of Bolingbroke. It is
certain that he did not die as shown in the play,
where Exton is represented as striking him down
while he is struggling with the servants who are commissioned to kill him; for some years ago Richard's
body was exhumed and no signs of a blow upon the
skull were discoverable. He might have been stabbed
to the heart, or starved to death, however, and on the
whole we may believe the latter was his fate. Bolingbroke would not have the stain of actual blood upon
him. He would not kill Richard outright, but would
let him die, a more quiet and king-like way of reaching the desired end. For death was inevitable. There
is no room on earth for a king uncrowned by force.
He is a constant source of danger to the reigning
monarch, a centre around which will gather those
discontented and daring spirits to whom peace has
no prizes, and upon whom established order has no
claim.

There was a story with which our Shakespeare seems
to have been unacquainted, that Richard escaped from
prison and lived for many years in hiding in the
Scottish marches. If this had been so, he would undoubtedly have been summoned from his obscurity by
Northumberland, Percy, and the Scotch in the rebel-

lion of Henry IV.'s reign, and willy-nilly have become a contestant for his own throne. But there is
no smack of truth to the story. Richard died and
Henry of Lancaster reigned in his stead. The ambition of perhaps a lifetime was achieved, but to what
a bitter end!

When we come to consider the events of Bolingbroke's reign as treated by Shakespeare in the first
and second parts of Henry IV., it will be seen that
the sceptre even of England might be too dearly
bought. We will discover that Bolingbroke was perfectly conscious of the treachery of his course, and that
he accepted the many sorrows of his life as a well-
earned retribution. We will find also the nobles, who
raised him one round on the ladder of power and
dignity above themselves, recalling Richard's prophecy
to Northumberland.

> Northumberland, thou ladder wherewithal
> The mounting Bolingbroke ascends my throne
> The time shall not be many hours of age
> More than it is, e'er foul sin, gathering head
> Shall break into corruption : thou shalt think,
> Though he divide the realm and give thee half,
> It is too little, helping him to all.
> And he shall think that thou which know'st the way
> To plant unrightful kings, will know again,
> Being ne'er so little urged, another way
> To pluck him headlong from the usurped throne.·

If all is granted concerning the alleged evils of Richard's mismanaged government, and the parliamentary
decree to depose him from the throne for cause is ad-

Act V., Scene 1.

judged fair, still Bolingbroke may not be relieved of the crime of usurpation.

He claimed the throne in right of descent from Edward III., of whom it is true he was the grandson. But Richard failing for whatever reason, the crown belonged to Edmund Mortimer, Earl of March, lineal descendant of Clarence, third son of Edward III.; while John of Gaunt, Bolingbroke's father, was fourth son, and out of the line of succession. This Edward was but ten years of age. Of his claim could be said, as was said of the unfortunate Richard by Langland, "Woe to thee, O land, when thy king is a child."

Again, we must consider that, granting Richard's incompetency, the nobles and parliament had precedent (in the case of King John over Arthur of Brittany) for preferring to place the sceptre in the strong hands of a man rather than in the weak grasp of a child. It was not his usurpation to the throne that disturbed Henry of Lancaster, usurpation though it was; it was remorse for the steps he took to mount so high. "Heaven knows," says Henry the Fourth, with his very latest counsel to the son he loved:

> Heaven knows, my son,
> By what by-paths and indirect crooked ways
> I met this crown : and I myself know well
> How troublesome it sat upon my head :
> To thee it shall descend with better quiet,
> Better opinion, better confirmation.
> For all the soil of the achievement goes
> With me into the earth.[1]

[1] II. Henry IV., Act IV., Scene 5.

It has been already noted that the play covers but a short two years of Richard's reign. This is in dramatic keeping with the idea hitherto thrown out, that the decline and fall of the House of Plantagenet is the theme of these eight dramas between king.John and Henry VIII., in relation to which continued story, the former stands as prologue and the latter as epilogue.

It is in these last two years that the seeds of the final dissolution of that House are sown, in those historic events which brought about the internecine rivalry of the families of York and Lancaster. This will be more clearly developed as the story of succeeding reigns unrolls before us on the superb canvas of our great poet.

The character of Richard is the *tour de force* of the drama. So large a space is devoted to the development of his personality that the play is better regarded as a poem than as an acting drama. As Coleridge says : " But in itself, and for the closet, I feel no hesitation in placing it as the first and most admirable of all Shakespeare's purely historical plays."

The student will note how clearly the chief elements in Richard's education, circumstances, and character are indicated in the first scenes of the play : whereby the attention of the reader is attracted, and his mind prepared for all that follows. He is in the midst of treasons and plots and conspiracies. He deals with them not with a masterful hand, but with a sort of shifty, cunning policy, which must o'erreach itself in the end. We cannot agree with those historians who give to Richard any deep or large sense of the royal dignity. While patriotism and love of country is one of the themes of the play (as of all of the English histories), Richard himself seems to value his crown for its glitter; his realm as a source of revenue; and his anointment as the "deputy elected of the Lord" as a matter of course, requiring no stewardship on the one hand, or accounting for on the other. In his day of humiliation he sees more clearly than before, but it stirs no kingly fire, and arouses no princely courage. While to the last he resents the illegality of his deposition, in his heart of hearts he accepts its moral fitness.

There would be more to say of the character of Bolingbroke if his story ended here. Over him also comes a change when once the cares as well as the glories of kingship are upon him. In the last Act (V., sc. 4) we note that anxiety over his son's courses which shows a father's yearning love creeping from beneath a noble's o'erweening ambition, and his gentle treatment of the rebellious Aumerle is not such as would be naturally expected of high-mounting Bolingbroke. By these signs of a finer realization of *noblesse oblige*, we are prepared for the wide difference between usurping Bolingbroke and the reigning monarch Henry IV., a contrast which the poet sets forth in the succeeding play.

As to the historic period in which the drama finds its setting, as already briefly noted, it was an important epoch of England's internal life. Richard coming to the throne upheld on the shield of powerful barons, saw not the cloud arising in the sky little larger than a man's hand, the growing power and influence of the people. The Commons had no hand in Magna Charta, but they had benefited by it. In the reigns of Henry III. and the great Edward, mutterings of uneasiness and dissatisfaction began to be heard. In this last year of the fourteenth century the old feudal tyranny was beginning to give way. The revolt which placed Bolingbroke in Richard's seat was not of the nobles only, but of the Commons also. This was the political situation and environment, a stage of transition, with which Richard, a product of the old feudal life, had to deal.

But there was another, a religious phase, which differentiated Richard's England from that of his predecessors. This phase is marked by the name of Wyckliffe, "the rising sun of the Reformation," and the spread of his doctrines.

We cannot fail to note that, as we trace the weakening of feudalism to the Magna Charta of King John, although it was gained by the feudal power, so we find the germs of the later Reformation in the famous interdict which the Pope laid upon the England of King John. Kings and popes did well in those days to join hands in the suppression of heretics, for heretics in religion were the stuff of which rebels in state affairs were made.

Wyckliffe died in 1384, but his Bible in the English tongue remained a charter of spiritual, as the Magna Charta was of political, freedom. Civil freedom gained a step, and a great one, in the deposition of Richard II. For in that event, while it seemed that the bad ambition of one man used the deep yearnings of the people to accomplish his own plans, in reality Bolingbroke was the unconscious instrument of that power, greater than baron, priest, or king, the power slowly gathering force and courage and hope under the rude homespun of the yeomanry of England.

Literature, too, was trimming her lamps and filling her vessels with oil. Chaucer and Gower by birth, and Froissart by adoption, uttered the first real notes of that Anglo-Saxon strain which has moulded the feelings, broadened the mind, made glad the heart, and strengthened the soul, of the whole human race.

The art of printing was yet to come, but when Guttenberg drew the first proof-sheet damp from his imperfect press, he drew a veil over the world's real infancy and darkness, and turned the face of the whole earth toward the promise of manhood and light ; a promise that has since been gloriously fulfilled, and never in so large a way, or by a more transcendent genius, than in the method and by the works of Shakespeare, poet and prophet, historian and seer.

some reforms which bore hardly on the aristocracy. The confederate leaders who had paved the way for one of their own number to the dizzy height of royalty, were especially aggrieved at his evident determination to reign independently, and even to curb the influence and crop the comb of feudalism.

Many circumstances conspired to trouble the peace of the House of Lancaster, but at their head and front was this civil discontent.

Shakespeare paints the death throes of feudalism with a master hand. The shadow of its passing enshrouded the whole reign of the first Lancastrian.

It was plainly inevitable in the nature of things, that the prophecy of the Bishop of Carlisle should be literally fulfilled :

> And if you crown him let me prophesy
> The blood of English shall manure the ground
> And future ages groan for this foul act.[1]

Richard's own warning to Northumberland :

> Thou ladder wherewithal
> The mounting Bolingbroke ascends my throne ![2]

must inevitably be established. The peers, of whom Northumberland was chief, felt themselves strong enough, if good reason should appear, to pull down whom they had set up. In those turbulent times good reasons were always within the reach of mailed hands.

It was inevitable also that the plain people of England should stand by the new king for the same reasons that had caused them to espouse his cause. He

---

[1] Richard II., Act IV., Scene 1. [2] Richard II., Act V., Scene 1.

was as nearly a democrat as the first part of the fifteenth century could produce. If not in heart, he was one in policy. The people, slow to change, were steadfast in their likes and dislikes, and they formed the real strength of the Lancastrian dynasty established by Henry IV., deepened and secured by Henry V. The break with his chief nobles thus threw Henry back upon the Commons and made way for the breaking down of the feudal system, which is the chief historic event writ large and illustrated in the two parts of this play. We see the process of disintegration in its first and most important stages. The real death-blow was struck when Henry defeated the combined force of the great nobility at Shrewsbury. After this the feudal system dragged on an impotent existence until, when the last of the Plantagenet kings died like a wild boar on Bosworth field, and Henry, first of the Tudors, came to the throne, there were but twenty-nine lay nobles to take their places in his first Parliament.

It will be noticed later on, how this passing of feudalism harmonizes with the introduction of Falstaff, and how the whole comedy movement of the play of which he is the centre, illustrates, not broad farce, but scathing satire.

Leaving the comedy for further consideration in its appropriate place, we notice that there are again three centres of historical importance about which the poet weaves the illustrations of his genius.

These are in order: I. The battle of Shrewsbury. II. The broken compact. III. Death of Henry IV., and accession of Prince Hal.

I. The events that led up to the battle of Shrewsbury, in which the royal forces were victorious, and the power of the great nobles well-nigh crushed, are vividly illustrated in the beginning of the play. It opens with news of the defeat and capture of Mortimer by the Welsh rebels under the "irregular and wild Glendower," and a great victory in the north over the Scotch by the king's men under the powerful Northumberland and his son, Harry Hotspur. In regard to the former event Shakespeare commits the anachronism of identifying Mortimer with his nephew, the Earl of March, who was the legitimate heir to the throne after Richard, by his descent from an older branch of the royal family than could be claimed for Henry IV.[1] The heirship to the throne would lie in young Mortimer, and Shakespeare is thus justified in treating one of the family name as an opponent whose influence the king had to fear, especially in alliance with the Northumberland party, owing to the fact that Hotspur's wife was the uncle Mortimer's sister. It was even reported that Richard had declared the Earl of March next heir to the throne. The usurper may have been led by these dangers to the security of his own claims, to see too readily in Mortimer's defeat and marriage with Glendower's daughter a treasonable plot. For Hotspur, rising in wrath at Henry's refusal

---

[1] The claim of Mortimer was through Lionel, Duke of Clarence, third son of Edward III. The claim of Bolingbroke, Henry IV., was through his father, John of Gaunt, fourth son of Edward III. Mortimer was the legal heir after Richard, who died without children. Misled by his chronicle authority, Shakespeare confuses the uncle and nephew Mortimer (vide Act II., Scene 3), where Hotspur's wife calls the Mortimer of the play her brother, as he was, and Act III., Scene 1, where Mortimer calls Hotspur's wife aunt, which of course she was not. See table of kings in Appendix.

7

to ransom Mortimer, having heard the report of Richard's declaration, cries out:

Nay, then I cannot blame his cousin-king
That wished him on the barren mountain starve.[1]

But that Henry had some excuse for looking askance upon his possible rival to the throne apart from personal considerations, is seen in the fact that Mortimer settled back so comfortably into his captivity as to marry his captor's daughter.

The battle of Holmedon, on the other hand, gave Northumberland and his family great prestige, and exalted still more that independence among the feudal lords, in which lay the sharpest thorn of Henry's crown. The play well illustrates this. Flushed with these victories, the old Duke, his brother Worcester, and his son Hotspur, hold themselves haughtily enough in the king's presence when he demands the prisoners taken in battle, which Hotspur declined with lame excuses, but finally consented to yield, on condition that Mortimer, his brother-in-law, be ransomed from the Welsh. Henry's refusal to ransom one whom he chooses to esteem a traitor, widens the breach with his once devoted ally, and here we have all the conditions for rebellion.

It is necessary to glance forward over the whole play to extract the reasons, as set forth in their dramatic order, which were deemed sufficient for the rebellion of the great lords, so soon after placing Henry on the throne.

The personal animus of the Percys is on the surface, and probably influenced the course of events to a con-

[1] Part I., Act I., Scene 3.

siderable extent. Feudal pride was touched by the en-
actions of Henry's first Parliament, which sought, as
has been already noted, to curb the power of the great
vassals of the crown.

Cries Hotspur indignantly, retailing the favors his
father had done Henry, when he was but

> A poor unminded outlaw sneaking home,
>
> .   .   .   .   .   .
>
> And now forsooth takes on him to reform
> Some certain edicts and some straight decrees
> That lay too heavy on the commonwealth,
> Cries out upon abuses : seems to weep
> Over his country's wrongs :— [1]

These petulant sarcasms of Hotspur were levelled at
acts of the king "which tended," as Knight says, "to
lead the people to think that the reign of justice had
come back." The innovations were chiefly on the side
of parliament and people. Among others were those
narrowing the scope of treasonable offences, and giving
parliament authority to declare them. They forbade
the star-chamber process of governing by packed com-
mittees instead of in open assembly. Notably, they
"tried to restrain the quarrels of the great nobles, by
forbidding any person except the king to give liveries
to his retainers." This was the crucial point. It
tended to build up a king's party, and to disintegrate
the vassalage by which the feudal barons were kings
and laws unto themselves.

It is probable, also, that Shakespeare is historically
correct in attributing some of the discontent to a feel-

[1] Part I., Act IV., Scene 3.

ing on the part of the nobility that they had been
tricked into seating Bolingbroke upon the throne.
— "You swore," says Worcester,

> And you did swear the oath at Doncaster,
> That you did nothing purpose 'gainst the state,
> Nor claim no further than your new fall'n right,
> The seat of Gaunt, Dukedom of Lancaster.
>
> .   .   .   .
>
> Whereby we stand opposed by such means,
> As you yourself have forged against yourself,
> By unkind usage, dangerous countenance,
> And violation of all faith and troth,
> Sworn to us in your younger enterprise.[1]

All that Henry has to offer are fair words and gra-
cious promises. But the logic of the situation was
terribly against him. When, later on, the king con-
fides in Warwick the prophecy of Richard (already
quoted), Warwick, in the endeavor to soothe his fears
by removing the warning from the field of prophecy to
that of clever guess-work, says, with keen philosophic
insight that could scarcely, however, have been reas-
suring:

> There is a history in all men's lives,
> Figuring the nature of the times deceased:
> The which observed, a man may prophesy,
> With a near aim, of the main chance of things
> As yet not come to life, which in their seeds
> And weak beginnings lie intreasured.
> Such things become the hatch and brood of time;
> And by the necessary form of this
> King Richard might create a perfect guess

[1] Part I., Act V., Scene 1.

That great Northumberland, then false to him,
Would of that seed grow to a greater falseness,
Which should not find a ground to root upon,
Unless on you.[1]

In other words, as Henry's crown was the gift of discontent on the part of the nobles, the discontent of the
nobles might place it somewhere else. So the rebellion was invoked, and the tactics of Bolingbroke turned
against Henry IV. But notwithstanding the griev-
ances of the nobles, the justice of their charges against
the king, and the added strength of Welsh and Scotch
alliances, their cause was weak, and the seed of its
disastrous failure sprouted long before Shrewsbury
battle-field. Northumberland and his immediate
friends could assemble armies of their vassals, but the
people as a whole were for the king. It will be remembered that he courted them successfully at the
time of his banishment, and he had never lost their
favor. They saw in this new rebellion, not resistance
to tyranny and weakness and oppression, but the envy
and jealousy of an aristocracy that blew hot or cold according to its own prosperity. If it had been right and
necessary to depose Richard and seat Henry, it was
treason and criminal to undo that work. They remembered how the appeals of Richard had been con-
temptuously flaunted by the Northumberland faction,
and were not to be deceived now by such demagogic
appeals as that of York's

With the blood
Of fair King Richard, scraped from Pomfret stones.[2]

[1] Part II., Act III., Scene 1.   [2] Part II., Act I., Scene 1.

Nor could the warrior-like Archbishop shift the respon-
sibility of a second revolt upon the shoulders of the
people, as when he attributed to the Commons the
very attitude of the malcontent nobles.

> The commonwealth is sick of their own choice,
> Their over greedy love has surfeited.
>
> .   .   .   .
>
> O thou fond many ! With what loud applause
> Did'st thou beat heaven with blessing Bolingbroke,
> Before he was, what thou wouldst have him be ?
>
> .   .   .   .
>
> O, thoughts of men accurst !
> Past and to come seems best : things present, worst.[1]

Another source of weakness was the heterogeneous
nature of the alliance against the king. The English
faction headed by Northumberland, but inspired and
animated by his son, brave Harry Percy, was the chief
factor, with whom were associated Owen Glendower
on the part of Wales, and the Earl of Douglas on the
part of Scotland. Percy and Douglas had but recently spent "a sad and bloody hour" together at
Holmedon, in which the "ever valiant and approved
Scot" had met with severe defeat. Such wounds are
not soon healed. Glendower was a romantic half-bar-
barian, although he had been "trained up in the English court." As the educated savage frequently falls
back into barbaric ways, in spite of the polishing of
grammar and rhetoric, so it is to be feared that Glendower was but a veneered courtier, after all. He was
the natural product of the hard life amid Welsh fastnesses ; the superstitions of a people whose ancestors

[1] Part II., Act I., Scene 3.

had perhaps been the pupils of the Druid priesthood; and an implicit belief that he held so important a place in the creative scheme that at his nativity, not only

> The goats ran from the mountains and the herds
> Were strangely clamorous to the frighted fields,

but

> The front of heaven was full of fiery shapes
> Of burning cressets : . . . .
> The frame and huge foundation of the earth
> Shak'd like a coward.[1]

Glendower was a poet, and a chieftain of men who were equally at home with the harp and chant, with the mixing of magic potions, with clever devices in the torture of prisoners, and in the wild irregular sallies and retreats which made up their idea of warfare. Glendower was a gentleman also, as will be observed in his intercourse with the brutal wit of Hotspur, and his tender thoughtfulness and care for women. But he was not a soldier nor a diplomat. He could and did defend his mountain caverns for many years, but he could not direct or command armies.

For a time the rebellion throve apace. The English party were buoyed up by hopes of cutting the royal crest; the Scotch by desire for revenge; the Welsh, with the idea that they were not as common men, and could not be defeated. Mortimer, the husband of Glendower's daughter, and the brother of Hotspur's wife, was the movable pawn of all the combinations, and it is not improbable that, had Henry IV. been defeated, the Earl of March might have ascended the throne.

[1] Part I., Act III., Scene 1.

The conspirators throve apace and even parcelled out the land they expected to win by their sword-blades. Of course, over this partition they quarrelled. One of the cleverest, and best worth reading scenes of the First Part of Henry IV. is Sc. 1 of Act III., in which Hotspur, Glendower, and Mortimer are set forth as not only counting their chickens before they are hatched, but parcelling out the mother hen and her nest.

While his malcontent subjects are thus occupied, Henry is not altogether sure of the outcome of these affairs. In the armed hosts of his enemies, to whom

> These promises are fair, the parties sure,
> And our induction full of prosperous hope,[1]

he saw the hand of a melancholy fate. The king's name was a tower of strength, but the king's soul was faint within him. He was not a mere demagogue this man who played sometimes the demagogue's part.

When we have allowed for the sympathy which Shakespeare conjures up about the last scenes of the life of Richard II., and are out from under the wizard's spell cast over the failing and pathetic fortunes of the deposed king, we can see that Bolingbroke has some noble characteristics which intensify as he looks with sad eyes from the gilded throne he sought with such a vain and fond ambition. As the troubles thickened about him, no one was quicker than himself to see their origin. He had planted the seed, and shock of battle at Shrewsbury was the harvest. Henry's greatest weakness lay in his guilty conscience. If not the blood, at least the unhappy fate, of Richard lay heavy

---

[1] Part I., Act III., Scene 1.

on his soul. In his last words to the son who was to
lift England to a higher pitch of glory and renown
than she had ever known, the careworn, remorseful
king confesses:

> Heaven knows, my son,
> By what by-paths and indirect, crooked ways,
> I met this crown, and I myself know well
> How troublesome it sat upon my head.
>
> . . . .
>
> How came I by the crown, O Heaven forgive!
> And grant it may with thee in true peace live.[1]

Henry's conscience was thus a perpetual menace to
the success of his efforts. Along with this was the
shadow flung upon the future fortunes of his house by
the careless life of Prince Hal, his oldest son and heir.[2]
The historic truth of this domestic trouble between
the king and his son is undoubted.

That the wild Prince was not quite the gentlemanly
scoundrel of Shakespeare's portrait, is quite true, but
that there was quite enough in his conduct to warrant
the gravest fears on Henry's part, we may be assured.
The king likened his heir to

> The skipping king who ambled up and down
> With shallow jesters and rash bavin wits,[3]

[1] Part II., Act IV., Scene 4. 5

[2] There is a touching line in one of the king's speeches, that conveys with
vividness an image of the lonely heart he bore beneath the majesty of
royalty.

> For thou hast lost thy princely privilege
> With vile participations: not an eye
> But is a' weary of the common sight
> *Save mine, which hath desired to see thee more.*
> —Part I., Act III., Scene 2.

[3] Part I., Act III., Scene 1.

And until the need appeared the king had cause for fear. But Hal was at Shrewsbury, and before that had assured his father's heart.

Prince H. This, in the name of God I promise here,
  The which if he be pleased, I shall perform.
  I do beseech your majesty may salve
  The long grown wounds of my intemperance :
  If not, the end of life cancels all bands :
  And I will die a hundred thousand deaths
  E'er break the smallest parcel of this vow.
King H. A hundred thousand rebels die in this
  Thou shalt have charge, and sovereign trust in this.[1]

And now the battle of Shrewsbury is fought. Hotspur leads the malcontent nobles, and Henry IV., with his sons and faithful peers, after a vain attempt at conciliation, defends the crown. Hotspur is defeated and slain—not as in the play at the hands of Hal, for dramatic proprieties are not always as artistically observed in battle as on paper. The power of the great nobles received a shock from which it never entirely recovered. The grandson of Bolingbroke met it, or rather was dominated by it, in the person of Warwick the King Maker. But in the case of Warwick the feudal power was largely personal and not of a class. Warwick was *sui generis.*

Feudalism as a system in England never lifted its head to more than hiss defiantly after Henry IV.; its blows were feeble and its sting drawn.

But in addition to that slow development of the English people of which Shrewsbury was a logical link, there were some natural reasons for the defeat of

[1] Part I., Act III., Scene 2.

the rebellion which Shakespeare indicates with historic
fidelity and poetic charm. Hotspur and the Douglas
engaged the king's forces before the Welsh under
Glendower, and the army under Northumberland, could
join them. Some have attributed this to Hotspur's
impatience and headlong zeal to fight wherever he saw
an enemy, without looking to the consequences. This
was partly the case, and Glendower's failure to arrive
in time was another element of disaster. But this
was unavoidable, owing to the surprising speed with
which King Henry and Prince Hal united their forces
and forced a battle. The king's army had been orig-
inally levied to aid Northumberland against the Scotch.
Hal had been making a campaign against Wales. The
news of the open revolt caused the two national armies
to speedily join forces, and Shrewsbury was thus almost an accident, as Agincourt was in the next reign.

Northumberland, whose name more than his vassals
was the tower of the rebels' strength, was "crafty
sick." He marched but slowly southward after his
impetuous son, sending messages of his inability to
proceed faster. If there were but this single campaign by which to judge the elder Percy, there might
be said much in extenuation of his failure to appear at
Shrewsbury. But unfortunately for his reputation, his
whole career was marked by the same sort of loud profession and little performance. He accomplished most
in helping to seat Bolingbroke. But the times were
with him then; before and after Shrewsbury they
were against him. His name was a great power in
that he was practically king of northern England
through the working of the feudal system. In his

name the revolt was planned, under his fostering boast and promises it took shape. Doubtless he hoped, by virtue of his former success, to draw the English nobility about his standard, and place Henry back as naked of influence and power, as when first he landed, a returned outlaw, at Ravenspurg. He was only partially successful in this attempt, not having taken into account the growth of a king's party, loyal first of all to the throne, not with a loyalty primarily subservient to the will of the feudal chiefs.

Hotspur realized how fatal this vacillation of his father's was :

> Sick now? droop now? this sickness doth infect
> The very life blood of our enterprise,
> 'Tis catching hither even to our camp.[1]

His endeavor to take courage from the fact that Northumberland's army, not being on hand, would be a good refuge in case of defeat, is cautiously overthrown by his uncle Worcester :

> But yet, I would your father had been here.
> .   .   .   .   .   It will be thought
> By some that know not why he is away
> That wisdom, loyalty, and mere dislike
> Of our proceedings, kept the Earl from hence.[2]

Hotspur tries to comfort himself in vain. The battle was fought and lost, and Northumberland hearing the news, dispersed his forces and retired to his castle at Warkworth. Henry did not force his submission too far, and for a time the revolted nobles and their dough-

---

[1] Part I., Act IV., Scene 1.   [2] Ibid.

ty chief lay quiet. With this battle the first part of Henry IV. concludes, and before discussing the desultory warfare of the next period we may profitably consider one or two of the characters already engaged, especially the contrasted types of Prince Hal and Harry Percy, called Hotspur.

It is too early yet to dwell upon the wild Prince Hal, save in those points wherein his father and others were prone to compare him with Hotspur, and usually to the heir apparent's disfavor. Shakespeare invariably links together the five dramatic epochs of his great national epic, from Richard II. to Richard III., by causing the titular hero to share our interest with his successor. In this way the figure of Bolingbroke casts a shadow forward from Richard II., Prince Hal from Henry IV., and Richard Gloster from Henry VI. It is as if to remind kings that in the evolution of affairs they must pass, while their kingdoms remain. This is one of the great and noble lessons which the poet-historian sought to teach. England was greater than any personage who might for the time rule or misrule from her throne. The royal policy of this or that sovereign might seem at any stage of national progress to be the one policy. But underneath the ripples of change, the surface commotions of man's passions and greed, the calm tide of nationalism rose and fell, obeying higher laws than the edicts of kings or parliaments.

From Canute downward, this tide has been controlled for men and not by men.

The delineation of the young Prince Hal in the first part of this play is thus not only a following out of the poetic and dramatic habit of Shakespeare, but is a logical necessity of the historical situation. The Prince is as important a figure on the stage where his father plays the chief part, as was his father in Richard II.'s time. We must keep our summing up of his character for the next chapter, where he appears in the full glory of his noble manhood, but a few words are necessary here as to the comparison usually instituted between him and Harry Hotspur. Shakespeare is responsible for these comparisons, since he leaves the inference to be drawn that they were of about equal age. Cries Henry IV., in the first part of this play :

> O, that it could be proved
> That some night tripping fairy had exchanged
> In cradle clothes, our children where they lay,
> And called mine Percy—his Plantagenet.[1]

Now, Harry Hotspur was contemporary with Bolingbroke himself, and old enough to be Prince Hal's father. This is ignored by the poet, but the drama gains by the poetic license. We have the king and his powerful noble, Northumberland, opposed to each other in the persons of their respective sons, who are drawn as types of the young manhood of those days. The one, a gay young gallant ; fond of taverns and low company ; careless of dignities ; apparently careless of honor. The other a warrior pure and simple, trained in camps instead of courts, despising the amusements and life of his rival, whom he at first scorns as :

> " The nimble-footed, mad cap, Prince of Wales,"

[1] Part I., Act I., Scene 1.

but whom he learns to respect for his deeds of valor when :

> Harry to Harry shall—hot horse to horse
> Meet, and ne'er part, till one drop down a corse.[1]

For the Prince of Wales, even in the play, is not the careless pleasure - seeker he seems on the surface. Presently we will discuss him more at length, but as contrasted with Hotspur he shows not unfavorably. The latter thinks scorn of his rival on idle report. Hal uses a nobler measure wherewith to gauge his father's foe. Addressing Worcester, the Percy's uncle, he says :

> Tell your nephew,
> The Prince of Wales doth join with all the world
> In praise of Henry Percy.
> I do not think a braver gentleman
> More active valiant, or more valiant young,
> More daring or more bold, is now alive,
> To grace this latter age with noble deeds.

Hal confesses that :

> For my part I may speak it to my shame,
> I have a truant been to chivalry.[2]

But even here a woman's judgment would decide for the wild boy, rather than for the steady, cold-natured man, as we must judge Hotspur to be in his domestic relations, however merry, ardent, and impulsive as a soldier. In the interviews given between Hotspur and his wife, the Lady Percy chides him for his absence of mind, his carelessness of her feelings, his utter absorption in affairs with which she is unac-

---

[1] Part I., Act IV., Scene 1.   [2] Part I., Act V., Scene 1.

quainted. The soldier in him speaks first to his servants, ordering them to saddle his horse, and as she continues her tender, anxious questioning, finally responds :

> Away,
> Away you trifler. Love? I love thee not.
> I care not for thee, Kate : this is no world
> To play with mammets and to tilt with lips.
> We must have bloody noses and cracked crowns,
> And pass them current too. God's me, my horse.
> What say'st thou, Kate? what would'st thou have with
>   me?

Lady. Do you not love me? do you not indeed?
> Well, do not then, for since you love me not,
> I will not love myself. Do you not love me?
> Nay, tell me if you speak in jest or no.

Hot. Come, wilt thou see me ride?
> And when I am on horseback I will swear
> ... thee infinitely. But hark you, Kate :
> ... have you henceforth question me
> ... reason whereabout.
> ... to conclude,
> ... Kate.

> But yet ...
> No lady close.
> Thou wilt not utter ...
> And so far will I trust thee, ...
>
> .   .   .   .   .   .
> Not an inch further.[1]

... is a good deal idealized. He has fine and ... ions. He is of heroic mould. His sar- ... as in the scene where he recounts

... Act II., Scene 3.

the visit of the fop to the battle-field of Holmedon, demanding prisoners. In anger he is magnificent, as in his outbreak at Henry IV. who refused to ransom Mortimer. In brutal jesting he is *facile princeps*, as in his interviews with Glendower, who deserved courtesy from a soldier and comrade-in-arms, not the sneering mockery and jibing to which his ally treated him. To sum up, Hotspur is a magnificent animal. He is not a leader among animals even. He is a soldier, not a captain. His heady temper brought about the defeat at Shrewsbury. He was a perfect type of the titled bravado. He fought valiantly, and died on the field of battle honorably, but not all the glamour of poetry thrown over him by the power of genius, can make him an ideal man.

Of Glendower we have already treated in a few strokes briefly indicating his character. Born in the caves of Wales; educated in the courts of kings; resigning his easy and luxurious life in London for the manlier and harder career of chieftain among his own race; he carried on a long warfare after the battle of Shrewsbury and died among his beloved hills, the idol of his rough retainers. He believed in all the superstitions of his times; saw visions and dreamed dreams; was often hunted from shelter to shelter; lay on barren mountains by night, and lifted his chant of defiance by day. A hard life; yet an easier one than that of Henry Bolingbroke vainly wooing sleep on his silken couch, with the uneasy head upon which lay a golden crown.

The second point of history marked by these two parts of Henry IV. is that already noted as the Broken

Compact. Although it occupies some space in the second part of Shakespeare's play, it needs here, for purposes of the story, to be barely mentioned. The poet huddles together his events for dramatic effect. The purpose seen in the two parts of the play is the Passing of Feudalism, and with the battle of Shrewsbury the first and most decisive blow at the system is struck. The events that follow it, until the final and complete victory over the rebellious nobles, in the breaking of Northumberland and Bardolph's power, were as follows: Shrewsbury's date is 1403. Shakespeare continues his story as though the nobles were entrapped by the broken compact at once. But it was after a turbulent two years, in 1405, that Prince John, of Lancaster, brother of the.Prince of Wales, together with some of his leading captains, made a treaty with Worcester on the part of the Northumberland party which the poet touches on as follows:

Westmorland, who has conducted the King's side and presented to John of Lancaster the articles of complaint for which the nobles asked redress, says:

> Pleaseth your grace, to answer then directly
> How far forth you do like their articles?
> *P. John.* I like them all, and do allow them well,
> And swear here by the honor of my blood, ·
> My father's purposes have been mistook;
> And some about him have too lavishly
> Wrested his meaning and authority.
> My lord, these griefs shall be with speed redressed.
> Upon my life they shall.
> *Arch.* I take your princely word for these redresses.
> *P. John.* I give it to you and will maintain my word.[1]

[1] Part II., Act IV., Scene 2.

So the compact was made; but the moment the nobles' army was disbanded, the leaders were arrested
for high treason; the pledges annulled, and those who
had relied upon the princely word were executed as
traitors.

But not yet Northumberland. A curious contrast
may be drawn between him and the wavering Duke
of York, in Richard's reign. After the death of his
son, the elder Percy had withdrawn from active life.
The new revolts had his sanction, but again at critical moments he failed to come to the front. That he
realized his own baseness the poet finely indicates.
When his wife would restrain him from action he
cries:

> Alas, sweet wife, my honor is at pawn
> And but my going, nothing could redeem it.

Hotspur's widow bitterly reminds him:

> The time was, father, when you broke your word,
> When you were more endeared to it than now.
> .   .   .   .
> Never, oh never, do his ghost the wrong
> To hold your honor more precise and nice
> With others, than with him.[1]

Northumberland's response is indicative of the remorse that must have filled his breast when he reflected, that but for his "crafty sickness," Hotspur
might be alive, and the Earl of March upon the
throne:

> Beshrew your heart,
> Fair daughter. You do draw my spirits from me

[1] Part II., Act II., Scene 2.

> With new lamenting ancient oversights.
> But I must go and meet with danger there,
> Or it will seek me in another place,
> And find me worse provided.[1]

This proved to be true. He dawdled with fate and was overwhelmed at last. He did not join the nobles who were tricked by the broken compact, and for the time escaped, but afterwards was up in arms with some of his friends, comrades-in-arms, chiefly Lord Bardolph, and was overthrown in the battle near Tadcaster in 1407, dying on the field.

In the play news of this is brought to the king upon the heels of that of the execution of the nobles with whom the truce was broken, although two years had elapsed :—

> *Harcourt.* From enemies heaven keep your majesty,
> And when they stand against you may they fall
> As those that I have come to tell you of.
> The Earl of Northumberland and the Lord Bardolph
> With a great power of English and of Scots
> Are by the sherif of Yorkshire overthrown.[2]

The poet links this happy news of the final suppression of rebellion with the last hours of the king, although six years elapsed before his death in 1413. The last half of the last scene of Act IV. is a perfect picture of these closing years of the king's reign, although it dramatically comprises but a few hours before his death. In this part of the play, we have to do with the third historic event of our analysis—Henry's death and the accession of Prince Hal.

[1] Part II., Act II., Scene 2.   [2] Part II., Act IV., Scene 4.

The king feels that his hour has come and desires to be led into his chamber to die.

History recounts that after the rebellions were crushed, the king desired to make his oft-intended journey as a Crusader to the Holy Land, as a sort of compensation for the sins of his royal policy. At the shrine of Edward the Confessor in Westminster Abbey, when he went to take his vows, he was taken ill and conveyed to an apartment near at hand called the Jerusalem chamber. A reference to this will be made presently. The king speaks upon recovering from his swoon:

> I pray you take me up and bear me hence
> Into some other chamber, softly, there.[1]

He asks for the crown to be placed upon his pillow near at hand, as though to lay to heart the vanity of that for which he had entered such torturous and devious ways. The Prince of Wales entering, finds his father asleep and alone, and fascinated by the appearance of the golden bauble, apostrophizes it:

> O, polished perturbation, golden care![2]

Then follows that much misunderstood scene where, as he soliloquizes, the prince lifts the crown from the pillow and puts it on his own head. A noise occurring he quickly leaves the room. His father awakes, and being told that only the Prince had been with him while he slept, cries out bitterly:

> The prince hath ta'en it hence, go seek him out.
> Is he so hasty that he doth suppose

---

[1] Part II., Act IV., Scene 4.   [2] Ibid.

My sleep, my death?
Find him, my lord of Warwick, chide him hither.[1]

Now, it has been too superficially argued that Prince
Henry was so eager to secure the crown that he could
not wait until he had assurance of his father's death;
so indeed the king argued:

> Thy wish was father, Harry, to that thought
> I stay too long by thee, I weary thee.
> Dost thou so hunger for my empty chair?[2]

But read the scene carefully. Note how careful a psy-
chologist the poet is. The emotions that stir the
Prince, contemplating the wasted face of his dying
sire, and the gleaming sign of royalty close to the
head it had uneasily adorned, are natural to the finest
shade of thought. He has no vulgar lust for what it
symbolizes:

> Sleep with it now,
> Yet not so sound, and half so deeply sweet
> As he whose brow with homely biggin bound,
> Snores out the watch of night.

He thinks his father dead:

> This sleep is sound indeed, this is a sleep
> That from this golden rigol hath divorced
> So many English kings.[3]

He knows, too, how much more than Richard, his
father valued the royalty for which the crown was sign
and seal. He knew the plottings and contrivings that
would ensue to challenge his own right to it. Surely

---

[1] Part II., Act IV., Scene 4.   [2] Ibid.   [3] Ibid.

he was no hasty bauble-loving roisterer, but his own father's son, who, as it were, with mechanical thought-fulness, putting the crown on his head, says:

> Lo, here it sets
> Which heaven shall guard. And put the world's whole
>   strength
> Into one giant arm, it shall not force
> This lineal honor from me.[1]

These musings are entirely in the vein of his father's last charges to him, when once reassured that the son is not vulgarly anxious to put on the "polished perturbation."

Henry's final words to the heir apparent throw light upon his life, and usurpation of the crown. In the hot zeal of youth, spurred on by acknowledged wrongs, touched also by an ambition for which the times were as responsible as his own temperament, Henry had reached for the chiefest thing in the world for a strong and masterful Englishman of that day.

He had some grounds of right, the strongest of which was least acknowledged by his age, but after all the most powerful, namely, the will of the common people. It was in lack of this factor, that Northumberland and those with him failed to snatch the crown from the head of him whom they believed themselves to have made. Literally, too, in those days successful force made a legal title. Bolingbroke ascended the throne an actual usurper: he died a legitimate king; as he says:

> For what in me was purchased
> Falls upon thee in a more fairer sort.[2]

[1] Part II., Act IV., Scene 4.   [2] Ibid.

And yet he knows too well the power of the old feudal nobility which he had fatally scotched, and with the breadth of statesmanship and grasp of policy, that always characterized his public career, laid out the best course for his son to pursue, in order to prevent or discourage the rebellion, which had embittered so large a part of his own reign.

> Yet though thou standest more sure than I could do
> Thou art not firm enough, since griefs are green,
> And all my friends, whom thou must make thy friends,
> Have but their stings and teeth newly ta'en out :
> By whose fell working I was first advanced,
> And by whose power, I well might lodge a fear
> To be again displaced. Which to avoid
> I cut them off ; and had a purpose now
> To lead out many to the Holy Land
> Lest rest, and lying still, might make them look
> Too near unto my state. Therefore my Harry
> Be it thy course to busy giddy minds
> With foreign quarrels.[1]

How thoroughly the prince entered into this mind of his father's, how admirably he appreciated its wisdom and statesmanship, and how successfully he carried out its suggestion, the next reign will give us ample illustration.

That Henry cherished remorse for his course toward Richard is clearly evident throughout this play. Remorse, it must be noted, however, not for the act, but for the method of usurpation. His confessions of the inmost secrets of his soul to the Prince of Wales, have no word of regret for the seizure of the crown.

[1] Part II., Act IV., Scene

As times went there was no room for regret. But
for the hard cruelty to his kinsman Richard, and for
the violent death of that discrowned monarch, for
which he was morally if not legally responsible, remorse and regret manifest themselves plainly.

One last reference to Henry's career, already briefly
alluded to, is to be noted in the lines :

K. Henry. Doth any name particularly belong
      Unto the lodging where I first did swoon ?
War. 'Tis called Jerusalem, my noble lord.
K. Henry. Laud be to heaven ! Even there my life must end.
      It hath been prophesied to me many years
      I should not die but in Jerusalem,
      Which, vainly, I supposed the Holy Land.
      But bear me to that chamber, there I'll lie
      In that Jerusalem shall Harry die.[1]

We remember that the crusades had been a bright
ideal always before Henry Bolingbroke. With such a
pilgrimage he proposed to wash the stains of usurpation from his guilty hands, and after his conquest
of the revolts, the crusades again occurred to him as a
useful means of employing the activity of the barons,
who might otherwise annoy him with further rebellions
at home. The crusades of the fourteenth century, and
thereabouts, were an escape-valve for all sorts of
humours. Kings took the cross to win distinction
against the Turk ; nobles to gain added laurels for
their pennons ; soldiers to push their fortunes ; bank-
rupts to fill their purses ; even beggars drove a good-
lier trade with the palmer's staff.

After the first freshness of the holy wars wore off,

[1] Part II., Act IV., Scene 4.

the chief object of their beginnings was lost sight of. The sepulchre of the world's Redeemer was forgotten, or made the pawn of worldly knights and bishops. All sorts of quarrels were given the dignity of crusades and the privileges of crusaders were awarded to cut-throat swash-bucklers of noble or common name.

That Henry was really stirred to intended service under the Cross, we know from the fact that in the last years of the Greek Empire, when it was hemmed in by the Mohammedan power, its Emperor Manuel visited England to beseech aid for a Christian empire against the enemies of the Cross. He was received and feasted by Henry, who had but just ascended the throne, and under this inspiration the Lancastrian assumed the Cross, although he put off the actual campaign until better times.

Gibbon, in his " Decline and Fall of the Roman Empire," dismisses the event as of no importance, saying that " if the English monarch assumed the Cross, it was only to appease his people, and perhaps his conscience, by the merit or semblance of this pious intention." [1]

Gibbon is not infallible authority on details of the religious motives, and we may give Henry the benefit of the doubt, it being certain that the chroniclers credited him with the intention declared in the beginning, and repeated at the end, of Shakespeare's play, that, had the times permitted he would have fought against Turk and Saracen in the Holy Land. So passed from life one of the strong men who have held the sceptre of England.

[1] Decline and Fall of the Roman Empire, Vol. V., Chap. 66, p. 300.

Whatever his faults of personal ambition, he saw the evil that lay curled about the root of England's noblest development—the feudal system—and struck it such a deadly blow as finally destroyed it. The people first in his reign grew to look upon their king as their natural leader, rather than upon their feudal lords. It was a great step in advance, as transforming England from an aggregation of small camps each clustered about the pennon of some noted baron, into a powerful host under a common commander, to whom was owed supreme homage. One great blot upon this reign is unnoted in the play. Henry IV. was the first English king to put a subject to death for his religious opinions. His father had protected Wyckliffe and the incipient reformers. The son was first of Englishmen to light the torch of religious persecution.

From a contemplation of the decline of feudalism under Henry, we turn to consider one important element in these two plays concerning which, in an historical study, we might seem to have little to say.

I have abstained from touching upon the comedy of the drama for two reasons : First, save in one particular, it has nothing to do with English history ; second, it deserves a chapter entirely devoted to it, as the richest vein of Shakespeare's humour. In one particular, however, Falstaff and his ragged crew have a very vital connection with the phase of English history marked by the passing of feudalism. What Shakespeare always intended to accomplish by the introduction of specific characters, and the grouping of them, we may not be sure. What he did accomplish he that runs may read. There are many theories for the introduction of the comedy of Henry IV. centering about that richest and most unctuous of rogues, Jack Falstaff.

With these, except two, the student need not be troubled.

First, the dramatic materials for two plays were very slender, and as in the foundation play, Falstaff and his friends are used for what is vulgarly called "padding," to extend the plays to the regulation length, while at the same time offering the necessary dramatic contrast of comedy to the blood and brutality of the tragedy— so Shakespeare used them in the two parts of Henry IV. Second, which is equally obvious, although not so generally received : namely, that Falstaff, Pistol, Bardolph, and all their horde of petty followers with loud braggadocio and easily pricked cowardice, are set forth as a travesty upon the highborn but pseudo-chivalry, then on its last legs, and destined soon to pass away entirely. Chivalry had lived its noblest long before. The thing that masqueraded under its name is roughly typified in Falstaff with his shrewd knavery, his animal appetite, his gross trading on the name and title of gentleman ; above all, his self-admitted knowledge that he was in certain important ways a humbug. Hear him, for example, soliloquize on honor.[1] But he is not the arrant coward and time server he would have us believe. He speaks here very much in the spirit of Falconbridge, quoted in the chapter on King John, when he determines to make the "vile commodity" his god. In these words we may read a

---

[1] Part II., Act V., Scene 1.

commentary on the boasted chivalry of the fourteenth
century. It was a painted simulacrum of the fair
original.[1]

Observe too the attitude of Prince Hal toward these
"lewd fellows of the baser sort," with whom he found
his lot cast for a while. The careful reader of these
plays will readily note that while the wild Prince was
often in Eastcheap Tavern, he was never of it. He
is banished by his own restlessness from the solemn
ceremonies of his father's court. He has no part nor
lot with his eminently proper and respectable brothers.
He seeks in dissipation, which it will be noted is
never more than reckless and indifferent, never vile,
the change such natures amidst such surroundings
have ever sought; more's the pity. But he looks on
the antics of his pot-room companions with a heavy
heart and forced smile, valuing them, and through
them the shams they represent in higher quarters, at
their true worth.

In proof of this attitude of the Prince the whole of
Act V. might be quoted.

Great are the misgivings with which his accession
to the throne is greeted. The poet cleverly adds to

---

[1] While Shakespeare was thus occupied in satirizing the English chivalry
of this period, Cervantes was putting forth his immortal travesty of middle-
age knight-errantry in the adventures of Don Quixote. And Francia Sac-
chetti, the Italian, quoted by Dr. Burckhardt in the *Renaissance in Italy*,
wrote toward the end of the fourteenth century, "Every one saw how all
the work people, down to the bakers, how all the woolcarders, usurers,
money-changers, and blackguards of all descriptions, became knights.
. . . How art thou sunken, unhappy dignity! Of all the long list of
knightly duties, what single ones do these knights of ours discharge? I
wish to speak of these things, that the reader may see that knighthood
is dead."

this apprehension by picturing the puffed-up joy of Falstaff, as he contemplates the elevation of his tavern companion to a throne :

What, is the old king dead? . . . Away, Bardolph: saddle my horse : Master Robert Shallow, choose what office thou wilt in the land, it is thine. Pistol, I will double charge thee with dignities. . . . I know the young king is sick for me. Let me take any man's horse : the laws of England are at my commandment. Happy are they which have been my friends, and woe unto my Lord Chief Justice.[1]

This same Lord Chief Justice, so the tradition runs, had committed the young Prince for some fault, and had been assaulted by him. Certainly Falstaff and his cronies were joyous in the hope that their enemy, the law of the land, impersonated in its chief administrator, would suffer by the changing of kings.

"Let vultures vile seize on his lungs also," is the comment of Poins.

Meanwhile at court there are long faces and heavy sighs. Doubtless for his own purposes, Shakespeare has painted in the dark shadows of the young Prince's character with a free hand, and there is warrant in all the chronicles for a certain degree of wildness and profligacy. The old play hints at this, and Shakespeare enlarges upon it for two reasons: first, to lay in a background for the artistic working out of a finer character for his chief hero—chief of all his heroes— and second, to give a more delicate shading to his comedy scenes.

But wild, Prince Hal was, and the Lord Chief Justice

[1] Part II., Act V., Scene 3.

was quite justified, from what he knew of his future king, in saying to the sympathetic Warwick :

> I would his majesty had called me with him,
> The service that I truly did his life,
> Hath left me open to all injuries.[1]

The general feeling that Henry V. will be ruled by tavern ministers, is voiced in the spiteful speech of his brother Clarence :

> Well, you must now speak, Sir John Falstaff fair,
> Which swims against your stream of quality.[2]

The new king, upon whom the " gorgeous garment majesty sits not so easy," is well aware of this feeling against him, and speedily answers it in a way that sends joy chasing the care from noble cheeks and brows.

> Brothers, you mix your sadness with some fear.
> This is the English, not the Turkish court.
> Not Amurath an Amurath succeeds,
> But Harry, Harry.[3]

This was good news, for Amurath the Turk signalized his accession to the throne by butchering the friends and relations of the preceding monarch and all who could be possible successors of himself. One by one the young king addresses and wins his court. His brothers, his barons, even the chief justice, whom he mischievously keeps upon the rack a moment, only to

[1] Part II., Act V., Scene 2.   [2] Ibid.   [3] Ibid.

release him with higher honors than he had yet worn,
all are made to see the truth of the wild heir's words :

> Let me but bear your love, I'll bear your cares.
>
> .   .   .   .
>
>   I survive
> To mock the expectation of the world,
> To frustrate prophecies.[1]

To the astonishment of the realm, nobles, and people,
the wild Prince Hal is transformed into the buoyant,
hopeful, splendid king, under whose rule England sang
her supremest song of triumph as a nation for many
a day.   Even Falstaff fell, and in his fall lies the one
stain, or apparent stain, upon the dramatic character
of Henry V.   The scene seems cruel in which he renounces and exiles the man who had been his resource
for wit and sympathy in the arid days of banishment
from court.   It is pathetic, the eager, turbulent, boastful haste with which the fat old knight scrambled to
throw himself in Henry's way.

> My king ! my jove ! I speak to thee, my heart.[2]

The king's scornful reply even did not penetrate the
thick crust of his well-grounded conceit :

> I know thee not, old man : fall to thy prayers,
> How ill white hairs become a fool and jester.
> I have long dreamed of such a kind of man,
> So surfeit swelled, so old and so profane :
> But being awake I do despise my dream.
>
> .   .   .   .

---

[1] Part II., Act V., Scene 2.   [2] Part II., Act V., Scene 5.

HENRY V.

The Famous Victories of Henry V., Containing the Honorable Battell of Agincourt, last half, afforded Shakespeare a slight groundwork for this play as for the preceding. Hall's Chronicle is the principal source of its history, however, and for the comedy Shakespeare is entirely responsible.

The date of this play is (probably) the middle of the year 1599. The only copy of it printed in the author's lifetime was a miserably imperfect and garbled one, which was surreptitiously published, made up from notes taken in the theatre during a performance.

It was first published, complete and unmarred, in the First Folio.

CHRONOLOGY OF HENRY V.

1413. Henry crowned upon the death of his father. He allays still further the domestic troubles of the kingdom by reconciling to his cause the young Earl of March, and the Percy family.

1414-15. France distracted by internal feuds. Charles VI., the king, subject to fits of insanity. Government carried on by his brother, Louis of Orleans, and his cousin, John of Burgundy, who were bitter rivals. Henry V. takes advantage of this state of affairs to make extravagant demands upon France, embracing certain provinces, the hand of the Princess Katharine, a large sum of money—finally the crown itself, in right of his descent from Edward III.

1415. These terms rejected, Henry determines to invade France. A domestic conspiracy is discovered between the Earl of Cambridge, Lord Scrope, and Sir Thomas Grey, in behalf of the claims of the young Earl of March, to the throne (although probably without his knowledge). Conspirators arrested and executed. Henry and his army lay siege to Harfleur, which capitulates September 22d. Henry moves toward Calais, October 8th. Battle of Agincourt, October 25th. Henry returns in triumph to London, November 23d.

1416. France still distracted. Burgundy allies himself with Henry. Desultory warfare.

1417. Henry again lands in France, meeting with small successes.

1418. Burgundy allies himself with the queen-regnant against the Dauphin and the Orleans faction.

1419. Henry and the Burgundy faction have a meeting, but negotiations fail on account of the former's excessive demands. Burgundy makes overtures to the Dauphin, who during a meeting causes the duke to be assassinated. The new

Duke of Burgundy breaks off negotiations with the Dauphin, and brings his party (including the queen and Princess Katharine) to Henry V.'s allegiance.

1420.   Treaty of Troyes (May 21), by which the King of England was to receive the hand of the Princess Katharine ; to be immediate regent of the kingdom; and to be recognized as successor to the crown on the death of Charles VI.

Henry marries Katharine, June 2.

1422.   Henry V. dies.

CHAPTER V.

Sources of the play.—Its epic character.—The use of the chorus.—One great historical event its theme.—The battle of Agincourt.—Events leading up to this triumph of English arms.—The long Franco-English duel.—Internal broils of France at Henry's accession.—Restlessness of the English nobles.—Attitude of the clergy.—Henry's pretentions to the French crown.—The Salic law.—Defiance of the "tennis-balls."— Misinterpretation of the frivolous youth of Henry.—Use made of the comedy element.—Conspiracy of the nobles, "gilt with French gold." —Divided French opinions as to Henry's ability.—The siege and fall of Harfleur.—Catholic make up of the English army.—Henry's with-drawal toward Calais.—The eve of Agincourt.—Hopes and fears of England.—Night scenes before the battle.—Henry among his troops.— The battle of Agincourt and total defeat of the French.—Henry's re-turn to England.—Interregnum of war.—Alliance of Burgundy and England.—Treaty of Troyes.—Henry acknowledged heir of the French crown.—The Dauphin continues desultory war.—Marriage of Henry and Katharine.—Character of Henry as further developed.—A type of England's ideal of royalty—The fallacious glory of foreign conquest.

In the epilogue to Henry IV. we have an indication of the scope of this play. We are promised a cam-paign in France, an introduction to the fair Princess Katharine, and perhaps further escapades with Fal-staff.

The poet fulfils his promises to the letter, save in the latter particular. Of Falstaff we read only con-cerning his death. It is a dramatic touch. The king's old life is dead in the person of his former boon com-panion. The Henry who fares forth with gallant armies to strike at the ancient foe of England is no

longer the Hal who consorted with the amateur high-
waymen of Eastcheap.   The close-fitting crown of his
father, subdued and solemnized, as well as exalted, the
one time roisterer in taverns.   The character of the
prince formerly "neighbored by fruit of baser quality "
growing " like the summer grass, fastest by night " had
been perfected.   With Falstaff passed the shadow from
his career.   We now behold him as the central figure
of a great epic, for epical in its character the play of
Henry V. is, as taken altogether as one production the
whole series is.   We have war now on a grand scale.
No little contention is this between barons, no spear-
thrusting of civil factions; but war in its most glorious
aspect, if war can ever be glorious.   In the chorus
which speaks between the acts of the play, the story
of this war is epitomized and explained.   It is the
first use in these plays of this literary form patterned
after the classic model.   It is used as an interpreter
and illustration of what precedes and follows it.
Chorus paints broadly what the acts and scenes depict
in detail.   It served to whet the appetite of an English audience for the feast of victory and triumph to be
spread before it.

One great and shining historical event is the central
motif of this play—the battle of Agincourt—fit successor to English arms, of Cressy and Poitiers.

The play summarizes in dramatic clearness, and
with much historic faithfulness, both the events that
led up to this point, and the results which flowed from
it.

England and France had long been rivals.   The
duello between the two great powers was perennially

taking active form. By the treaty of Edward III.,
after Cressy, a truce had been patched up, unsatisfac-
tory because insincere. The fatal persistence of English kings in claiming foreign provinces since the time
of King John, kept hot and feverish the terms of
peace between the two countries. When Henry V.
came to his throne in 1413, France was rent asunder
by internal broils. Two great parties strove for the
mastery, the king's party and that of the Duke of
Burgundy. The king was insane; his wife not quite
capable of dealing with great affairs ; the Dauphin, or
heir-apparent, a young man, liable to be influenced by
the factions which divided his future heritage, and held
in check by a partisan, the Count Armagnac.

As if this were not enough for the unhappy people
of France to face and deal with, a claim is put forth
by Henry V. of England for the throne, in right of
inheritance from Edward III.

Shakespeare discusses the question of Henry's right
to the French crown in a very learned and apparently
satisfactory manner :

> His true title to some certain dukedoms,
> And generally to the crown and seat of France,
> Derived from Edward his great grandfather.[1]

But the claim seems really to have been a shallow one.
By the treaty of Edward III. England was entitled to
certain possessions in France, notably the duchy of
Normandy, and Touraine, the earldoms of Anjou and
Maine, and the duchy of Brittany ; but the treaty had
never been fulfilled ; England had been actually de-

[1] Act I., Scene 1.

frauded of the spoils of war granted under that treaty, and these were the provinces to which Henry V. had some show of right to lay claim. But these did not constitute a shadow of a right to the crown itself. Indeed Henry did not at first—before the campaign preceding Agincourt—pretend to the throne, although he made a vague renewal of the old claim of Edward III., which was scouted. He then demanded these provinces only. But with them he made some extra territorial requests which were sure to arouse the ire of the French, namely, the hand of Katharine in marriage and two millions of crowns hard cash.

We quote here the careful historian, Knight: "The French Government consented to give up all the ancient territories of Aquitaine and to marry the daughter of Charles VI. to Henry, with a dowry of six hundred thousand crowns, afterwards increased to eight hundred thousand, . . . and the demand of Henry for the cession of Normandy, Maine, and Anjou was rejected. The French then sent an embassy to England, when Henry demanded Normandy, and all the territories ceded by the peace of Bretigny, under the threat that he would otherwise take arms to enforce his claim to the crown of France."[1] This was the state of affairs when the play opens, early in the year 1414.

France was broken in two by factional broils. The hated English were looking on with greedy and ambitious eyes. Henry V. was the centre of interest. What would he do? To understand the king's position we may revert to the previous play, and quote

---

[1] Knight's History of England, Vol. II., Ch. 1., p. 17.

again the wise words of Bolingbroke on his death-bed,
to the son who was to succeed him :

> Yet though thou standest more sure than I could do,
> Thou art not firm enough, since griefs are green.
> And all my friends, whom thou must make thy friends,
> Have but their stings and teeth newly ta'en out,
> By whose fell working I was first advanced,
> And by whose power I well might lodge a fear
> To be again displaced. Which to avoid
> I cut them off; and had a purpose now
> To lead out many to the Holy Land,
> Lest rest, and lying still, might make them look
> Too near unto my state. Therefore, my Harry,
> Be it thy course to busy giddy minds
> With foreign quarrels.[1]

The nobles about Henry's court were, as ever, restless.
War was their chief delight, their prime occupation.
The playful description of Hotspur's appetite for
strife in the previous play is hardly exaggerated from
the real attitude of the English soldier, noble, and
man-at-arms of the times. "I am not of Percy's
mind," cries Hal, who was so like to Percy afterward
in the craving for battle, "I am not of Percy's mind,
the Hotspur of the north ; he that kills me some six
or seven dozen Scots at a breakfast, washes his hands
and says to his wife, 'Fie upon this quiet life, I want
work.' 'O, my sweet Harry,' says she, 'how many
hast thou killed to-day?' 'Give my roan horse a
drench,' says he, and answers an hour after, 'some
fourteen; a trifle, a trifle.'"[2] The characteristic of

---

[1] Henry IV., Part II., Act IV., Scene 4.
[2] Henry IV., Part I., Act II., Scene 4.

the brawny Englishman, whose idea of amusement is
said to be to go out and kill something, has a bit of
historic truth in it. Certainly the lords who were
gathered about the young King Henry were pining for
the smell of blood and the clash of arms. Failing in
this as against their foreign enemies, they were sure
to find some cause for buckling on the sword at home.
Bolingbroke's advice was in the line of broad statesmanship, and Henry the Fifth was fully aware of its
value. The failure of France, due, perhaps, largely to
her own internal trouble, to keep the truce of Bretigny,
was reason, or at least occasion, for the busying of
giddy minds with foreign quarrels. Already treason
was hatching, centering in the pretension of the young
Earl of March to the throne, although Henry had released him from prison, and he himself was not moving in the matter.

And now the king found an unexpected spur given
to his warlike plans. The attitude of the clergy of his
realm was in his favor. It must be remembered that
we are reading of the days of John Huss (1415) and
the Council of Constance (1414). The stirrings of
Reformation were troubling the peace of the Church.
The state, its stout ally, and often obedient servant,
was looking curiously and enviously into the enormous
and well-filled treasuries of bishop and abbot. In the
previous reign a bill had been proposed in Parliament
which would have passed,

> But that the scambling and unquiet time
> Did push it out of further question.[1]

[1] Act I., Scene 1.

And this bill, the Archbishop of Canterbury com-
plains to the Bishop of Ely in the opening scene of
this play,

> If it pass against us,
> We lose the better half of our possession.
> For all the temporal lands which men devout
> By testament have given to the Church,
> Would they strip from us.[1]

This was not only drinking deep, but drinking cup
and all, as Canterbury puts it. There must be something done, for this self-same bill is now proposed
again. It was to the interest of the Churchmen that
Henry and his restless nobles should be occupied
abroad. Anything seemed a noble quest that would
seek quarry elsewhere than in the Church. The one
thing lacking to, and needed by, Henry in his foreign
wars was money. It were better

> to give a greater sum,
> Than ever at one time, the clergy yet
> Did to his predecessors part withal,[2]

than to lose forever half their estates. But more than
this did the clever Churchmen do for the foreign wars.
They succeeded in making them not only respectable
but obligatory upon the conscience of the king.

It is not at all certain that Henry was over-con-
scientious in the matter of pushing pike and exchang-
ing shots with his insane royal brother across the
Channel. Hudson's eulogy of Henry's motives and
scruples here is altogether strained.[3] It is the fault of

---

[1] Act I., Scene 1.   [2] Ibid.
[3] Hudson's Life Art and Characters, Vol. II., p. 124.

even the best of critics, and Hudson ranks as one of
the best, to see no faults in their heroes. That Henry
was glad to have the voice of the Church on his side
goes without saying ; that he would have stayed his
purpose without it, we may doubt.

The argument of the chorus in Scene 2 of Act I. is
appropriately used by the dramatist to mark the fact
that Henry must have presented his claims to France
in a formal and legal document. It reads in the play
like the result of a lawyer's struggle to embalm his
brief in blank verse.

The stumbling-block is the Salic law, which barred
inheritance through the female line, and Henry's claim,
if any just claim he had, was through Isabella, Queen
of Edward II., daughter of the French Philip the Fair,
from whom he was fourth in direct descent. Isabella's
two brothers both died. The crown fell, under the
provisions of the Salic law, to Charles, the younger
brother of Philip, and his descendant was now upon
the throne.

The apostrophe to the Archbishop of Canterbury to
beware of wresting the truth in order to establish the
English claim to French sovereignty, is one of those
fine bursts of eloquence with which the whole play is
charged, and which Shakespeare delighted to put in
the mouth of the favorite hero.

> And God forbid, my good and faithful lord,
> That you should fashion, wrest, or bow your reading,
> Or nicely charge your understanding soul
> With opening title miscreate, whose right
> Suits not in native colors with the truth :
> For God doth know how many now in health

Shall drop their blood in approbation
Of what your reverence shall incite us to.
Therefore take heed how you impawn our person
How you awake our sleeping sword of war.[1]

It must be noted here, in behalf of the truth of history,
that those who take their history from Shakespeare
should have before them in this and like passages the
large and broad conception the poet had of poetic
license. There is nothing on record to cause us to
think that Henry V. was more conscientious in his
international policy than other rulers before and after
him. All that Hudson draws his inference from, such
as this and similar speeches; his thanksgiving to God
for victory ; his *Non nobis* and *Te Deum* after Agincourt ;
might be paralleled in the career of most monarchs of
those days. Religious phrases were very current, not
as cant but as familiar daily speech. The Church of
the pre-Reformation period was the most real of all
institutions to an Englishman. A man was a Christian as he was a citizen. The king in this play is no
more conspicuously pious than the majority of people.
There is a grace and tenderness about the poet's favorite conception of the kingly character, and a glamour
upon the page which portrays him to us. But history
is one thing and poetry another. Henry was a manly
prince, noble and generous, and after the fashion of his
age pious; but we need not be called upon to believe
that he was endowed with any supernatural qualities.

The Salic law is reasoned away by the learned
Archbishop in a clever manner.[2] The argument is a

---

[1] Act I., Scene 2.   [2] Ibid.

puzzling one. Even Courtenay, the most painstaking of delvers, gives up its solution. We need not attempt to unravel it, briefly quoting a few lines of the ingenious Churchman's explanation:

> The land Salique is in Germany,
> Between the floods of Sala and the Elbe;
> Where Charles the Great, having subdued the Saxons,
> There left behind and settled certain French,
> Who, holding in disdain the German women
> For some dishonest manners of their life,
> Established then this law: to wit, no female
> Should be inheritrix in Salique land;
> Which Salique, as I said, 'twixt Elbe and Sala,
> Is at this day in German called Meisen.[1]

Henry is easily convinced by all this array of facts and inferences that the Salic law was not a bar to his just claims. The conviction was borne in upon him with the sanction and express commission of the Church. The Old Testament is quoted in behalf of "unwinding the bloody flag."[2] There is another obstacle, however, an obstacle often in England's way, the fear of a Scotch invasion. Says the king:

> For you shall read that my great-grandfather
> Never went with his forces into France
> But the Scot on his unfurnished kingdom
> Came pouring like the tide into a breach.
> With ample and brimfulness of his force,
> Galling the gleaned land with hot essays,
> Girding with grievous siege castles and towns.

---

[1] Act I., Scene 2. [2] Numbers xxvii. 8.

Westmoreland drops into ancient and poetical tradition :

> But there's a saying, very old and true :
> "If that you will France win,
> Then with Scotland first begin." [1]

The ingenious archbishop once more comes to the res-
cue in these puzzled counsels, and in one of the famous passages of the play delivers his parable of the
bees, the moral of which is that the state is divided,
like a swarm of bees, into different classes with divers
functions, therefore :

> Divide you happy England into four,
> Whereof you take one quarter into France,
> And you withal shall make all Gallia shake.
> If we, with thrice such powers left at home,
> Cannot defend our own doors from the dog,
> Let us be worried. [2]

The king now resolves upon the war, and having prepared himself by argument, and what was of more
importance, with the sinews of war furnished by the
large gift of the clergy, he receives an embassy from
the French court.

In all this was Henry more ambitious than conscientious? Shakespeare hints at the former while declaring the latter :

> France being ours, we'll bend it to our awe,
> Or break it all to pieces :   .   .   .
>
> .   .   .   .
> Either our history shall with full mouth
> Speak freely of our acts : or our grave

---

[1] Act I., Scene 2.   [2] Ibid.

Like Turkish mute, shall have a tongueless mouth,
Not worshipped with a waxen epitaph.[1]

Here speaks the proud ambitious monarch. So far,
and not to his discredit relatively, he was a product of
his times.

He meets the French embassy, and in this meeting
the poet cleverly pictures how the Nemesis of Henry,
in the shape of ghosts from his wild youth, rise up
now to check his pride. At home and among his own
people these ghosts had faded away. The wild prince
was forgotten in the gallant king. But his reputation abroad had yet to be cleansed of the stains that
marked the Falstaffian period. In answer to his claims
upon the French crown, the ambassador of Charles
VI. says bluntly and somewhat indiscreetly :

The prince our master
Says that you savor too much of your youth,
And bids you be advised there's naught in France
That can be with a nimble galliard won :
You cannot revel into dukedoms there.[2]

And forthwith presents the astonished and offended
king with a set of tennis-balls as a more appropriate
occupation for his talents. This episode of the tennis-
balls is taken from the old play, whence it was adopted
from the Chronicles.

Henry acknowledges the bitter mockery and returns
a manly reply :

And we understand him well,
How he comes o'er us with our wilder days
Not measuring what use we made of them.

.   .   .   .

[1] Act I., Scene 2.   [2] Ibid.

10

But tell the dauphin I will keep my state,
Be like a king and show my sail of greatness
When I do rouse me in my throne of France.

.   .   .   .

And tell the pleasant prince this mock of his
Hath turned his balls to gun-stones : and his soul
Shall stand sore charged for the wasteful vengeance
That shall fly with them.

.   .   .   .   .   .

His jest shall savor but of shallow wit
When thousands weep more than do laugh at it?[1]

With Act II., warned by the chorus, we are brought
now to look upon the seamy side of the English court.
A conspiracy is brooding, and although Shakespeare
makes no mention of the actual cause, sufficiently indicating his idea that the conspirators were " gilt with
French gold "—the real occasion for it doubtless was
some attempt to unseat Harry in favor of the Earl of
March, who, whether knowing to the scheme or not,
was now a trusted officer in the royal army.

On the threshold of his French campaign the king
is thus reminded of the words of his dying father, that
the wounds of his own usurpation were yet green, and
the stings but newly taken out.   Scene 2 of Act II.,
reveals the unravelling of the conspiracy against the
king's life, showing that French intrigue had much to
do with it, but personal ambition more.   Henry's address to the guilty nobles, especially to Lord Scroop,
is most affecting :

Thou that didst bear the key of all my counsels,
That knewest the very bottom of my soul,
That almost mightst have coined me into gold,

[1] Act I., Scene 2.

Wouldst thou have practised on me for thy use?
May it be possible that foreign hire
. Could out of thee extract one spark of evil
That might annoy my finger?[1]

But the whole evil of this transaction lay not in the single fact of a conspiracy, discovered in time and its purpose headed off. It must have to an extent unsettled the minds of those who were loyal and faithful and devoted to their king's interest, making them suspicious even of each other and fearful of what treason might fall out. The poet intimates this in the sad words of Henry, in this same address:

> Such, and so finely bolted didst thou seem,
> And thus thy fall hath left a kind of blot,
> To mark the full-fraught man and best indued,
> With some suspicion.[2]

However, the conspiracy once exposed and its members executed, the king drops all thought of domestic troubles, trusting in a large way to the general good faith in his people, the exciting pleasures of a popular war, and the high hopes of a great victory to settle all internal broils. Now:

> Cheerily to sea the signs of war advance,
> No King of England, if not King of France.[3]

With this watchword Henry set forth from Southampton in the midsummer of 1415.

We may pause here to notice the use of the comedy element in this play, in so far as it illustrates the his-

---

[1] Act II., Scene 2. [2] Ibid. [3] Ibid.

toric situation. It is distinctly lower comedy in one
set of characters and higher in another, than that
which centred about Falstaff in Henry IV. The old
knight's companions are all in these wars, and represent the attitude of the rascal element of England's
population toward the warlike spirit of England's king.

> Now all the youth of England are on fire,
> And silken dalliance in the wardrobe lies.[1]

But what of Nym, Pistol, and Bardolph? They, too,
are all on fire. There is a stir in the tavern parlor.
There is a bringing out of rusty swords, a shaking out
of stained armor. "We'll be all three sworn brothers
in France,"[2] in spite of quarrels and grudges at home.
But not I fancy because "honor's thought reigns solely
in the breast of every man."[3] Pistol will go so far as
to pay his debts, though he is of the opinion "Base is
the slave that pays."

> For I shall sutler be
> Unto the camp, and profits will accrue.[4]

And cries again:

> Let us to France, like horse-leeches, my boys,
> To suck, . . . the very blood to suck.[5]

The war was thus approved by the stained brava-
does. There was nothing to lose, and possibly much
to gain. They could afford to dissolve ancient
grudges, knowing each other's rascal nature, and the
advantage of union in a common cause. We may not

---

[1] Chorus to Act II.   [2] Act II., Scene 1.   [3] Chorus to Act II.
[4] Act II., Scene 1.   [5] Act II., Scene 3.

say there was not some lagging sense of loyalty to the king. Many have the finer feelings deeply encrusted with sordid actions. Perhaps, on the whole, the philosophic Gower sums up this phase of English life as aptly as could be, in discoursing of ancient Pistol with his friend Fluellan :

Why, 'tis a gull, a fool, a rogue, that now and then goes to the wars to grace himself at his return into London under the form of a soldier. And such fellows are perfect in the great commanders' names. And they will learn you by rote where great services were done : at such and such a sconce, at such a breach, at such a convoy : who came off bravely, who was shot, who disgraced, what terms the enemy stood on : and this they can perfectly in the phrase of war, which they trick up with new-tuned oaths : and what a beard of the general's cut and a horrid suit of the camp will do among foaming bottles and ale-washed wits, is wonderful to be thought on.[1]

Meanwhile in France there are searchings of heart, but under the influence of an impression that Henry is to be lightly esteemed on account of his wild days, there is no movement to heal internal divisions.

Shakespeare does not attempt to follow accurately the real embassies that passed between the two kingdoms any more than he professes to give the actual words that were spoken. And there is no need, for purposes of gathering the true spirit of the history of those times, that we should seek to identify occasions. In the scene in the French king's palace,[2] Burgundy is represented as being present. But he was at this very time hostile to the king, and the active enemy of the Orleans party, of which the king was nominal head.

---

[1] Act III., Scene 6. [2] Act II., Scene 4.

The duke did, however, send troops to the aid of his king, at first, to repel English invasion. He considered it patriotic and politic. Afterward, as we shall see, he withdrew his aid, and even joined forces with the English. This scene is valuable as noting the existence of two parties among the French, the one despising, the other estimating at their full value, the worth of English armies.

The old king in one of his fits of sanity urges :

> To line and new repair our towns of war
> With men of courage and with means defendant :
> For England his approaches makes, as fierce
> As waters to the sucking of a gulf.[1]

The Dauphin barely grants that " the sick and feeble parts of France " should be looked to, and scorns any serious show of fear :

> No, with no more than if we heard that England
> Were busied with a Whitsun morris-dance,
> For, my good liege, she is so idly kinged
> Her sceptre so fantastically borne
> By a vain, giddy, shallow, humorous youth,
> That fear attends her not.[2]

The king is mindful of the past, as well he might be. He knows the strain of blood in Henry is the same

> That haunted us in our familiar paths,
> Witness our too much memorable shame,
> When Cressy battle fatally was struck.
>
> .   .   .   .   .   .
>
> This is a stem of that victorious stock.[3]

---

[1] Act II. Scene 4.   [2] Ibid.   [3] Ibid.

But the Dauphin's mind was the mind of all young France, and fatally young France paid for it.

We are next before Harfleur. The chorus that introduces the third act is a rare example of poetic genius dealing with otherwise dry details. Dr. Johnson could see nothing in this introduction of the chorus but a clumsy device. We wonder how he could have failed to perceive both its use and beauty, especially this one and that in Act IV.

We are now greeted by the noble strain :

> Once more unto the breach, dear friends, once more,
> Or close the wall up with our English dead ; [1]

a strain unworn by constant quotation, unhackneyed by trite allusions. Like the splendid harmonies of a master-musician it throbs and thrills us as we read, in spite of the déclamations of the school-room and the parsing exercises of childhood.

Harfleur was not won offhand. For more than a month the English army battered at its walls, undermined its towers, lay leech-like in its trenches, sucking its life-blood. In vain the besieged looked for relief. It never came. France was distracted in her head and members. Factions were warring with each other, while a populous city begged in vain for help against the common foe.

Harfleur fell, and Henry gave thanks for the victory in the church of St. Martin, which he entered barefoot and in humility. His position was a curious one. By his own profession he appeared to the French people not as a destroying conqueror who sought their dis-

---

[1] Act III., Scene 1.

tress, but as a faithful sovereign, shuddering at the civil dissensions of Burgundians and Orleanists. He presented himself as the savior of France, her rightful king, protecting her from her erring and quarrelsome sons.

But with the conquest of Harfleur Henry found himself in desperate straits. His army had wasted away by fevers, by wounds, by death. It was a costly victory he had won. He might hold the city for a time, but to what advantage? It seemed as though he must go back to England with his reduced army, with little booty and no glory, save that of storming and carrying a town he could not hold. He was urged by the fainthearted to return at once by sea. A few days would restore the army to its home. A few hours' journey by sea would take them out of the toils into which they had so gallantly plunged, and place them again in the silken dalliance they loved. But Henry saw not affairs so. He was urged to another course, both by personal pride and the sure and certain knowledge of how frail a hold upon the throne his would be, did he fail now to satisfy the English thirst for glory and foreign conquest. He would not yield to the cry of his council to return. He determined to march to Calais. Just what the king expected to gain by this march, history does not tell. It was not that he expected or wanted the pitched battle which was the actual result of this campaign. Probably it was a leap in the dark, a trusting to Providence, and, as the old chronicler writes, "relying upon the divine grace and the righteousness of his cause, piously considering that victory does not consist in multitudes." Action of some sort was demanded of him, and whether his course was prudently taken, it was justified in its result. Like the charge at Balaklava its rashness was forgotten in its success, and its tentative foolishness in its practical wisdom, as events fell out.

So Harfleur is left behind, and the weakened and at times discouraged army set forth amid clouds of darkness. They saw nothing before them but a dangerous journey with an uncertain end. But before them was a glory that paled not before any after-achievement of English arms. Shakespeare is here again the interpreter of that thought with which all these English plays are charged; that kings are but pawns and knights but common men, in the great sweep of national movements. As none could look forward from Harfleur to Agincourt, so none from the bright glories of Henry's triumphant fields could perceive the clouds hanging low over England in the reign of his son.

We may examine here the other and different side of the comedy element of this play, which we have noted as being of a higher character than that in the two parts of Henry IV. The Nym, Pistol, and Bardolph coterie is contrasted with that of Fluellen, Macmorris, and Jamy, petty officers in the royal army. These add a lighter vein to the story while not dropping to the vulgar level of Eastcheap. But as *dramatis personæ* they have an historical significance also, in indicating the catholic make-up of the English ranks. Fluellen is a Welshman, and perhaps had fought against the king's father under the irregular and wild Glendower. Macmorris is an Irishman, one of those " rug-headed kerns," possibly, against whom the English sovereigns were perpetually making campaigns, as in Richard II.'s time. Jamy is a canny Scotchman, and the Scotch, as the beginning of this play sufficiently indicates, were always in a state of revolt. And yet here they were together, weaving the feather, the shamrock, and the thistle into one common emblem against the common foe. It was significant of the growing solidarity of the English people emerging from the petty statecraft of feudalism. It was significant of the growing homogeneousness of the English people, by whatever local name they might be called. It was a fulfilment of the prophecy of Bolingbroke's last words, that occupation for a common glorious cause abroad must tend more than anything else to prevent the breaking out of small revolts against the house of Lancaster at home. It is true that the most savage of civil wars was yet to come, but the catholic comprehension of Henry V.'s army before Harfleur and at Agincourt were symbolic of that oneness of national purpose which was to close the wounds of civil war with the death of the last Plantagenet, never again to be reopened for reasons of state. For after Bosworth field the internal feuds of England were theological and ecclesiastical in their inception, not civil.

On the march now toward Calais; the poet noting from time to time by alternate scenes from the French and English head-quarters, the state of feeling, the hopes and fears, the boastings and brave words of both. "God of battles," cries the Constable of France,

> Where have they this mettle?
> Is not their climate foggy, raw, and dull?
> On whom, as in despite, the sun looks pale.[1]

[1] Act III., Scene 5.

And yet he accurately estimates the bedraggled condition of the English troops:

> Sorry am I his numbers are so few,
> His soldiers sick and famished in the march;
> For I am sure when he shall see our army
> He'll drop his heart into the sink of fear.[1]

And to speak truth, the French brag and bluster had a strong basis whereon to flourish. Henry's army was in a desperate strait. Still it marched on as soldiers march who believe in their leader. And Harry's troops believed in him, although he lacked no discipline, and punished offences among his own men in a way that boded ill for his enemies.

Anent which we come once more, and for the last time, across the rogue Bardolph. Fluellen addresses the king, who has asked him what the losses were among his soldiers: "Marry, for my part I think the Duke hath lost never a man but one that is like to be executed for robbing a church, one Bardolph, if your majesty know the man: his face is all bubukles and welks and knobs and flames of fire: and his lips plough at his nose."[2]

So the poet used the historic fact of a man's stealing a pyx, recorded by the chroniclers, to speed the prince's former companion to a fitting end.

With the chorus to the Fourth Act we join the rival camps on the eve of Agincourt.

> Now entertain conjecture of a time
> When creeping murmur and the poring dark
> Fills the wide vessel of the universe.

[1] Act III., Scene 5.   [2] Act III., Scene 6.

> From camp to camp, through the foul womb of night,
> The hum of either army stilly sounds.[1]

In the English camp there is realization of great impending danger: "The greater therefore should our courage be," cries the king.

> There is some soul of goodness in things evil,
> Would men observingly distil it out,
> For our bad neighbor makes us early stirrers,
> Which is both healthful and good husbandry.[2]

But Henry does not confine himself to encouraging the leaders:

> For forth he goes and visits all his hosts,
> Bids them good-morrow with a modest smile,
> And calls them brothers, friends, and countrymen.[3]

And as he talks now to this one, now that, the bragging Pistol, the sententious Fluellen, the king uncovers in a modest, noble way that which must be the grief of great men, on whom lesser men depend: "I think the king is but a man as I am: the violet smells to him as it doth to me; the element shows to him as it doth to me; all his senses have but human conditions; his ceremonies laid by, in his nakedness he appears but a man; and though his affections are higher mounted than ours, yet when they stoop they stoop with the like wing."[4]

Again, in protest against the common habit of laying all sins at the king's door, especially the death of

---

[1] Chorus to Act IV.   [2] Act IV., Scene 1.
[3] Chorus to Act IV.   [4] Act IV., Scene 1.

soldiers in battle, he protests, unknown to the common soldier with whom he holds the conversation:

> The king is not bound to answer the particular endings of his soldiers; the father of his son; nor the master of his servant; for they purpose not their death when they purpose their services.[1]

But while he makes the protest he realizes of how little weight it is:

> Upon the king, let us our lives, our souls,
> Our debts, our careful wives,
> Our children and our sins, lay on the king.
> We must bear all.
> O hard condition. Twin-born with greatness.
>
> . . . .
>
> What infinite heart's ease must kings neglect
> That private men enjoy.[2]

So with preparations in prayer, and masses, and restless sleep, and reliance upon God and king, the English camp awaits the dawn soberly, quietly, grimly, in patience and with hope.

The Frenchmen, on the other hand, are not like-minded. They infallibly believe in their success on the morrow. They even grieved that the English were so few, as it would tend to taint the glory of their arms.

> There is not work enough for all our hands,
> Scarce blood enough in all their sickly veins,
> To give each naked curtle-axe a stain.[3]

The night is passed in revelry, dice-throwing for the morrow's ransoms, boastful longings for the rising

---

[1] Act IV., Scene 1. [2] Ibid. [3] Act IV., Scene 3.

sun. The truth is somewhat distorted here, although the spirit of the scene is well preserved. The French were confident and full of braggadocio. They had a genuine contempt for their adversary, based perhaps upon a knowledge of how weak the Harfleur campaign had left him. But Shakespeare, in his whole treatment of the French side here, as afterward in Henry VI., shows a too strong patriotic bias to be entirely fair. It was the cue of the Elizabethan playwright to belittle and besmirch both France and Spain. The shillings of the groundlings rolled in more merrily to such tunes. But this provincial spirit is fatal to art. True, our poet but copied the chronicles. But as poet and artist he should here, as elsewhere, notably in King John and Henry VIII., have decanted the spirit and left the old wine bottles out of sight. We must decide that in his handling of the French attitude in this play he was the Englishman before he was the artist—a grave fault, yet forced upon him to an extent by the limitation of his age.

The shock of arms and Agincourt is over. An accidental meeting, not a preordained pitched battle, it reflected the highest glory on the English arms, and, in its effects, pitched the highest note of England's greatest song of warlike triumph in any age.

The march was resumed to Calais, and late in October Henry landed in England, the idolized monarch of a great people, every man of whom who had remained at home regretted it bitterly; while every soldier who returned found free quarters on all sides and a welcome on all lips.

The humility of the king's *Non nobis* and *Te Deum*

found slight echo in the towns and villages of England. Unto Henry and themselves was the chief glory and the great renown. "His bruised helmet and his bended sword" were far more thought of than his humble "Not unto us but unto God."

There is an interregnum now of two years, during which affairs in France go from bad to worse. The Emperor Sigismund occupied himself in making an empty effort to secure terms of advantageous peace between his royal brothers of England and France.

Burgundy carried on a desultory war with the Orleans or Armagnac faction. Brigandage, on a greater or less scale, ravaged the fair country of France from end to end. Charles VI. was crazy most of the time, of which advantage is taken by the hostile duke. Henry V. lands once more on foreign soil and proceeds to the final conquest of his ancient enemy. Burgundy turns traitor to his king and makes alliance with the English. Henry, pushing on from one success to another, occupies a large slice of French territory. The Count of Armagnac has in his control the young Dauphin : but Burgundy seizes the French queen, and wrests from her an appointment as governor-general of the realm. Burgundy, forgetting his alliance with Henry, was setting up, as ruler of France, his court at Paris; the Dauphin's was at Poitiers.

Henry besieges and reduces the great city of Rouen, whose inhabitants vainly looked for help from both the French leaders, who assumed to be the legitimate heads of government.

Events now marched with rapid step. Burgundy and the queen seek an alliance with Henry. It was broken off. Then the Dauphin seeks a reconciliation with Burgundy. It is proceeding favorably, when suddenly the young prince treacherously kills the duke. All hope of alliance between the French parties is now at an end. Philip the Good, son of the slain Duke of Burgundy, at once assumes his father's place and seeks out Henry of England. He ultimately brings the king and queen of unhappy France, and their chief supporters to a meeting with Henry V. and his nobles. This is at Troyes in Champagne. The Dauphin and his claims are disregarded. It is here, and after these stirring events, that Shakespeare, in Scene 2 of Act V., brings us face to face with his dramatic puppets.

It will be noticed that he passes over all allusion to the death of the elder Burgundy and carries on the story as though he were dealing with the personage of that name who figures in previous acts. It is, however, with his son Philip the Good, Duke of Burgundy we have now to do. There is a marriage in the air and peace in prospect. Henry demands his terms like a merchant, and insists upon them like a usurer. He listens to Burgundy's pathetic picture of poor France "losing both beauty and utility," and replies with the assurance of one who holds the cards of fate:

> If, Duke of Burgundy, you would the peace
> Whose want gives growth to the imperfections
> Which you have cited, you must buy that peace
> With full accord to all our just demands.[1]

With these terms and just demands we are already familiar. Henry abates no jot or tittle of the claims for

[1] Act V., Scene 2.

which he had "let loose the dogs of war." *First*, he will have Katharine to his wife. *Second*, he will be regent of the kingdom of France during the king's life; and *third*, he will receive the crown as his own upon the king's decease. This was the famous treaty of Troyes. The legal heir to the throne is entirely ignored. Henry is espoused to the fair Princess Katharine after a soldierly wooing, and the play ends with Henry's "prepare we for our marriage."

Surely Shakespeare, in his devotion to the character of Henry V., could not have selected a more brilliant ending for the life with which he has dealt in three successive plays. With all France his heritage, and all England his own, with a patriotic people who saw in him a fitting successor to the Black Prince, whose Cressy had been fairly outdone by Agincourt; with the gratified ambition of a soldier's life on his head as a crown, and a beautiful wife by his side as a helpmeet, the poet leaves, we cannot but believe regretfully, this chiefest and best beloved of all the children of his brain.

This character of Henry, now dramatically completed, deserves close study. Both as an artistic conception and as an interesting personality it must receive the palm over all the purely historic characters, and rank well up with those notable personages of tragedy to whom the genius of Shakespeare has lent their most transcendent lustre. We have noted, stage by stage, the gradual steps in the evolution of Henry's remarkable character. It is often observed that he was Shakespeare's favorite, and frequently claimed that the poet makes the gallant king the mouth-piece

11

of his own soul's meditation. That there is a general likeness is manifest. Both poet and prince spent an idle youth, at the same time nourishing the germs of a nobler manhood. Both were acquainted with taverns, and it is quite probable that wild Prince Hal borrowed his inns and roisterings, and acquaintance with low and wild phases of town life from the actor-author whose genius thus coined even his hours of idleness into gold. But here all likeness ends. One may read into the speeches of a great many of the poet's creations the sentiments of his own heart. Why Henry should be selected as their especial channel it is hard to see. I believe it may arise from a desire to feel better acquainted with Shakespeare himself. The details of his personal life are so meagre that anything which can possibly throw light upon it is eagerly welcomed.

The wish is father to the thought both in this character, and in the ever-recurring discussion of the auto-biographical character of the Sonnets.

We have seen Henry V. in all guises. He runs the gamut of all phases of a lad bred to fortune and to place. In all these manifestations we see something to admire, and from stage to stage of his development we trace the origin of each succeeding step.

It is as a lover only that, upon cool examination, he disappoints. He woos as Hotspur would have wooed. There is a lack of coherency in the character here. He is rough and uncouth. He rides rough-shod over a road he knows must lead to victory, because Katharine is one of the terms of his truce and treaty with her father. Although he asks, and even begs for consideration, there is a subtle laugh back of his pleading which he seems to enjoy as a huge jest. Katharine, from what little we see of her, is worth knowing better. She is charming, with her quaint old French and her broken and sometimes wilfully mistaken English. Her mother is a dignified figure-head, who plays her daughter's charms against a lover's supposed distraction, in order to gain a point in statecraft.

To return to the king and the question involved in his prosecution of the claims for the French crown. The high moral tone which Shakespeare adopts in setting forth this claim ; the assumption of Henry that it was for France's sake that he made these campaigns, is not borne out by the history, nor does Shakespeare, who is in the main faithful to the historic facts, succeed in maintaining it. It is on the very surface of this play that the young king, in order to prevent discussions over what some great nobles contended was his dubious title to his own crown, sets up a preposterous claim to the crown of a neighboring kingdom. For the greater glory of the English name an army is readily assembled for the purpose of maintaining this claim, in which the king is assisted by a clergy who fear too close an investigation into their own affairs.

An accidental battle occurring, during what was practically a retreat from a costly victory, throws the game entirely into his hands. With Agincourt back of him he dictates his own terms to a kingdom torn by internal dissension and ruled by a lunatic. He names his price for peace. Katharine as a bride, and the reversion of the French crown as an heritage.

This is all well done for the times, and Henry is

even conspicuously in advance of the semi-barbaric habits of his day in many of the customs of warfare, as noticeably in the order to his troops to abstain from pillage on the enemy's soil. But, after all, the French campaign was bad policy. Henry was a type of the prevailing English idea of glory, far more than if, in that day, he had won Ireland and Scotland and made them integral portions of an homogeneous empire. The English were but slowly to learn that their real strength lay not in foreign conquest, but in domestic prosperity. These wars were costly, although they made trade active and commerce thrive. Heine's bitter criticism we cannot accept entirely, although we may see the grain of truth under the cynic critic's chaff: "In truth," he says, "in those wars the English had neither justice nor poetry. For they partly concealed the coarsest spirit of robbery under worthless claims of succession; and in part made war as mean mercenaries, in the vulgar interests of mean merchants or shopmen."

But whatever the view of the modern student the English people rejoiced in Henry V.

They went wild with enthusiasm over Agincourt. The gay prince, for whom in his wildest days the people had a fondness, had justified himself, and spoiled the expectations of his enemies. And Shakespeare ends his play at just that point in his hero's career when there could be no regrets for his past, and the brightest hopes of greater glory for his future.

England had had her days of gloom, and was destined, as the result of these very famous victories, to have days of still deeper misery; but over the marriage of Henry and Katharine, there were no shadows. No birds of evil omen perched above the broad pennon of the warrior king. All voices joined in shouts of *Te Deum Laudamus,* and the poet sings his song of triumph clear and brilliantly, without a false note or jarring harmony, to the last bar, and, in spite of his own words, with no "rough and all unable pen,"

> Our bending author hath pursued the story,
> In little room confining mighty men.[1]

[1] Chorus ending Act V.

HENRY VI.

There is no known "foundation play" for Part I., the material for which is gathered from Hall's Chronicle.

For Parts II. and III. there are alleged to be originals, viz.: The First part of the Contention betwixt the two famous Houses of York and Lancaster, with the death of the good Duke Humphrey; and the Banishment and death of the Duke of Suffolk, and the Tragicall end of the proud Cardinal of Winchester, with the notable Rebellion of Jacke Cade, and the Duke of York's first claim unto the Crowne. London 1594. And, the True Tragedy of Richard, Duke of York, and the deathe of good King Henrie the Sixt, with the whole Contention of the two houses, Lancaster and Yorke, as it was sundrie times acted, etc.

Some of the critics hold (a) that Shakespeare wrote these original plays and afterward rewrote them in the form preserved to us through the First Folio. (b) That Shakespeare had nothing to do with them except to use them as he used other plays, for raw material. (c) That the two plays are surreptitious and therefore imperfect copies of the Shakespeare originals. Either theory is plausible ; neither is certain.

Dates of Shakespeare's plays 1592–94.

They are not mentioned by Meres, and first appear in their present form in the First Folio.

1422. Henry V. buried in Westminster Abbey. Henry VI. an infant. Duke of Gloucester (king's uncle) made Protector. Charles VI. of France dies (October). Duke of Bedford made regent (for Henry) over France. Duke of Burgundy maintains the English alliance. The son of Charles VI. crowned King of France at Poitiers, as Charles VII., in defiance of the treaty of Troyes.

1423. Battles of Crevant and Vermueil. French defeated.

1428-29. English siege of Orleans raised by Joan of Arc.

1429. Battle of Patay. Great defeat of the English. Charles VII. crowned King of France at Rheims.

1430. Henry VI. crowned King of France at Paris.

1430-31. Joan of Arc taken prisoner, tried and executed for sorcery.

1432. Burgundy deserts the English alliance.

1435. Death of the regent Bedford. Decline of English power in France.

1440. Arraignment of Eleanor Cobham (wife of the Protector Gloucester) for sorcery.

1445. Truce with France. Marriage of Henry VI. with Margaret of Anjou. Cession of French provinces to Charles VII., causes dissatisfaction in England.

1447. Murder of Duke of Gloucester. Death of Cardinal Beaufort. Henry VI. under the influence of Queen Margaret and her favorite the Duke of Suffolk.

1450. English practically lose all foothold in France. Internal dissensions in England. Banishment and violent death of Suffolk, the queen's favorite. Insurrection throughout England. Jack Cade's rebellion. His rise, temporary successes, defeat and death.

1452. Overt beginning of the wars of the Roses in the factional strifes between the Duke of York and the Lancastrian Duke of Somerset.

1454. During King Henry's serious illness York made Protector.

1455. First battle of St. Albans. Not an act ostensibly against the crown on the part of the Duke of York, but factional between the interests of York and Somerset. York victorious. York makes pretensions to the crown, by right of descent from the third son of Edward III.

1460. An act of Parliament declares York the true heir to the crown after Henry VI., ignoring the claim of Henry's son by Margaret of Anjou. Battle of Wakefield (December). Defeat and death of York, whose son Edward (afterward Edward IV.) succeeds to his claim.

1461. Victory of Yorkists at Mortimer's Cross (January). Battle of St. Albans, defeat of Yorkists (February). In spite of this Edward proceeds to London, is welcomed by the people, and assumes the crown as Edward IV. (March). Battle of Towton (March 30). Great victory for the Yorkists. Henry VI. flies to Scotland, and Margaret to France.

1464. Alliance between Margaret and France. Battle of Hexham. Lancastrians again defeated. Henry imprisoned in the Tower. Marriage of Edward IV. with Lady Elizabeth Grey. Estrangement of Warwick from the Yorkist cause.

1469. Marriage of George, Duke of Clarence, the king's brother, with Isabel, daughter of Warwick.

1470. Warwick and Clarence, driven out of England by the king's jealousy, ally themselves with Margaret of Anjou and the Lancastrians.

1470. October 6, Edward IV. driven from the throne, and Henry VI. restored as the result of this alliance.

1471. Edward IV. returns to England. Battle of Barnet and death of Warwick. Battle of Tewkesbury and final defeat of the Lancastrians. Death of Henry VI.

CHAPTER VI.

HENRY VI.—THE WARS OF THE ROSES.

Authenticity of this play, especially Part I.—Vital connection between the
three Parts.—Historic centres of action as noted in the three divisions.
—Part I.: French wars and episode of Joan of Arc.—Part II.:
Civil dissensions and Jack Cade's rebellion.—Part III.: Warwick,
the "King-maker," and triumph of House of York.—Confusion of details in the play as in the chronicles.—England's song of triumph
turned into a wail of woe.—The dauphin crowned, and France, *sans*
Burgundy, renounces English rule.—Siege of Orleans, and Joan of Arc's
marvellous career.—Faction of the red and white roses.—Burgundy
deserts the English and joins his king.—Capture of the Maid.—Her
trial and execution.—Character and position of the Maid in romance
and history.—Treaty of peace.—Margaret of Anjou betrothed to
Henry of England.—Division and parties among the English nobles.
—(a) King's party, with Suffolk as prime favorite.—(b) Gloucester,
the Protector, a patriot, resenting the French treaty.—(c) Somerset,
and Buckingham, representing the selfish opposition to the king.—
(d) The Yorkist party, and Warwick's ambition.—Warwick holds the
key to the situation.—Cabals of Gloucester's enemies.—His wife's ambition.—Her arrest for sorcery, and penance.—York's title to the
throne advanced.—Jack Cade's rebellion.—Fifteenth-century socialism.
—Cade's progress and defeat.—The Wars of the Roses in full fury.—
The first agreement.—Henry to be succeeded by York.—Margaret goes
to war for her son, ignoring Henry, who becomes a shuttlecock between two or three parties.—Margaret's victory.—The horrors of civil
war.—York dies and his claims taken up by Edward, his son (afterward Edward IV.).—Edward on the throne.—Margaret a suppliant at
the French court.—Warwick appears for Edward.—News out of England —Warwick's wrath at Edward's slight treatment.—Margaret and
Warwick strike a treaty, and with help from Louis set forth to depose Edward.—The combined forces defeat Edward temporarily and
restore Henry.—Battle of Barnet and death of the "King-maker."—
Tewkesbury and the downfall of the Lancastrian cause.—Imprisonment and exile of Margaret.—Edward IV. reigns undisputed.—The
anti-French spirit of Shakespeare.

THE reign of Henry VI. forms the most confused
part of English history after the days of legend and
tradition that mark Anglo-Saxondom. All writers are

uncertain and all students puzzled. Shakespeare, both as writer and student, appears to have shared in these historical perplexities, and his contribution to a knowledge of the times is as far from accuracy as to details, as it is faithful, on the whole, to the general character of the age.

The first part of the play has few friends for its Shakespearean authorship. But if he is not the author of this as well as of Parts II. and III., there are reasons for inferring that he is at least the editor or adapter, to as great an extent as may be claimed for him in the play of King John. These reasons are :

First, The significance of the last Chorus of Henry V., in which the events of this Part I. are indicated after the same fashion as the Chorus is employed throughout that play.

Second, The introduction of the dead King Henry at its beginning, and the historical and dramatic connection thus established with the preceding play.

Third, The anti-French spirit of this Part, in harmony with Shakespeare's method and custom throughout the play.

Fourth, The fact that these three Parts were alike attributed to Shakespeare by the editors of the First Folio, who were in better position to judge of the matter, not only than the critics of our own day, but of the critics of their own day. They were Shakespeare's friends, managers, and business associates. Better than any one else in England they must have known what came from the poet's pen. There is a vital connection, too, between the three Parts. The foreign affairs of England treated in Part I., are necessary to

an understanding of the domestic troubles with which
Parts II. and III. are occupied. We conclude, therefore, that for purposes of historical study, at all events,
this Part I. is necessary to Parts II. and III., and that
in all probability the hand that penned the latter had
a large share, at least, in the composition of the former.

The play as a whole covers the whole reign of Henry
VI., from the death of his father, in 1422, to his own
death, in 1471, and includes also a portion of the reign
of Edward IV., first king of the rival house of York.

The three pivots around which the discordant order
of events revolve, are marked by three names:

I. *Joan of Arc,* and the loss of the French conquests
of Henry V.; II. *Jack Cade,* as one of the moving
springs of civil dissension ; and III. *Warwick the King-
maker,* the last of the great barons, who in his own
powerful person revived for a time the fading glory of
Feudalism, and with whose death at Barnet it expired
forever.

It is in vain that we attempt to unravel the anachronisms in these plays. For dates and accurate notation
any English history may be read. It is our place and
purpose only to show how brilliantly the poet illustrates the spirit of the age he treats, although often
at the expense of the letter of history. One should not
read Shakespeare for the history, but having read the
history Shakespeare seems to make us understand it
the better. The author of the popular history of the
English people pays this tribute to the poet anent the
period we have now in hand : " It is a story well known
to the English people, for it has been told in the dramatic form by a great historical teacher. History,

strictly so called, the history derived from Rolls and Statutes, must 'pale its ineffectual fire' in the sunlight of the poet."

In the opening scene of the play we catch the muffled sound of a dead march rolling through the aisles, and rising in moaning melody to the vaulted roof of Westminster Abbey. The body of the hero of Agincourt, the conqueror of the French, lies in state. His son, a babe but nine months old, holds in his weak hands the heavy sceptre of two kingdoms. Shakespeare, the artist and hero-worshipper, is at his best in the conception, if not in the execution, of this dramatic touch. England's song of triumph is turned into a wail of woe.

> Hung be the heavens with black, . . .
>
> .　　.　　.　　.　　.　　.　.　　.
>
> England ne'er lost a king of so much worth.[1]

Two short years only of undimmed glory abroad and at home after the treaty of Troyes, did Henry V. enjoy. In these he completed the practical conquest of France in alliance with the Duke of Burgundy. Shortly after his death the feeble Charles of France also passed away, and under the treaty of Troyes, which we saw signed in the last chapter, the infant Henry VI. succeeded, not to the regency, but to the actual crown of France. For a time the Duke of Bedford as regent easily maintained the English claim, but it was an unnatural state of affairs that could not last. The Dauphin proclaimed himself as Charles VII., and be-

[1] Part I., Act I., Scene 1.

gan that struggle for his hereditary throne to which the name of Joan of Arc lends such romance.

The first act of Henry VI. is a forecast of the whole play. In the very lamentations of churchmen and nobles over the body of their late king, and growing out of the death of him who alive had bound all together by a strong hand, we hear the notes of mutual suspicion, and anon the clashing of factions. While Exeter and Gloucester boast of the glory of arms, lamenting the king's " brandished sword," and " arms spread wider than a dragon's wings," the Bishop of Winchester declares: " The church's prayers made him so prosperous." To which the soldier returns a cutting retort. Bedford, who was regent of France, as the proper dramatic mouth-piece, is forced to cry : " Cease, cease these jars and rest your mind in peace." Then follows messenger after messenger from France bringing the intelligence which for the first few years of Henry VI.'s minority was wafted with every wind across the Channel from French fields to English ears. The Dauphin was proving himself the worthy descendant of a long line of kings. The people of France who had yielded to the prowess of a great soldier and gallant prince, the husband, moreover, of their own fair princess, Katharine, irked under a foreign yoke when held in place by a babe in arms. They began to renounce the English domination and to return to their natural allegiance.

Burgundy could not control all France for England, although for a time he fought alongside of the successors-in-arms of the English prince to whom he had sworn fealty.

And Bedford had been at first successful. He had

pushed the English pennon into many a corner of France where the fleur-de-lis alone had waved for sovereignty. He was hampered in his movements at first by a quarrel between the Duke of Gloucester and the Duke of Burgundy. But this settled, and with Burgundy once more to aid him, he pursued his aggressive policy, and sat down with ten thousand troops before Orleans.

Charles VII. was at his wit's end to retain the city. He was so weakened that he could not move. France, from gradually beginning to take heart of hope, was almost in despair for means to combat the English and Burgundian allies. What should be done? The answer came from a quarter as remote as unexpected.

The peasantry of France suffered as no other class from the unnatural divisions of her great nobles and the strides of horrid war. Within the heart of the common people lay shame and sorrow over the English rule and the Burgundian alliance. The words of the Maid of Orleans to the duke, when persuading him to forsake the enemies of his country and cast in his lot where both patriotism and piety beckoned him, fairly, and with no exaggeration, expressed the mind of the people upon whom lay the burden, and in whose sides were the wounds of war, while they had none of the glory that attended camps and courts.

> Look on thy country, look on fertile France,
> And see the cities and the towns defaced
> By wasting ruin of the cruel foe;
> As looks the mother on her lovely babe
> When death doth close her tender dying eyes.
> See, see, the pining malady of France,

Behold the wounds, the most unnatural wounds
Which thou thyself hath given her woeful breast.
O, turn thy edged sword another way,
Strike those that hurt, and hurt not those that help.[1]

So thought and felt, doubtless, the mass of the French
people. In the countryside lived a simple maid who
"saw visions and dreamed dreams." She felt the
shock and saw the miseries of war. Her soul was in
arms for her country. What could she do, a child, the
daughter of a shepherd, without credit, without interest. What she did do is one of the marvels of history.
It is the greatest of all pities that Shakespeare read his
chronicles too closely, and in this instance especially,
transferred from their naturally biased pages, a picture
of Joan of Arc, so grossly untrue and unfair, that one
is reconciled to the theory that he did not conceive the
Joan of his drama, and perhaps even softened down
the ruder strokes of another brush. The genius which
could analyze the grief of Constance, open the infinite
depths of a woman's heart as in Katharine of Aragon,
and exploit the shining tenderness of Portia, could apparently see nothing in the mission of Joan of Arc,
save what he caught through the narrow and distorted
view of insular prejudice and the hateful anger of a
people against a despised but victorious foe. In the
whole treatment of Joan there is little to indicate her
true historic character. She came up from her village
and sought her king. Despised at first, the superstitions of the age finally gained her a hearing. At the
head of an army she relieves Orleans. At the head of
another she leads the Dauphin to Rheims where he is

[1] Part I., Act III., Scene 3.

crowned and anointed King of France. Then she
would withdraw, but her name had become an inspiration to the army, and the king holds her to his service.
The haps of war varied now. The Duke of Burgundy
pursued some small successes against Charles, but Joan
had revealed to the king and people of France their
own strength. The contest is a stubborn one. In the
midst of it, and while on the whole favorable to France,
the Maid of Orleans is taken prisoner by a band of
partisans; is sold to Burgundy; is sold by him in turn
to the English, and by the English, after a year's imprisonment, tried and condemned for sorcery, is burned
at the stake, while an English cardinal stands by con-
senting to the shameful act. History has crowned her
with the crown of martyrdom. " We have burned a
saint," cried out one of the soldiers who stood about
the burning stake. And still her place in history is
not a settled one.[1] Note now, as worth study, the
character-drawing of the English poet.

In her introduction to Charles of France, she is made
to assume an arrogant and boastful tone, even as re-
gards her personal appearance, totally at variance with
the modest faith of one who believed herself inspired
of God to do her country service. Of the vision of the
Virgin, Joan says :

> In complete glory she revealed herself,
> And whereas I was black and swart before,
> With those clear rays which she infused on me,
> That beauty am I blessed with which you see.
> Ask me what question thou canst possible
> And I will answer unpremeditated :

[1] The Church of Rome has but recently canonized her.

> My courage try by combat, if thou dar'st,
> And thou shalt find that I exceed my sex.
> Resolve on this, thou shalt be fortunate
> If thou receive me for thy warlike mate.[1]

And again she is made to boast:

> Now am I like that proud insulting ship
> Which Cæsar and his fortunes bare at once.[2]

The English were taught to look upon the maid as a witch; no difficult matter in those times, and for some generations later. Shakespeare expresses this feeling, which undoubtedly laid fast hold upon the imagination of the soldiery, officers and men alike, in Talbot's savage apostrophe:

> Here, here she comes, I'll have a bout with thee,
> Devil, or devil's dam, I'll conjure thee!
> Blood will I draw on thee, thou art a witch,
> And straightway give thy soul to him thou serv'st.[3]

And the Duke of Bedford, regent and general in chief of the English troops, thus speaks concerning Charles, the French prince, whom Joan crowned at Rheims:

> Coward of France, how much he wrongs his fame,
> Despising his own arms' fortitude,
> To join with witches, and the help of hell.[4]

There is a contemptible assumption all through the play, also, that the Maid was not pure in her honor. Scene Fourth of the Fifth Act, in which she is made to confess the shamefullest of all shameful things for

---

[1] Part I., Act I., Scene 2. [2] Ibid.
[3] Part I., Act I., Scene 5. [4] Part I., Act II., Scene 1.

woman's lips, is a brazen violation both of decency and of historic truth. But we can fancy the pit of an Elizabethan theatre ringing with applause at the atrocious falsehoods.

The scene[1] in which the Maid has an interview with fiends, in which even they, familiar spirits of darkness, forsake her, is a fitting prelude to the language she is made to use concerning both her allies and her enemies, after she is taken prisoner.

The Duke of York makes an insulting speech concerning her and the French prince which would have turned the real Maid speechless with shame and pale with horror ; the poet's Joan answers in kind :

> *Puc.* A plaguing mischief light on Charles and thee,
> And may ye both be suddenly surprised
> By bloody hands in sleeping on your beds.
> *York.* Fell, banning hag. Enchantress hold thy tongue.
> *Puc.* I prithee give me leave to curse awhile.[2]

Now this is not the Joan of Arc of history nor of poetry. It is an English tradition above which apparently the dramatist could not rise on account of his audience.

We must not suppose, however, that Shakespeare is without apologists for his treatment of the Maid of Orleans.

Charles Knight, who speaks with authority, declares that the poet idealizes the character from what is found in the chronicles concerning her. And up to the scene already alluded to, when she makes the inconsistent and contradictory assertions about her honor, Knight calmly alleges, " But in all previous scenes Shakespeare has

---

[1] Part I., Act V., Scene 3.   [2] Part I., Act V., Scene 3.

drawn the character of the Maid with an undisguised sympathy for her courage, her patriotism, her high intellect, and her enthusiasm. If she had been the defender of England and not of France, the poet could not have invested her with higher attributes." [1]

Knight's rapturous admiration is buttressed by one argument as follows:

"Neither the patriotism nor the superstition of Shakespeare's age would have endured that the Pucelle should have been dismissed from the scene, without vengeance taken on imagined crimes, or that confession should not be made by her which should exculpate the authors of her death. Shakespeare has conducted her history up to the point where she is handed over to the stake. Other writers would have burned her upon the scene." [2]

This is a refinement of distinction without difference which seems to me to have few equals as a bit of special pleading. Her honor is stabbed, her modesty travestied, her humility veneered, her firm faith in God as her inspiration turned into an incantation scene with fiends, and because to this is not added that she is literally burnt at the stake on the scenic stage, we are to believe that the English poet was above and beyond the harsh spirit of his age in the delicacy with which he treats her dramatic career.

Again Mr. Knight says, in extenuation of his adoration of Shakespeare, "It is in her mouth (Joan's) that he puts his choicest thoughts and most musical verse." [3] But surely this is not a legitimate deduction. He puts

---

[1] Knight's Studies of Shakespeare, Bk. IV., Ch. 4, on Henry VI.
[2] Ibid.   [3] Ibid.

in the mouth of one of the basest of English kings that
fine outburst against the usurped authority of Rome,
beginning:

What earthly name to interrogatories
Can task the free breath of a sacred king?

The same king gave away the crown and honor of England to the pope, and received it back as a fief of the
Holy See. Shakespeare's estimate of Joan's character
must be found in her own words concerning herself,
her mission, and her deeds. And judged by that
standard we fail to find a basis for Knight's laudatory
comment. The real reason was, as we have already
noted, the state of the English mind, the demands of
the patrons of the theatre, and the evident purpose of
Shakespeare to put upon the stage, plays that would
fire the English heart with enthusiasm, and draw shillings from the English purse. This is not a hard view
to take if we look upon Shakespeare as a man ; if we
conceive of him as a demigod who could do no weak
or faulty thing, the criticism, of course, falls to the
ground.

We pass over hastily the other points treated in this
section of the three-part drama of Henry VI.

Burgundy finally deserted his English allies, although not as in the play, at the interposition of Joan
of Arc.

The infant Henry VI. was crowned in Paris, but it
was an empty ceremony. France had risen in her
mighty wrath, and shook the invaders one by one from
her soil. The glory of Agincourt faded away. The
English possessions were reduced to Normandy, a por-

tion of Anjou, and Maine. Fourteen years after Joan
of Arc was burned at the stake, her work was all but
accomplished. Rene, Duke of Anjou, gave his daughter
Margaret in marriage to the young Henry VI., and in
return received a cession of the two provinces, Anjou
and Maine, which were, as is said in the play, the keys
to Normandy. This was with the advice and consent
of Charles VII. A *sortie* now and then, after this, was
made upon French soil by English troops ; but in 1453,
of the brilliant conquests of Edward III. and the
Black Prince, and of the "famous victories" that
followed Henry V., and the "honorable battle of Agincourt," there was but one remnant left to grace English
arms, and the little town and fortress of Calais was the
sole reward for all those costly wars. England was
humiliated and felt her humiliation. But she was
slowly learning the lesson, which one of the chief
events of the despised King John's reign should have
taught her, the lesson Shakespeare was patiently teach-
ing that Elizabethan England, which had its dreams
of foreign conquest too.

With the dimming of the fleur-de-lis on the fair
pattern of England's royal robe arose civil dissensions,
due partly to the popular rage against the administra-
tion of affairs which had lost France ; partly to the
mutterings of socialism against Church and State, and
partly to the quarrel, now coming to a head, of the rival
houses of York and Lancaster for the throne. In
our treatment of the French wars we have dealt mainly
with the course of English policy abroad. That, as
we have seen, ended in the loss of all that had been
won to the greater glory of the English name by

Henry V. This was not due wholly to the inspired bravery of a village maiden, the valor of French arms, or the weakness of the English generals. Bedford and Talbot, especially the latter, were names to conjure with as warriors in England and France for many years. With reference to the First Part of Henry VI.,[1] possibly the poet Nash wrote in his " Pierce Penniless," date of 1592, " How it would have joyed brave Talbot, terror of the French, to think that after he had lain two hundred years in his tomb, he should triumph again on the stage, and have his bones new embalmed with the tears of ten thousand spectators at least (at several times) who in the tragedian that represents his person, imagine they behold him fresh bleeding."

If Talbot and his companions - in - arms had been properly supported at home, it is possible that the song of triumph and the wail of woe had not been so close together. But there were dissensions within the English court resulting from the struggle for possession of the young king, and the prestige of power that went with his person. At the outset of the play one of the messengers who brings bad tidings from France, says :

> Amongst the soldiers there is muttered
> That here you maintain several factions,
> And whilst a field should be despatched and fought,
> You are disputing of your generals.[2]

This was too true. Passing over for the most part the internal history of England during the progress of the French disasters, above recorded, we note one

---

[1] Act IV., Scene 7.   [2] Part I., Act I., Scene 1.

phase of these home disputes, before taking up the state of affairs at the opening of Part II.

While "cropped are the flower-de-luces in their arms," the buds of the white and red roses, are opening among the nobility into the blossoms of civil war. For that scene [1] in the Temple Garden, where over "some nice sharp quillet of the law," the cause of the Yorkist branch of the house of Plantagenet is espoused by the farseeing and ambitious Warwick, there is no known historic basis. How, when, or where the roses were assumed as party badges is not known. Probably it was an accident. The causes of the roses lay in English history. When Richard II. threw his warder down, first banished, and then seized the estates of Bolingbroke, making a clear way for that usurping sovereign, the possibility of civil strife over the title lay in the existence of a child, the legal heir before Bolingbroke, to the throne. It was prophesied then, and Warwick, in the spirit of that prophecy, declares in the Temple Garden :

> This brawl to-day,
> Grown to this faction in the Temple Garden,
> Shall send between the red rose and the white,
> A thousand souls to death and deadly night.[2]

In Act II., Scene 2, the scene between Mortimer and his nephew Plantagenet (soon to be made Duke of York) is contained the historical argument which we have been tracing in these chapters.[3] In a few words, we may indicate exactly the position of the hostile families. The Richard Plantagenet, afterward

---

[1] Part I., Act II., Scene 4.   [2] Ibid.
[3] See Appendix, p. 307.

Duke of York, of this play, is the lineal Yorkist heir to the English throne, through the third son of Edward III. Henry VI. is the Lancastrian occupant of the throne, tracing his lineage to the fourth son of Edward III. Lancaster has three unbroken reigns in succession, and the strong claim of possession. York has undoubted right to the title by strict law of primogeniture. Warwick throws himself now upon the side of the Yorkist family and wears the white rose. To fight this brawl out means more than to continue a quarrel over some quillet of the law begun in the Temple Garden. The great mass of the people who took part in these civil wars were not learned in questions of primogeniture and what constituted a legal title to the crown of England. They fought for the red rose or the white. They looked for fighting orders to their captains. A whole generation grew up while the hideous wars were in progress. Act II. of Part II. of the play gives a vivid picture of what the fancifully named strife actually meant in the homes of those who supported this or that king on the throne. But the nobles knew for what they were fighting. The house of York was making a desperate effort for a great crown; the Yorkists were for the spoils of the crown. The house of Lancaster, after a brilliant career of three reigns, was on the wane, and was putting forth every effort, not so much to revive its former glory as to maintain its present place secure.

There were good and bad on both sides. Humble men and ambitious men faced each other on the battle-field and lay down together in the camp. But all the time the sun of Lancaster was setting, and that of

York rising. Warwick, who was the English states-man of his day, sagaciously cast in his fortunes with the Yorkist house.

To return now to the opening of the Second Part, and the state of affairs in England at the time it marked. Out of the mystifications and confusions of the chronicles we draw the threads of at least four distinct factions.

The king's party, of which Suffolk was head and prime favorite with Henry, owing to the successful issue of his efforts for the union of the king with Margaret of Anjou. Cardinal Beaufort's interest lies here also.

Gloucester, the good Duke Humphrey, who was pro-tector of the realm during Henry's minority, a genuine patriot, head of the war party, and deeply resenting the treaty with France, of which Margaret had been the price.

Somerset and Buckingham, representing the selfish opposition to Gloucester and the king, envious and hot against the protector, and fearing Cardinal Beaufort, as deep schemers fear those who rival them in craft. Somerset says :

> Cousin of Buckingham, though Humphrey's pride,
> And greatness of his place, be grief to us,
> Yet let us watch the haughty cardinal ;
> His insolence is more intolerable
> Than all the princes in the land beside ;
> If Gloucester be displaced he'll be protector.[1]

The fourth faction was that of the *Duke of York*, with whom was allied Warwick, whose policy it was to fo-ment disturbances, and fire the embers of discontent

[1] Part II., Act I., Scene 1.

already heaped up in great quantity, in order that every advantage might be taken against the Lancastrian occupant of the throne.

All these parties, with perhaps the exception of Gloucester, the good Duke Humphrey, were seeking their own advancement in the name, but with little reference to the rights of, the king. And Henry VI. was not the man for such rude times. A parallel is often traced between him and Richard II. There is a certain weakness, effeminacy in its least pleasant sense, in both characters. But in Richard it came from moral cowardice. He could not bear to face trouble. In Henry it resulted from overstrained piety. He could not bear the sight or knowledge of any wrong going on about him. Evil unmanned him. Simple-minded as a child, he trusted those about him without a shadow of doubt as to their perfect faith and honor. He had not a drop of the soldier blood in his veins, nor a spark of the warlike spirit in his soul. He was a strange son of such a pair as Henry V. and Katharine. Yet this was the prince in whose hand was borne the pennon of a falling house. Even about his marriage he does not seem to care deeply.

> " I shall be well content," he says, " with any choice
> Tends to God's glory and my country's weal." [1]

But it was this marriage which saved his crown for many years. Margaret of Anjou was the complement of Henry VI. Had she possessed his sweet sincerity and humble piety she would have been a model queen ; Had he possessed her virile and resolute courage he

[1] Part I., Act V., Scene 1.

would have been a model king. As it was, Margaret of Anjou supplied the place of a man at the head of the house of Lancaster; and to her alone was due the prolonged struggle between the white rose and the red. When a victory for Henry's army is spoken of, it is always Margaret who is in the field; and it is Margaret who again and again, in spite of Warwick at first, and afterward in alliance with him, lifts Henry from a state of humiliation in which he meekly and contentedly rests, to an uncertain triumph, for which he does not care.

Gloucester, as protector of the realm, and the least selfish of all the nobles, is the chief object of attacks and cabals on the part of these court factions. Warwick, as the most powerful and richest among the aristocracy, with the reputation of feeding thirty thousand people daily at his board in times of revelry, holds the key of the situation. That is, men and money were the forces that carried most weight in the fifteenth century, and Warwick had both in excess of his fellows.

Gloucester is the centre of attack, because his positive influence at court is for the prosecution of the French war, and the reviving of the glory of English arms. Moreover, he is loyal to the king, and, to an extent, influential with him. As he reads over the French treaty, in which the conquests of the idolized Henry V. are ceded one by one to the Duke of Anjou, his faltering accent echoes a good portion of the national feeling outside of the court circle.

> Pardon me, gracious lord,
> Some sudden qualm has struck me at the heart,
> And dimmed mine eyes that I can read no further.

" Shall Henry's conquest," he cries to the nobles,

> Bedford's vigilance,
> Your deeds of war, and all our counsel die ?
> O peers of England, shameful is this league,
> Fatal this marriage, cancelling your fame,
> Blotting your names from books of memory.[1]

But the good Duke's words were of no avail. The majority seem to agree in his sentiments, but thirst for his removal.

The first three Acts of Part II. are taken up with the plots and scheming against the protector, of which plots and schemes Beaufort and Somerset are chief movers. He was first struck through his wife, known in history as Eleanor Cobham, of doubtful memory. That she was ambitious, a good hater, and determined to secure and maintain a lofty position at court we know from history, and her husband's warning to her indicates the part she had in his downfall:

> O Nell, sweet Nell, if thou dost love thy lord
> Banish the canker of ambitious thoughts;
> And may that thought, when I imagine ill
> Against my king and nephew, virtuous Henry,
> Be my last breathing in this mortal world.[2]

For Eleanor Cobham would have had him put forth his hand and reach at the glorious gold of Henry's diadem. She seeks the aid of witch and conjurer, not out of keeping with her age, and is finally by these means entrapped. To imagine the death of the king was treason, and to conjure evil spirits for information concern-

---

[1] Part II., Act I., Scene 1.
[2] Part II., Act I., Scene 2.

ing such a thing was worthy of death. The king pronounces by poetical license the sentence :

> Stand forth, Dame Eleanor Cobham, Gloucester's wife,
> In sight of God, and us, your fault is great,
> Receive the sentence of the law for sins
> Such as by God's book are adjudged to death.
> You four [addressing her confederates] from hence
>   to prison back again ;
> From thence unto the place of execution :
> The witch in Smithfield shall be burned to ashes,
> And you three shall be strangled on the gallows.
> You, madam, for you are more nobly born,
> Shall, after three days' open penance done,
> Live, in your country here, in banishment,
> With Sir John Stanley in the Isle of Man.[1]

Scene 4th of Act II. gives the pathetic picture of the penance. From a certain horror against the vain, cold woman, we grow under the spell of poetic genius to have a feeling of deepest pity and sorrow for her. It is one of the most touching scenes in all these plays. Robed in a white sheet, her feet bare, and a taper burning in her hand, she performs her penance through the open streets of London, to whom her husband comes :

> Come you, my lord, to see my open shame ?
> Now dost thou penance too. Look how they gaze,
> See how the giddy multitude do point
> And nod their heads, and throw their eyes on thee.
> Ah, Gloucester, hide thee from their hateful looks
> And in thy closet, pent up, rue thy shame,
> And ban thine enemies, both thine and mine.

[1] Part II., Act II., Scene 3.

But Gloucester's time soon comes, Eleanor's last words
to the good Duke Humphrey prove true.

> For Suffolk . . .
> .　　.　　.　　.　　.　　.　　.
> And York, and impious Beaufort, that false priest
> Have all limed bushes to betray thy wings.[1]

He will not believe it. Innocent of all charges save
that of loyalty, in a court honeycombed with self-seeking and shrewd treason, how should he believe it?
He is soon deprived of his honors, summoned before
Parliament to answer charges which are best understood by his answer to them :

> I never robbed the soldiers of their pay,
> Nor ever had one penny bribe from France,
> So help me God, as I have watched the night,
> Ay, night by night, in studying good for England.
> .　　.　　.　　.　　.　　.　　.　　.
> No ; many a pound of mine own proper store,
> Because I would not tax the needy commons,
> Have I dispersed to the garrisons
> And never asked for restitution.[2]

But proofs of innocence were not sought for on the
part of the powerful cabal which must have the good
Duke Humphrey out of the way. He was condemned
for treason, and died by violence. A cloud of suspicion rests upon Suffolk, Beaufort, and Margaret.
Warwick and his faction, holding aloof from these
practices against Humphrey Gloucester, stand ready
to make capital for the Yorkist cause out of them.
Henry protests against the crime. Yet Suffolk, under

[1] Part II., Act II., Scene 4.　　[2] Part II., Act III., Scene 1.

the protection of Queen Margaret, resents the charge and keeps a high hand over his fellow and rival nobles, until that great force, long suffering, but mighty when aroused, the common people, clamors at the palace-gates for vengeance.

Gloucester had been the people's friend, and they knew it. Suffolk had been their enemy, and they knew that. Doubtless they were subtly stirred up to the clamor point, and in this lay the connection of the people with the civil wars.

For while Gloucester is the person against whom the court cabals must work, the Duke of Suffolk becomes the object of popular hatred. He and Queen Margaret were close allies. He had been proxy for the king in the royal marriage, and there were dark whispers, to which scenes in the play give credence, of their more intimate relations.

The speech of Salisbury marks what was the feeling of the English masses against the noble whom they believed had dishonored their king :

> Dread lord, the commons send you word by me
> Unless Lord Suffolk straight be done to death
> Or banished fair England's territories,
> They will by violence tear him from your palace,
> And torture him by grievous lingering death.
> They say by him the good Duke Humphrey died.
> They say in him they fear your Highness' death.[1]

So Suffolk was banished, and in Scene 1 of Act IV. his strange fate is told. Leaving England for exile, doubtless dreaming of a return through Margaret's influence,

---

[1] Part II., Act III., Scene 2.

he was taken prisoner by an English war-ship, and disappeared forever.

The poet deals with him more savagely, and at the hands of the people, to indicate apparently that the people were the real cause of the powerful favorite's overthrow. And we are at once led by this incident to one of the great preliminary movements and active agents in promoting the strife of Lancaster and York, in the person of Jack Cade, and the socialism of the fifteenth century. Jack Cade is one of the strange figures of romantic history, whose cause after this lapse of time cannot be accurately judged. By some he was looked upon as a patriot; by others as a rebel; by many as a hero; by many as a rogue. The movement which he headed had for its object political reform. The closest investigation leads us to the conclusion that the religious ferment of Lollardry at the same time had nothing to do with Cade's rebellion. It was a rising of the peasants, under the leadership of a shrewd soldier, who called himself Mortimer, for the purpose of exciting feeling against the House of Lancaster, and perhaps at the instigation of the Yorkist faction, to prepare the way for the Duke of York's claim upon the throne, as heir of the Mortimers. The Kentishmen were dwellers in the manufacturing district, and the sudden cessation of the French wars had wrought them harm. The complaint of the commons of Kent, according to the chronicles, called for "administrative and economical reforms ; a change of ministry, a more careful expenditure of the royal revenue, and the restoration of the freedom of election."

These were not excessive claims surely. A victory

over the royal troops, a quick march upon London, and the execution of Lord Say, gave Cade and his insurgents prestige. The Royal Council yielded in form to their demands, and against Cade's advice the malcontents disbanded. He still carried on the war, and opened jails for his soldiers, but the undisciplined host quarrelled among themselves, and deserted in numbers. Cade was finally killed by a civil officer, and the revolt came to an end with no advantage to the commons of Kent or of England.

Shakespeare touches upon but one side of this rebellion, its absurd and illogical side. He was sorely in need of comedy for the tragic drama of Henry VI. and pitched upon the social and political heresies of fifteenth century socialism to provide it.

Flippantly as he thus seems to treat a movement of respectable proportions and for desirable ends, we cannot fail to read in the speeches of these lath-carrying heroes, a good deal of the bathos and lurid rhetoric with which our own times are more or less familiar. We need not find in this use of the Cade revolt an argument, as many do, to buttress the position that Shakespeare was an aristocrat, despising the people. It is too large a subject to more than advert to here. But while in this instance he does not even state Cade's side fairly, he does, what he doubtless intended as an artist, relieve the gloom of his drama; and as an historian, presents one true, if absurd, side of the movement.

Jack Cade's preposterous claim to a royal pedigree, descendant of the Plantagenets and Mortimers, did not deceive his allies ; the very making of it was a stul-

13

tification of the words of his followers that "there never was merry world in England since gentlemen came up."[1] We notice that as soon as the rebel leader comes to power he is as arrogant as the bluest-blooded noble, and will strike a man dead for not addressing him as Lord Mortimer. This savors of modern times. Position and money make even anarchists conservative of their own—which is anarchistic heresy. As always, the unthinking people believe all things of all men if only they can have a try at upsetting the standing order of things. "Be brave, then," cries Cade, "for your captain is brave and vows reformation. There shall be in England seven halfpenny loaves sold for a penny, the three-hooped pot shall have ten hoops, and I will make it felony to drink small beer."[2]

A bright thought occurs to Dick the butcher. "The first thing we do, let's kill all the lawyers." And Cade's answer, extravagantly expressed as it is, does most curiously indicate the mental attitude of the peasantry of that day, and of all people who think little and read not at all, toward instruments and institutions of whose origin or *raison d'être* they are in total ignorance. "Is not this a lamentable thing, that of the skin of an innocent lamb should be made parchment? that parchment, scribbled over, should undo a man?"[3]

The demagogue has the ignorance of his audience on his side. He has in behalf of his appeals that sullen jealousy of the masses who are conscious of classes, that

---

[1] Part II., Act IV., Scene 2.   [2] Part II., Act IV., Scene 2.

[3] Ibid.

is, of a caste above them and more accomplished. That a man can write and read and cast accounts is monstrous to the peasants who never hold a book save in awe, or a pen without fear of sorcery. So Cade's main charge against Lord Say, who was the chief noble sacrificed in this uprising, is hardly exaggerated: "Thou hast most traitorously corrupted the youth of the realm in erecting a grammar school; and whereas, before, our fathers had no other book but the score and the tally, thou hast caused printing to be used; and contrary to the king, his crown and dignity, thou hast erected a paper mill. It will be proved to thy face that thou hast men about thee that usually talk of a noun, and a verb, and such abominable words as no Christian ear can endure to hear."[1]

There was no escape from death when such charges were treason, and Lord Say died. But such revolts also die of their own fevers and wounds. Cade moralizes over the fickleness of his followers in a strain with which again we are made familiar throughout these chronicle plays: "Was ever feather so lightly blown to and fro as this multitude? The name of Henry V. hales them to a hundred mischiefs, and leaves me desolate."[2]

Meanwhile the Yorkist cause begins to lift its head

---

[1] Part II., Act IV., Scene 7.   [2] Part II., Act IV., Scene 8.

NOTE. A century later, in 1671, Sir William Berkeley, Governor of Virginia, wrote home to England, "I thank God there are no free schools or printing, and I hope we shall not have them these hundred years. For learning has brought heresy and disobedience and sects into the world, and printing has divulged them and libels against the best government. God keep us from both."—Douglas Campbell's "Puritan in Holland, England and America," vol. i., p. 32.

above the troubled surface of the nation's life. The York faction was accused of using Jack Cade to foment discontent and make people familiar with the name of Mortimer, through whom the Duke of York claimed inheritance. Shakespeare notices this in Scene 2 of Act IV., when Stafford says: "Jack Cade, the Duke of York hath taught you this," and although Cade answers in an aside, "He lies, for I invented it myself," it is not conclusive. It is altogether probable that as York used the death of Gloucester, the attainder of Suffolk, and the quarrels of the Churchmen of the period, so he used these discontents of the people to foment dissension and further his own schemes.

Poor Henry VI. is in a constant state of lamentation. He is no sooner well rid of Cade than the dire news comes of York's march with the Irish troops, to ostensibly remove the Duke of Somerset from power, but really to assert his own claims to the throne.

> But now is Cade drawn back, his men dispersed,
> And now is York in arms to second him.[1]
>   .   .   .   .
> Was never subject long'd to be a king
> As I do long and wish to be a subject.[2]

This was literally true. Henry has more fire and force in the play than he had in history. But he was not fit to govern the England of the fifteenth century. He would have found his place in the nineteenth rather. Royalty for its pomp and show and power was never dear to him. His books and his beads were more precious than sceptre and crown. He realizes this, and

---

[1] Part II., Act IV., Scene 9.   [2] Ibid.

dimly, too, as Shakespeare hints, he feels that his fee-
bleness is hurtful to the realm :

> Come, wife, let's in and learn to govern better,
> For yet may England curse my wretched reign.[1]

We can but briefly touch upon the details of the furi-
ous wars that culminated in these last days of Henry
VI., although they were brewing as far back as Richard
II. On the one hand is the House of Lancaster with
Henry VI. and his son Edward, Prince of Wales, the
centre of a group of nobles, whose interest, ambition,
and loyalty cause them to wear the blood Red Rose of
the reigning house. The martial spirit of this party
is Margaret of Anjou, patient, revengeful, terrible ; fascinating and attractive for her high courage and splendid hope.

On the other hand is Richard Plantagenet, Duke of
York, with his sons, Edward (afterwards the Fourth),
Edmund Rutland, who dies early in the strife, George,
afterwards the " false, fleeting, perjured Clarence," and
ablest, most unscrupulous, self-contained of all, Richard
Gloster, the hunchback duke, afterwards known to in-
famy as Richard III. The guiding spirit of this house,
among a host of others who wore the milk White Rose
of York, was Warwick, well named the King-maker.

When once the shock of battle is joined, Henry VI.
drops out of the actual contest, save as he is taken up,
first by one and then the other of these factions, who
shrouded their own ambitions beneath his robe of royalty. He is simply a shuttlecock. Margaret and Warwick are the master-hands in this game of war. The

[1] Part II., Act IV., Scene 9.

claims of York are urged upon Henry and Parliament, after various skirmishes and battles in which the pretender to the throne is usually worsted. The Parliament of 1560 at length came to a compromise as the only way of settling a question that promised to distract the land interminably. This was that Henry should reign for life, and that York and his heirs should succeed to the crown. We can imagine the maternal fury of Margaret, who was away from London when this grave matter was discussed and settled. By this pact her son was robbed of his rights forever. She loses no time, but flies to arms, and in the battle of Wakefield the Duke of York is slain, and his son Edward succeeds to his pretensions. Margaret let slip the fruit of her victory to indulge her revengeful nature in some executions, and the young Edward, dropping the mask of loyalty to Henry VI., marches upon London, is proclaimed rightful king, and once more the fierce contention comes to shock of battle, at Towton. Here Warwick for the Yorkists won a great battle, one of the bloodiest in English history. Henry and Margaret fled away. Edward IV. was crowned king, and but for a feeble struggling moment or two of seeming power afterwards under the powerful banner of Warwick who now opposed them, the Lancastrians passed into obscurity. The House of Plantagenet was still upon the throne, but the usurpation of Bolingbroke was avenged, and the York branch resumed the seat which belonged to it of hereditary right.

Edward is variously described as a soldier and a voluptuary. He was a mixture, not strange, of both. That he fought bravely ever is beyond doubt. That he was ever fond of "silken dalliance" is equally so. Warwick had made him, and literally had placed him on the throne. He deserved some consideration, but Edward thought he asked too much.

While the great baron is at the court of France suing for the hand of the French princess for the English king, Edward takes the bit in his royal teeth, and marries off-hand a lady of the court whose modest beauty charmed and captivated him.[1] Margaret and Warwick are both suppliants now before the throne of Louis of France, but in what different case. Margaret a discrowned queen, her husband a willing hermit in exile, her son, for whom she pleads, a beggar at her side. She has little enough to offer in the way of alliance with the proud French sovereign. Warwick, on the other hand, is empowered to offer the hand of one of the greatest kings of Christendom to the daughter of France. Margaret sues with tears and promises; Warwick with gallant smiles and gold. What wonder Warwick wins. It was an age when on the surface of things might made right.

But just at the moment when this "proud setter-up and puller-down" is carrying all before him, Margaret has a strange and unexpected victory. News out of England. Edward's light marriage with the Lady Grey. "King Louis," cried Warwick to that angry and misused monarch,

> "I here protest in sight of Heaven,
> And by the hope I have of heavenly bliss,

[1] Nothing is historically certain concerning this episode except that Edward married the Lady Elizabeth Grey. Shakespeare's delineation is taken from Sir Thomas More.

That I am clear from this misdeed of Edward's,
No more my king, for he dishonors me.

  .   .   .   .

I here renounce him and return to Henry.
My noble queen, let former grudges pass,
And henceforth I am thy true servitor."
Mar. Warwick, these words have turned my hate to love,
And I forgive and quite forget old faults,
And joy that thou becom'st King Henry's friend.[1]

So the mother and the queen drops out of account her personal indignities, for the sake of her exiled husband and her youthful son :

My mourning weeds are laid aside,
And I am ready to put armor on.[2]

Yet Warwick was no lover of the Lancastrian. His pride is touched at Edward's treachery to himself, and

Not that I pity Henry's misery,
But seek revenge on Edward's mockery,[3]

is his watchword for that bloody campaign, whereof Margaret's was husband and son, king and prince.

Again the rude shock of war. The powerful King-maker once more pulls down a king, and seats the old-time occupant. Then follows Barnet, and Warwick dies. Tewkesbury follows, and the final downfall of Henry of Lancaster, who returns thankfully to his Tower prison, while Margaret is first imprisoned and then exiled from the country.

---

[1] Part III., Act III., Scene 3.
[2] Ibid.   [3] Ibid.

The House of York is seated firmly on the throne. The troubled Margaret of Anjou retires to France and her father's toy kingdom, after a feeble and futile attempt to rally the lost cause of the Red Rose. The murder of her son, which is dramatically told by the poet, is historic only as to the fact; but Margaret's lament over him[1] is a just apostrophe upon those savage times.

There were fine points in Margaret's character. We must ever bear in mind that Shakespeare was unable to do her the justice which the great Scotchman does in his novel, "Anne of Geierstein," where is pathetically told the story of her last days. Our poet gives the mob judgment of Margaret, the English mob judgment at that. It is well to remember in making up our minds as to the truth of Shakespeare's character study, that he was pronouncing it upon the chieftain of a defeated house, of a broken dynasty, and a French woman, to whom directly and indirectly was traceable a good deal of England's humiliation. We shall come upon her ghost, as it were, in the play of "Richard III.," where, after a strange fashion, the poet commits the greatest of his many anachronisms by her introduction, and at the same time points his moral and adorns his tale the better for his historic untruth.

Those scenes in which are introduced the conjurer Bolingbroke, the witch Margery Jourdan, and the two quarrelling bourgeois, Horner and his apprentice,[2] as well as that in which the impostor Simpcox is exposed,[3] will well repay careful reading. Together with

---

[1] Part III., Act V., Scene 5.   [2] Part II., Act II., Scene 3.
[3] Part II., Act II., Scene 1.

the Jack Cade incident they pour floods of light upon the social life of the England of this period.

With the close of Part III. we begin to have glimpses revealing the nature, ambitions, and evil heart of Richard Gloster, afterwards Richard III. and last of the House of Plantagenet. The interview with patient old King Henry, which ends in his violent death at the hands of his nephew, gives us the key to that character which, next to that of Hamlet, seems the least resolvable of all Shakespeare's work. Over the dead body of his former king and kinsman, the wild beast in Richard growls :

> If any spark of life is yet remaining
> Down, down to hell and say I sent thee thither,
> I, that have neither pity, love nor fear.
>
> .   .   .   .
>
> Clarence, beware, thou keep'st me from the light,
> But I will sort a pitchy day for thee,
> For I will buzz abroad such prophecies
> That Edward shall be fearful of his life,
> And then to purge the fear, I'll be thy death.
> King Henry and the prince his son are gone.
> Clarence, thy turn is next, and then the rest.[1]

And while these dark clouds and steaming mists of bloody plots are thus rising over the soul of the king's youngest brother, that king is in the midst of his loyal friends, with his family about him, resting from the toils of war.

> Once more we sit in England's royal throne.
>
> .   .   .   .
>
> Come hither, Bess, and let me kiss thy boy.
> Young Ned, for thee thine uncles and myself

---

[1] Part III., Act V., Scene 6.

Have in our armor watched the winter's night,
Went all afoot in summer's scalding heat,
That thou might'st repossess the crown in peace ;
And of our labors thou shalt reap the gain.[1]

Poor young prince, the Tower looms up before thee,
though thou seest it not ; and the shadow of it falls
upon thy young life, lying in thy mother's lap, cast by
the baleful eyes of him who cries in affected loyalty :

And that I love the tree from whence thou sprangest
Witness the loving kiss I give the fruit.[2]

[1] Part III., Act V., Scene 7.   [2] Part III., Act V., Scene 7.

RICHARD III.

THE source of this play is Sir Thomas More's "Life of Richard III." More was a member of the household of the Bishop of Ely of the play, and must have had the best of opportunities for getting at the real facts. His history was incorporated into Hall and Holinshed's "Chronicle." Shakespeare follows him with great faithfulness, particularly in his description of Richard's person, and acts upon the hints of More in charging Richard's several crimes upon him.

Two other plays on the same subject were in existence, having only few things in common with Shakespeare, and these mainly of such a nature as could be secured by any biographer.

One of these, in Latin, by Dr. Thomas Legge, was said to have been acted at Cambridge in 1579.

The other was in English (anonymous) : *The True Tragedy of Richard III., Wherein is shown the death of Edward IV., and the smothering of the two young princes in the Tower.*

Shakepeare's "Richard" is mentioned by Meres, having been published in 1597, and was issued in five quarto editions, besides the First Folio.

from
CHRONOLOGY OF EDWARD IV. (FROM 1471), EDWARD V., AND RICHARD III.

(Shakespeare includes these all under the title-play of "Richard III.")

1471. Edward IV. reigning in peace.

1473. Richard Gloster marries Anne Neville, daughter of Warwick, who had been either married or betrothed to the son of Henry VI., slain at Tewkesbury.

1475. Invasion of France under Edward IV., which results in the treaty of Picquiney. Under this treaty Edward was given a large sum of money ; a marriage was arranged between his daughter and the son of Louis XI.; and Margaret of Anjou was released from her confinement to find a home with her father, King Rene.

1478. The Duke of Clarence arraigned and executed for treason. His family attainted.

1483. Death of Edward IV. (April 9). Edward V. (his son, aged 12½ years) enters London (May 4). The peers swear fealty. Richard Gloster chosen Protector. The queen mother seeks sanctuary through fear of the Protector. Richard denounces the queen's relations as traitors. The Duke of York (younger brother of Edward V.) removed from "sanctuary," under promise of life and good treatment. June 22, Dr. Shaw's sermon at Paul's Cross, declaring the illegitimacy of Edward V. and the Duke of York. June 25, an assembly of prelates and nobles (not a parliament) declared the fact of illegitimacy. June 26, Richard acknowledged by the peers as King of England. July 26, Richard and Anne crowned. The young princes disappear from English history, the public rumor being that they were murdered. Oct.– Nov., revolt of the Duke of Buckingham. Earl of Richmond (last of the Lancastrian family) driven off by a storm from an attempted descent upon England.

1485. Henry, Earl of Richmond, sails from Harfleur to lay claim to the throne of England. Richard III. meets him and is defeated and slain at Bosworth Field (Aug. 21). Richmond crowned as Henry VII. on the battle-field.

CHAPTER VII.

RICHARD III.—THE LAST OF THE PLANTAGENETS.

Essential difference between "Richard III." and the other historical plays.
—Why Richard is treated with more severity than other historical
characters equally depraved.—The political situation at the beginning
of the play.—The queen's party *versus* the nobles with Buckingham at
their head.—Three great historical events marked in the drama.—(I.)
The death of Edward IV.—(II.) Richard's successful usurpation of the
throne.—(III.) Bosworth Field and Richmond.—Events between the
death of Henry VI. and that of Edward.—The clearing of the field for
Richard's ambitious plan.—The seizure of Clarence.—The unspeakable
wooing of Anne by Richard.—The clashing of rival court factions.—
Underplay of Margaret's fury.—Her artistic introduction in the drama.
—Edward IV. effects a hollow reconciliation between the queen's fac-
tion and the nobles.—Edward's death.—Struggle of the rival factions
to gain control of the young king.—Richard and Buckingham win.—
Fall of the queen's kindred.—The princes lodged in the Tower.—
Buckingham saps the popular loyalty by hinting at the illegitimacy of
both Edward IV. and his sons.—Gloster's "scruples" overcome.—
Gloster's ambition attained and he is crowned with Anne as queen.—
The thorn in Richard's crown.—The falling away of Buckingham.—
Death of the young princes.—Richmond's star begins to rise.—First
revolt against Richard is crushed.—Richmond unable to land, and
Buckingham defeated.—Anne dies, and Richard schemes for the hand
of his niece Elizabeth.—This princess is pledged to Richmond by the
faction opposed to Richard.—Gathering of the discontented nobles.—
Night before the battle of Bosworth.—Visions of the rival command-
ers.—Their moral *raison d'être*.—The day of battle; defeat of Richard and crowning of Richmond as Henry VII.—End of the Wars of the
Roses.—Encouragement to literature under Edward and Richard.—
Progress of the commons.

THE curtain rises now upon the last act of the epic
drama depicting the rise and fall of the House of Plantagenet and, incidentally, the decay of the feudal sys-

tem which had been the backbone of English life from the days of William the Conqueror.

There is a very great difference between the handling of the incidents in " Richard III." and the method followed in the other historical plays. It is a character portrait. One figure dominates the movement of every scene and moulds the arrangement of every detail.

From King John to Henry VI. we have a series of panoramic views. The stage is crowded with figures of considerable importance. There are currents of movement apart from the titular hero.

But in Richard III., from the moment of his introduction in the famous sarcastic soliloquy :

> Now is the winter of our discontent
> Made glorious summer by this sun of York,[1]

until he dies fighting against fate on Bosworth Field, the subtle devil in the hunchback's heart plays with the other persons of the drama, and dominates their every movement. "I am myself alone," these words of the man self-exiled from sympathetic intercourse with his fellows express his character, and form the key-note of the whole bloody tragedy.

All readers approach this play with preconceived ideas, for which Shakespeare himself is largely responsible. There have been other historical personages as bloody and villainous as Richard, but few have been treated with such critical severity. The reason is that Richard is made the mouth-piece of his own depravity.

[1] Act I., Scene 1.

Ordinary villains have an excuse, however poor, for their villainy, which is their mask to the outer world, and which not unfrequently deceives themselves. We are able to trace this in the case of Henry VIII., who argues himself learnedly and conscientiously into the loathsome act of divorcing Katharine of Aragon that he may marry Anne Boleyn. But Richard makes no excuses. To the woman he seeks to marry for the great property she has, he declares that he did kill her husband and her father. To his criminal intimates, for he had no others, he is quite barefaced in his proposals of new crimes. He bargains bluntly for the death of his brother, and treats the murder of his nephews as an ordinary commercial transaction.

Whatever Richard was in his life, this is the verdict of history upon him : that he was a villain so unnatural as to be almost supernatural, and Shakespeare, taking this portraiture directly from the chronicles, exaggerated it upon the screen of his tragedy. So long as men put forth extenuating circumstances for their crimes, so long it is always possible to drop the mantle of charity over their misdeeds. But when they glory in guilt, this cannot be done. Richard glories in his deviltry, and takes posterity into his confidence through those soliloquies of the poet which are psychological studies in shamelessness. The soliloquies in "Richard III." are a dramatic necessity. We could not get at the real man without them. But in the mouth of Richard the soliloquies are far more than instruments of dramatic art ; they are in keeping with the character Shakespeare seeks to lay before us. There was absolutely no soul in whom Richard could confide. To first this one, then that, of his subordinate allies, he divulges certain acts to be performed, and in so far as Buckingham, for instance, is necessary to the working out of a scheme, he allows him to know that little corner of his mind. But confidant he has none. "I am myself alone" expressed his relation or lack of relation with his surroundings. He loves no one, trusts no one, strange to say, hates no one, but uses all. Now such a man must, as it were, think aloud; that is, he must crystallize his thoughts, emotions, instincts into concrete words, and confide in himself at all events. He must arrange and clarify his thoughts in order to proceed upon the orderly lines that lead to success in whatever undertaking.

Here we have, then, a self-revelation, not only as a rhetorical ornament and dramatic necessity, but as a psychological truth. Hence we have the naked villain, with nothing held back or shaded off, as it would be were he conversing with another.

The political situation at the beginning of the play is faintly indicated in the opening speech of Richard, who thus throws his baleful shadow forward over the future, in sarcastic jeering at his brother Edward's peaceful disposition, reflected, it will be remembered, in the last scene of "Henry VI. :"

> Grim-visaged War hath smoothed his wrinkled front :
> And now instead of mounting barbéd steeds
> To fright the souls of fearful adversaries,
> He capers nimbly in a lady's chamber
> To the lascivious pleasing of a lute.[1]

[1] Act I., Scene 1.

14

Affairs of state do not now engage the thoughts of Richard, but only his own relations to these "piping times of peace."

> I that am curtailed of this fair proportion,
> Cheated of feature by dissembling nature,
> Deformed, unfinished, sent before my time
> Into this breathing world, scarce half made up,
> And that so lamely and unfashionable
> That dogs bark at me, as I halt by them,
>
> .   .   .   .
>
> I am determined to prove a villain.[1]

Edward reigned in peace, after the exhausting and bloody war of succession. A mock campaign into France, which began with claiming the throne, and ended in receiving a pension to keep away from France, was the only semblance of war, if we omit the ever-recurring border troubles between England and Scotland.

From the wreckage of civil strife, a single waif tossed for awhile upon its troubled waters, and then washed upon the shores of Brittany, there to bide his time, the Earl of Richmond, was the only possible contestant with the House of York for the throne.

There were two parties grouped about the throne of Edward IV. The queen's, comprised mainly of her own family and their adherents lately taken from the untitled gentry, as she herself had been, and made over into earls and dukes — Rivers, Dorset, Grey. The old nobles' faction was headed by Buckingham, and quietly sympathized with by Richard Gloster.

[1] Act I., Scene 1.

The three events around which the action of the play centres are : (I.) the death of Edward IV.; (II.) the successful usurpation of Richard Gloster ; (III.) Bosworth Field and the coming of Earl Richmond.

After the death of Henry VI., Edward IV. reigned twelve years, years of peace and exhaustion. All England lay bleeding and gasping for the life that had been well-nigh drained from her system in the long duel of the White and Red Roses. This play covers a period of fourteen years from 1471 to 1485. One-half of the period is treated, in its essential points, in the first act, closing with the death of Clarence, which happened in 1478.

The first historical event which comes to our notice is the seizure of the Duke of Clarence, which is here somewhat advanced in point of time.[1] The poet took a hint of the chronicle, and upon it based this direct murder of Clarence by Gloster. Although the latter was certainly to benefit by Clarence's death, and we may readily suppose that he was not averse to it, still the simple truth is that Edward himself was afraid of his brother Clarence, and had him arrested on charges of sorcery similar to those alleged against the Duchess of Gloucester in the preceding reign. But before the death of Clarence, Richard Gloster, marrying Anne Neville, became his brother-in-law. Monstrous as this marriage seems, Shakespeare has made it almost plausible. Anne was the daughter of Warwick, the Kingmaker, the widow of Henry VI.'s son, who, if the battle of Tewkesbury had had another termination, would have succeeded his father upon the throne. To

[1] Act I., Scene 1.

woo the widow of one and daughter of another of his
victims within two years after their death would seem
the height of hateful audacity. Shakespeare makes
the contrast sharper by beginning and ending the gris-
ly courtship over the very coffin of Henry VI., as it is
borne to its place of burial accompanied by the weep-
ing Anne. This wresting of the historic fact has its
meaning, however. Two years had not passed when
the marriage was accomplished. The poet indicates
the judgment of mankind upon such an unnatural union
by declaring in fact that lapse of time could not sufficiently excuse it on Anne's part. If she consented after
two years she would have said yes over the murdered
body of her father-in-law.

It is the most unspeakable wooing of history or fiction, as Richard even was fain to confide to himself:

> Was ever woman in this humor woo'd?
> Was ever woman in this humor won?
>
> .   .   .   .
>
> What! I, that killed her husband and her father,
> To take her in her heart's extremest hate ;
> With curses in her mouth, tears in her eyes,
> The bleeding witness of her hatred by ;
> Having God, her conscience, and these bars against me,
> And I no friends to back my suit withal,
> But the plain devil and dissembling looks,
> And yet to win her, all the world to nothing.[1]

Now to understand the mental and moral attitude of
the Lady Anne under such circumstances we should
have the benefit of a woman's criticism. We search in
vain among the characters touched by the pen of Mrs.

[1] Act I., Scene 2.

Jameson and Lady Helen Faucit Martin. Anne is passed over. The masculine mind fails to plumb the depths of this feminine mystery. Courtenay decides offhand that Anne's complacency is proof that Richard was not actually guilty of that double murder at least, which is an admirable *petitio principii.* Hudson simply remarks that her " seeming levity in yielding is readily forgiven in the sore burden of grief it entails upon her," and that her nature is " all too soft to stand against the crafty and merciless tormentor into whose hand she has given herself."

To my mind there is one explanation and one only. Richard was the strong man of his times. Ugly, deformed,

> Nor made to court an amorous looking-glass,

still he was a powerful individuality. By sheer force of intellectual strength he dominated, and fascinated men as well as women. If by any chance Anne had come under the spell of Richard's magic winning power, she could easily proceed step by step, from hatred of his crimes and contempt for his person, to admiring his genius, and exulting that, even in seeming, the strong man was at her feet. She might not have really believed that her "beauty was the cause of that effect," but she must have been moved to hear it so alleged. In other words, Anne was in love with Richard, and all that sparring of the courtship scene is the resistance of one who expects to be captured and desires to be. It must be remembered of course that even with such a dissembler as Richard one interview would not accomplish all he achieved. Nearly two years' romantic pursuit, baffled again and again by the jealousy of Clarence, is crowded within the compass of these lines. Clarence had married Anne's sister, and did not wish to share the great King-maker's wealth with his brother.

Richard's object in the marriage was two-fold: first, to get Anne's enormous property, and second, perhaps, to unite himself ever so slenderly with the Lancaster family, in preparation for his future assault upon the throne. Clarence is now haled to his death. In the play Richard is made the head and front of his sudden taking off, while Edward the king holds back, and is only with difficulty induced to sign the death-warrant, which he laments in a beautiful passage in answer to an appeal to save the life of a courtier's servant:

> Have I a tongue to doom my brother's death,
> And shall that tongue give pardon to a slave?
> My brother killed no man, his fault was thought,
> And yet his punishment was bitter death.
> Who sued to me for him? [1]

There is no doubt that Richard saw Clarence's death with complacency, and perhaps helped the king to its commission, but because Gloster has the bad name, we may not excuse Edward from the darkest stigma of his brother's execution.

Intermingled with the plottings weaving about the doomed, "false, fleeting, perjured Clarence" are indications of a growing restlessness in the royal household and in the court.

[1] Act II., Scene 1.

The factions of, respectively, the queen and the old noble families are clashing hotly. It will be remembered that Edward's love-match with the Lady Elizabeth Grey had not been pleasing to the court, any more than to Warwick. In "Henry VI." the king argues with his nobles, endeavoring to placate them, but incidentally is shown his secret misgivings and their scarce repressed disgust.

The speedy exaltation of the new queen's sons and relatives, the intermarriage of her family with some of the old aristocracy of the realm, perhaps her own indiscretions, natural to newly created royalty, all had weight in intensifying this feeling. Gloster made use of it. He hints to Clarence on that unfortunate's arrest:

> Why, this it is when men are ruled by women.
> 'Tis not the king that sends you to the Tower;
> My Lady Grey, his wife, Clarence, 'tis she
> That tempers him to this extremity.
>
> . . . .
>
> The jealous o'erworn widow and herself,
> Since that our brother dubbed them gentlewomen,
> Are mighty gossips in our monarchy.[1]

The quarrels between these factions at court, out of which Gloster makes his capital by assuming that he has been injured in the king's eye by Elizabeth's representations, are made an occasion for the strangest historical anachronism, and yet most faithful interpretation of that stormy period.

The queen, smarting under unjust accusations and insults, replies after a long, quarrelsome discussion, in

[1] Act I., Scene 1.

which the different characters are set forth, revolving still about Richard and his schemes :

> My lord of Gloster, I have too long borne
> Your blunt upbraidings and your bitter scoffs.
> By Heaven, I will acquaint his majesty
> Of those gross taunts that oft I have endured.
> I'd rather be a country servant-maid
> Than a great queen with this condition,
> To be so baited, scorned, and stormed at :
> Small joy have I in being England's queen.[1]

And now appears, first in asides, unseen by the persons of the drama, and then openly, Margaret of Anjou. Actually she had at this time retired to her exile on the Continent, and was nursing her sad memories far from the shores where she had played a man's part battling for her rights. But potentially she was present at the factional quarrels of the English court, in a real and sensible manner. In one way she had been one of the occasions of the Wars of the Roses. Her marriage with Henry VI. had been accomplished at the cost of French provinces, won in glorious battle. She opposed the power of those English nobles who sought to hold her husband in tutelage. She had pinned the Lancastrian rose to her proud bosom in loyalty, and nourished its failing petals while others were falling away from the losing cause. She had kept the embers of civil strife alive, and to her indomitable perseverance in behalf of her husband and son England owed much of the miseries of the last days of Henry VI. But she had been fighting for a principle,

---

[1] Act I., Scene 3.

honorable and noble, against injustice, perjury, and wrong. She was defeated, her husband slain, her son deprived of his heritage. By poetic license she now comes back to the scene of her former triumphs and defeats, to gloat over the factional struggles of her enemies. One after another, in asides, she characterizes the quarrelling courtiers, the queen, Gloster, the memory of Clarence, "who did forsake his father, Warwick, and forswear himself," and finally breaks forth in their faces:

> Hear me, you wrangling pirates that fall out
> In sharing that which you have pill'ed from me.

But at once the chorus is turned upon the person of their common enemy. Their own quarrels are forgotten in the meed of cursing due this foreign interloper. "What," she cries,

> "Were you snarling all before I came,
> Ready to catch each other by the throat,
> And turn you all your hatred now on me?
>
> .   .   .   .
>
> Can curses pierce the clouds and enter heaven?
> Why, then, give way, dull clouds, to my quick curses.
> Though not by wars, by surfeit die your king,
> As ours by murder to make him a king.
> Edward, thy son, that now is Prince of Wales,
> For Edward, my son, which was Prince of Wales,
> Die in his youth by like untimely violence.
> Thyself a queen, for me that was a queen,
> Outlive thy glory, like my wretched self.
> Long mayst thou live to wail thy children's death
> And see another, as I see thee now,
> Decked in thy rights, as I am stalled in mine.
>
> .   .   .   .

Rivers and Dorset, you were standers by—
And so wast thou, Lord Hastings—when my son
Was stabbed with bloody daggers. God, I pray him
That none of you may live your natural age,
But by some unlooked accident cut off.[1]

We forbear to quote her awful curse upon Richard,
whom she instinctively recognizes as the real "troub-
ler of this poor world's peace." But it will be observed
that Margaret is introduced much after the fashion of
Chorus, a combination of prediction and commentary
upon the persons and events with whom her influence
is still powerful. This vindictive shade of Margaret
in the play is one of the great artistic and dramatic
triumphs of the poet. Absent in body, she is literally
still present in English intrigue and politics. As these
very factional quarrels proceeded from the victory of
the York faction over the Lancastrian, whose virile
chieftain Margaret had been, and whose wrongs had
been mainly involved, so the dramatic use of her restless ghost as the mouthpiece of vengeance is justified.
Her invocation was to be sorely and literally fulfilled.

At the end of this scene Gloster's soliloquy upon
his own hypocrisy is worth re-reading as the poet's
conception of his historic character :

I do the wrong, and first begin to brawl.
.   .   .   .

Clarence, whom I indeed have cast in darkness
I do beweep to many simple gulls,
Namely, to Stanley, Hastings, Buckingham,
And tell them 'tis the queen and her allies
That stir the king against the duke my brother.

[1] Act I., Scene 3.

Now they believe me, and withal whet me
To be revenged on Rivers, Dorset, Grey,
But then I sigh, and with a piece of Scripture
Tell them that God bids us do good for evil;
And thus I clothe my naked villany
With old odd ends, stolen forth of holy writ,
And seem a saint when most I play the devil.[1]

Most evil men seek to cast a decent veil of excuse over their real and inner life. But Richard drew no veils whatsoever. He simply played hypocrite, acted as a hypocrite might act, but only used hypocrisy as he used demagogism, to accomplish his personal ends for the moment. The act ends with the actual murder of Clarence at Richard's instigation.

We are now introduced to the bedside of the dying Edward, who had the end, somewhat unusual in his house, of dying in his bed. This scene of the apparent reconciliation of the two opposing parties of the realm is historic.

Well did Edward know the probabilities of a renewal of internecine strife. Well did he know Gloster's ambitious soul. Well, also, he must have known the rivalries between the newly made nobles and those of the old régime. To patch up a peace, and make them swear fealty to each other and to the young prince who was to succeed to the throne, was the only thing Edward could do, as, when brought face to face with death, he says :

I every day expect an embassage
From my Redeemer, to redeem me hence,

[1] Act I., Scene 3.

And now in peace my soul shall part in heaven,
Since I have made my friends at peace on earth.[1]

So died Edward IV., as strange a compound of king as ever sat upon a throne.

Bulwer-Lytton's novel, "The Last of the Barons," gives a very fair if not flattering portrait of him. At once soldier and voluptuary, with a good mind and a weak will; haughtily independent to the point of breaking his word with the King of France and the powerful Warwick, in order that he might marry a simple gentlewoman for love, yet easily led by his favorites; a patron of learning, yet loose of life. He had the weakness of Henry VI. without the gentle sweetness of soul that redeemed it. He will occupy a fair place in history, mainly because of a somewhat neutral reign sandwiched between the helplessness of his predecessor and the cruelty and ferocity of his virtual successor, for his son, Edward V., reigned but thirteen weeks. And now begins that struggle for a throne, none the less bitter and blighting because it did not appear upon the surface of events. Richard Gloster was in the north on some warlike errand for the crown, when he learned that Edward IV. had passed away. The hollow truce patched up by the dead king dissolves at once. Outwardly there is no opposition to the coronation of young Edward V. But his mother knows the perils of the way to a secure seat upon that throne where she had sat so fearfully, though held there by a royal hand. The queen's relations and friends feel instinctively that their fate is bound up with that of the child-king. The people have their thoughts, too, which

---

[1] Act II., Scene 1.

they express with bated breath. Says one citizen greeting another :

Doth the news hold of good King Edward's death?
.   .   .   .   .   .
Ay, sir, it is too true ; God help the while.
.   .   .   .   .   .
Then, masters, look to see a troublous world.
.   .   .   .   .   .
Woe to that land that's governed by a child.[1]

They knew, perhaps, of Richard II.'s childish grasp upon the sceptre, and they had felt the evils of Henry VI.'s babe-royalty.

There was no time lost by either side. The two young princes, Edward, now the Fifth, and Richard, Duke of York, were with their mother, guarded by Rivers, Dorset, Grey, upstarts in the eyes of Buckingham and his fellows. Richard Gloster moves to London to assist in his nephew's coronation, which was set for April 4th. Edward, surrounded by his mother's clan—Rivers, Vaughan, and Grey notably—proceeds from Ludlow Castle toward London. Rivers, on the part of the boy-king, meets Gloster at Northampton and is there arrested. The young king and his friends are joined at Stony Stratford the next morning by the ambitious duke with Buckingham at his heels to carry out his behests. The friends of the queen are arrested, and the boy-king surrounded by his enemies, who profess friendship and fealty, as well as thanksgiving at having rescued him from those who sought, as they said, to gain control of his person only to subvert the realm. This is the beginning of the

[1] Act II., Scene 2.

end.   The party of Gloster proceed, ostensibly yet for the purpose of celebrating the coronation, to London.

But meanwhile news of these rough measures had flown to the queen's ears.

> "Ah, me," she cries, "I see the ruin of my house;
> The tiger now hath seized the gentle hind,
> Insulting tyranny begins to jet
> Upon the innocent and aweless throne." [1]

She seizes upon what she believes is the last chance of safety for herself, and with the young Duke of York flies to the sanctuary of Westminster.

Now follows the swearing of loyalty to Edward V. by the nobility, with Richard, Duke of Gloster, as Protector of the realm.   The ambitious schemer has nearly reached the top round of his plotting.   He is in a position to reward his allies, which he does with a liberal hand, using his semi-royal prerogative to bind them closer to his interests.   Hastings was still with Richard and Buckingham, believing that in the arrest of the queen's friends he was but securing the best interests of the realm.   The young king is lodged in the Tower, awaiting the still delayed coronation.   The next move in the tragedy is set down by Shakespeare with unsparing fidelity.   It is a meeting of the Council : Hastings speaks :

> Now, noble peers, the cause why we are met
> Is to determine of the coronation.
> In God's name, speak.   When is the royal day ?
> .   .   .   .
> *Buck.*   Who knows the Lord Protector's mind herein ? [2]

---

[1] Act II., Scene 4.   [2] Act III., Scene 4.

Enters now Gloster, who after some light compliment to Hastings and a request that the Bishop of Ely should send for some notable strawberries, takes Buckingham aside :

> Cousin of Buckingham, a word with you.
> Catesby hath sounded Hastings in our business,
> And finds the testy gentleman so hot
> That he will lose his head ere give consent
> His master's child, as worshipfully he terms it,
> Shall lose the royalty of England's throne.[1]

The conspirators withdraw for consultation, but to speedily return for the acting out of their drama. Hastings, representing the loyal nobility, faithful to the throne and blood royal, rather than to this or that faction, stands in the way of their plot. Gloster bursts out wrathfully, addressing the Council :

> I pray you all, tell me what they deserve
> That do conspire my death with devilish plots
> Of damned witchcraft, and that have prevailed
> Upon my body with their hellish charms?[2]

With well-simulated rage he levels his malicious charges against Hastings, and exhibits his withered arm (which had been so from his birth) as though it were the result of sorcery. Slowly that innocent victim, who had been warned by Stanley of the approaching storm, realizes his doom and England's woe :

> Woe, woe for England, not a whit for me,
> For I, too fond, might have prevented this
> .   .   .   .

---

[1] Act III., Scene 4.   [2] Ibid.

> Oh, Margaret, Margaret, now thy heavy curse
> Is lighted on poor Hastings' wretched head.[1]

And this is the end of almost the only amiable and virtuous man who plays a man's part in this tragedy. The pitiful subterfuges of Gloster and Buckingham, that they had been suddenly attacked, the peace of the realm threatened, and the king imperilled by a plot against the Lord Protector, were all too successful, and the citizens of London were infected with the subtle poison of doubt concerning the legitimacy of Edward IV. and consequently of his sons.

The reputation of Edward as a loose gallant was a well-chosen basis of attack against his character. The mass of people are, on the whole, true to the domestic instincts, and resent their betrayal, especially by those who are set over them in authority. The homes of England have ever been the source of her real strength in courts and on battle-fields. Singularly enough, too, the most hated of vices is easiest of belief by those who detest it most. It was no difficult matter for Buckingham and his paid subordinates so to blacken the name of Edward that it reflected upon his sons. But that Richard stood by willing to defame his mother, in order to have the crown by a show of legitimacy revert to himself, would pass belief did we not know that like perversions of nature are of frequent enough recurrence in history to warrant the probable truth of this one.

Richard's partial betrayal of sentiment as he whispers his atrocious lies to Buckingham does not redeem him in our eyes.

[1] Act III., Scene 4.

> Yet touch this sparingly, as 'twere far off,
> Because you know, my lord, my mother lives.[1]

One line here of Richard's as he dismisses his hench-
men to their several tasks of preparing the people to
greet him as their king, brings up a point of much
historic interest.

> Go, Lovell, with all speed to Doctor Shaw.[2]

On June 22d was delivered at St. Paul's Cross, by the
Rev. Ralph Shaw, a sermon on a text from the Book of
Wisdom, "The multiplying brood of the ungodly shall
not thrive." A report of this sermon was made at the
time by Fabyan, the chronicler, as follows :

> By the mouth of the Rev. Ralph Shaw in the time of his
> sermon was there showed openly that the children of King
> Edward IV. were not legitimate, nor rightful inheritors of
> the crown, with many dis-slanderous words, in preferring of the
> title of the said Lord Protector, and of disannulling of the
> other.

This was based upon the story which was industriously
circulated and believed, that Edward had been secretly
married, before his union with Lady Grey, and that
this first wife, undivorced, was alive. Shakespeare intimates in the line just quoted that Dr. Shaw's sermon
was instigated by Richard, with how much truth is
not known.

The course of events is now indicated in the dialogue between Richard and Buckingham, and in the
famous scene where the former permits his scruples to
be overcome, and to assume the crown.

[1] Act III., Scene 5.   [2] Ibid.

15

Glos. How now, how now, what say the citizens?
Buck. The citizens are mum, say not a word,

      .   .   .   .

But like dumb statues or breathing stones
Stared each on other and looked deadly pale,
Which when I saw, I reprehended them,
And asked the mayor what meant this wilful silence.

      .   .   .   .

The mayor, evidently without relish, addressed the mob, and Buckingham continues:

When he had done, some followers of mine own,
At lower end o' the hall, hurled up their caps,
And some ten voices cried, " God save King Richard ! "
And thus I took advantage of those few :
"Thanks, gentle citizens and friends," quoth I.
" This general applause and cheerful shout
Argues your wisdom, and your love to Richard."
Glos. What tongueless blocks were they. Would they not speak ?
Will not the mayor, then, and his brethren come ?
Buck. The mayor is near at hand ; intend some fear ;
Be not you spoke with, but by mighty suit ;
And look you, get a prayer book in your hand,
And stand between two churchmen, good my lord,
For on that ground, I'll make a holy descant ;
And be not easily won to our requests.
Play the maid's part. Still answer nay, and take it.[1]

Now in these passages are indicated two historical facts. The people were slow to give up the cause of the young princes, and Richard's assumed austerity and pious demeanor, as well as his apparent reluctance to take the crown offered by his own claquers, were played off against the passions skilfully excited among

---

[1] Act III., Scene 7.

the people by tales of the late Edward's gallantry and looseness. "Alas!" cries Richard, pressed to take the crown,

> Alas! Why should you heap this care on me?
> I am unfit for state and majesty;
> I do beseech you, take it not amiss,
> I cannot, nor I will not yield to you.
> *Buck.* If you refuse it, as in love and zeal
> Loath to depose the child, your brother's son,
>
> .   .   .   .   .   .
>
> Yet know whether you accept our suit or no,
> Your brother's son shall never reign our king,
> But we will plant some other on the throne,
> To the disgrace and downfall of your house,
> And in this resolution here we leave you.
> Come, citizens, we will entreat no more.
>
> .   .   .   .   .   .
>
> *Glos.* Will you enforce me to a world of cares?
> Call them again. I am not made of stone,
> But penetrable to your kind entreaties,
> Albeit against my conscience and my soul.
>
> .   .   .   .   .   .
>
> But if black scandal or foul-faced reproach
> Attend the sequel of your imposition,
> Your mere enforcement shall acquittance me
> From all the impure blots and stains thereof;
> For God doth know and you may partly see
> How far I am from the desire of this.[1]

Richard Gloster is now crowned King of England. "In the first parliament thereafter," according to Knight,

"a statute was passed reciting that in a bill presented by many lords spiritual and temporal, and others of the commons in great multitude, the crown was claimed by Richard as his

---

[1] Act III., Scene 7.

father's heir, in consequence of a pre-contract of matrimony having been made by Edward IV. with dame Eleanor Butler, . . . by which his children became illegitimate, and that the line of the Duke of Clarence had been attainted." [1]

These were the legal grounds whereby Richard III. came into possession of the throne of England. We have noted how slowly, and as it were against their better judgment, the commons accepted this usurpation. Two reasons led them, doubtless, to acquiesce in it, once accomplished. One was a loathing of the bare idea of another civil war. A generation had grown up while the Roses were tossing above the pikes of St. Albans, Towton, Barnet, and Tewkesbury. Men were weary of drawing blood from their brethren. Peace at any price seemed honorable and the wisest patriotism. This is the first reason. It might not have held had there been a competent leader on the ground to dispute Richard's crown. The princes were boys. Their mother was deprived of the services of her family, all the leading spirits among them having been cast into prison. There was no Bolingbroke, no Hotspur, no Warwick, no Margaret of Anjou. True that far away in Brittany was the young Richmond of the House of Lancaster, grandson of Henry V.'s widow, the fair Katharine, of whom Henry VI. had said with the prescience of poetry :

This pretty lad will prove our country's bliss.
His looks are full of peaceful majesty ;
His head by nature framed to wear a crown ;
His hand to wield a sceptre; and himself

[1] Knight's History, Vol. II., Chapter VIII., page 166.

Likely in time to bless a regal throne.
Make much of him, my lords, for this is he
Must help you more than you are hurt by me.[1]

Richmond will presently stir into life, but at the critical moment when Richard mounts the throne of England he is too far off and perhaps forgotten, to be a
factor in the problem.   Both young princes are in the
Tower, from whence only their bones shall ever emerge
after more than two centuries of dispute and mystery
as to their fate.   Elizabeth, their mother, may not even
see them.

Eliz.   Master lieutenant, pray you, by your leave,
          How doth the prince and my young son of York?
Brak.   Right well, dear madam ; by your patience
          I may not suffer you to visit them ;
          The king hath strictly charged the contrary.
Eliz.   The king, who's that?
Brak.   I mean the Lord Protector.
Eliz.   The Lord protect him from that kingly title.
          Hath he set bounds between their love and me?
          I am their mother.   Who shall bar me from them?
Brak.   No, madam, no.   I may not leave it so.
          I am bound by oath and therefore pardon me.[2]

Now comes the messenger to Anne, who is with Elizabeth and sympathizing with her, to summon her to
her coronation, and thus Elizabeth feels the full thrall
of Margaret's curse.

"Nor mother, wife, nor England's counted queen."[3]

[1] Henry VL, Part III., Act III., Scene 7.
[2] Act IV., Scene 1.   [3] Ibid.

Once again this widowed mother, bereft of her children, who yet live, flies to the house of God for sanctuary, pausing but for a moment to utter her pathetic
adjuration to the Tower which holds her heart's beloved :

> Pity, you ancient stones, those tender babes
> Whom envy hath immured within your walls.
> Rough cradle for such pretty ones.
> Rude, ragged nurse, old sullen playfellow
> For tender princes, use my babies well.
> So foolish sorrow bids your stones farewell.[1]

Gloster's ambition is now attained. He is legally
seated on the throne, and Anne, daughter of Warwick,
is crowned his queen. It is always unsafe to infer
from a man's completed ambition, a life-long scheming
to attain it. And to simply read this play, or the
bare historic facts upon which it is founded, we are
led to suppose that Richard became a villain almost
offhand, that seeing the opportunity, he seized upon it
with a remorseless selfishness that counted no cost of
blood or bitter suffering in others. And this is another
reason why he appears the monster which he is depicted upon the stage. We see him in the full maturity
of his guilt. But without going farther than the facts
will warrant, we may trace in the previous plays a sort
of evolution of the character which blossomed into this
evil, tainted, Rose of York.

Theorists are reasonably fond of tracing the beginning of his wickedness to the sensitiveness of youth,
conscious of great powers of mind, encased in a deformed and ugly body.

[1] Act IV., Scene 1.

King Henry's speech expresses what Richard seems to have thought all the world believed :

> The owl shrieked at thy birth, an evil sign.
> The night crow cried, aboding luckless time.
> Dogs howled and hideous tempests shook down trees.
>
> .   .   .   .
>
> Thy mother felt more than a mother's pain
> And yet brought forth less than a mother's hope,
> To wit, an undigest, deformed lump.[1]

And Gloster gradually took this opinion bitterly to heart, and resolved to live accordingly. What men expected of him they should have. Without fault of his he had been made a sort of physical monster. He would be what he seemed. The world should have him at its own valuation.

> Then since the heavens have shaped my body so,
> Let hell make crooked my mind to answer it.[2]

At first sensitive and bitterly shy, he broods over it ; loathes every one about him, because he thinks himself loathsome to them. Then, as he appreciates his own intellectual strength and extraordinary mental capacity, he glories in his deformities as having the potency of unwelcome surprises for those who look down on him. He is *facile princeps*, after the death of Warwick, among the men of the court. We see in the play how he twists and turns the strongest of them to his will. It is quite conceivable that the idea of the throne was not at first present in his wicked schemings, that held no one sacred, no life secure, no blood

---

[1] Henry VI., Part III., Act V., Scene 6.   [2] Ibid.

precious. We remember the pleased, almost startled, surprise at his success in the wooing of Anne, and the resolutions it induced:

> My dukedom to a beggarly denier
> I do mistake my person all this while.
> Upon my life she finds, although I cannot,
> Myself to be a marvellous proper man.
> I'll be at charges for a looking-glass,
> And entertain a score or two of tailors,
> To study fashions to adorn my body.
> Since I am crept in favor with myself,
> I will maintain it with some little cost.[1]

Humorously exaggerated as this is, we trace the idea in Richard's mind and see how he carried it into effect as he mingled in the politics of the times. He finds himself able to lead, control, master, people. He will do this wherever it leads him, in revenge for nature's deprivation of those physical adornments which aided other men. Others used their natural parts and beauties to advance themselves. He will show advancement in spite of, even by means of, his deformities. (Note that scene in the council chamber at the arrest of Hastings, where he displays his withered arm.)

The wooing of Anne is thus a part and parcel of the evolution of Richard's character along these lines. So he surveyed the court, and measured the resources of its factions. In pure malignity, he pushed the dagger of his spite into first this one, then that, until he perceived the crown glittering before him. It came in his way, and he took it, grimly smiling doubtless at the

---

[1] Act I., Scene 2.

thought of what Warwick would have thought, or Henry VI., or Edward IV.

But once gained, there is a thorn in this crown. "Ha, am I King? 'Tis so, but Edward lives." That is disposed of without much trouble. The princes are slain and their bodies buried, only to be resurrected in comparatively modern times. But in this incident Shakespeare falls into a mistake concerning Buckingham, and so often an historical mistake which becomes a clever dramatic triumph. Buckingham's falling away was not on account of Richard's desire to have the young princes slain. It is one of the tangled mysteries of history, why he did fall away so soon, and after being loaded with benefits from the free hand in which he had helped to place the sceptre of England. But he was not the man to have uttered words at Richard's first suggestion of the murder that should cause the wily plotter to exclaim:

> High reaching Buckingham grows circumspect.[1]

But he was the man, as Shakespeare hints again, when the king grows cold toward him, to resent not having a full share of the spoils of the usurpation.

> My lord, I claim the gift, my due by promise,
> For which your honor and your faith is pawned.
> .   .   .   .
> I am thus bold to put your grace in mind
> Of what you promised me.[2]

And the king's dry, cold sneer:

> I am not in the giving vein to-day,

---

[1] Act IV., Scene 2.   [2] Ibid.

probably expressed his impatience at the importunities of one for whom he considered he had done enough and rewarded amply.

Buckingham probably failed to receive the consideration he thought his due. At all events, shortly after the coronation of Richard and Anne he is up in arms, and in active correspondence with the Earl of Richmond, who sets forth from Brittany, but by a storm is beaten back from the coast. The unfortunate Buckingham, deprived of his ally, is taken prisoner, and had to his share what he had so often awarded others, and on the scaffold cries :

> Thus Margaret's curse falls heavy on my neck.
> " When he," quoth she, " shall split thy heart with sorrow,
> Remember Margaret was a prophetess." [1]

And now Richmond is on the seas, and his star begins to rise. He is the last living direct heir of the Lancastrian line which was set aside when Edward IV. of York came to the throne. Henry, Earl of Richmond, was the son of Edmund, who was the son of Owen Tudor and Katherine, the widow of Henry V. He was also the lineal descendant, by Katherine Swynford, of John of Gaunt. He thus inherited in the Lancastrian line, although this line was debarred by Parliament from the throne. Queen Anne had died and her infant son. Richard was again " himself alone," not without suspicion, say the Chronicles, that he had murdered his wife. Before this he had paid such attention to his niece Elizabeth, Edward's daughter, as to create scandalous talk at court.

[1] Act V., Scene 1.

The poet represents him truly at this juncture, with a rising cloud in the sky of his prosperity, seeking marriage with his niece, in order probably to so unite the house of York upon the throne as to prevent the possibility of being disturbed by the last scion of Lancaster.

There is much dispute about Shakespeare's intention in that scene where Richard woos the young princess through her mother. History assures us both that Edward's Queen consented to this match, and at the same time had pledged her daughter's hand to the Earl of Richmond, which was an ideal political marriage from the standpoint of the nobles who hated Richard, and wished well to England. In the play, after a scene of cursing and cajolery very similar to that of the wooing of Anne, Elizabeth appears to yield to Richard's blandishments. We need not believe the poet intended it for more than seeming. He here means to indicate how Richard's intellectual cunning was beginning to o'erreach itself. The snare into which Anne had fallen he spread for Elizabeth, and fell into himself. The Queen hoodwinked him and intended to. "Relenting fool, and shallow changing woman," as Richard thought her, she was then in correspondence with Richmond, and destined once more to see happy days in the reign of her daughter as England's queen. Richard held a kingdom in his hand; swayed the councils even of his enemies; tossed human souls into eternity without effort; but he did not see into this wronged woman's ruse, nor know that love is stronger than arms and scaffolds.

Richmond is at the gates of his heritage. He has

not a large army. A few of the discontented nobles come to greet him. The friends of Edward IV. come out of their sorrowful retirement to gather about a Lancastrian who is preferable at last to their own White Rose. The ex-queen's friends flock to him, but the people are comparatively indifferent. There is no great uprising of the commons either for Richard or for Richmond. The people indeed are curiously and sullenly indifferent, except those who, with remnants of feudal attachment feel they are fighting the battle of their chiefs. Richard gathers his armies, also small in number. He holds his rival but cheaply, and calls him " Shallow Richmond."

It is the night before the battle of Bosworth Field.[1] The handling of this scene of the last act reminds us somewhat of the eve of Agincourt. Now we see Richmond confident that he is God's captain, yet alert in preparation against the wiles and stratagems of the " wretched, bloody, and usurping boar." Now we behold Richard, restless, anxious, " I will not sup tonight," drinking great bowls of wine, without somehow " that alacrity of spirit and cheer of mind he was wont to have." The busy preparations are all made. The night falls. Richard and Richmond sleep. To both come visions in that night before the day of fate. The poet may not be quarrelled with for introducing ghosts upon the mimic stage. The moral *raison d'être* of these spirits, who rise first to one and then to the other of the leaders, is unquestionable. In Richmond's dreams he is comforted and strengthened by assurance that his course is just. In Richard's he is tormented

[1] Act V., Scene 3.

and disturbed by the guilty deeds of his past, which now rise in judgment upon him. Those ghosts did truly represent the moral attitude of the two leaders in the last struggle between the houses of York and Lancaster.

> God and good angels fight on Richmond's side
> And Richard falls in all his height of pride.[1]

No use of soliloquies could here accomplish the end aimed at, to place the moral strength and weakness of this struggle before us. The feeble outburst of Richard as he rouses from his crime-haunted sleep, is evidence of this. That speech beginning, "Give me another horse, bind up my wounds,"[2] is wretched as compared with former soliloquies. It seems a poor bit of actor's fustian. The ghosts, on the other hand, may be inartistic, as is often objected, but they are powerful dramatic auxiliaries. Through their wailing moans we hear the last note of cold despair beginning to sweep across the soul of the usurping Richard. The memory of every crime lies heavy on his soul, as next day he met Richmond in the shock of battle, unnerving his courage and palsying his arm.

The battle of Bosworth Field ended in the victory of Richmond, who was triumphantly crowned king as Henry VII. It ended the wars of the Roses, and the life of the last Plantagenet King. He dies like a soldier, nobler in that moment than when he had reigned over all England. "Then truly," says the old Chronicle, "in a very moment, the residue all fled, and

---

[1] Act V., Scene 3.   [2] Ibid.

king Richard, alone, was killed fighting manfully in the thickest press of his enemies." So ended the wars of the Roses. Richmond was crowned king, upon the field of battle. Shortly after he was ratified in his prerogatives and kingdom by Parliament. He married Elizabeth of York, and the blood of the rival houses mingled in the veins of their son Henry VIII. Shakespeare has not touched with his pen the period between Richard III. and Henry VIII., but in his last chronicle play with the latter as its titular hero, he completes the story begun with the reign of King John.

One cannot turn from the tragedy of Richard III. with a true regard for its historic importance, without a word as to its women characters. Anne's sorrows and fate redeem in the eyes of sentiment her degrading folly. The old Duchess, mother of Richard, is well sustained both dramatically and historically.

Elizabeth, queen of Edward, mother of the princes of the Tower, is admirable. She may have been a light woman and indiscreet. She may have forwarded too busily the fortunes of her family, but this is a trait of human, not especially of woman, nature, and has its noble side. We must maintain that she overreached Richard in the end, by the keen unscrupulousness of a loving woman when those she loves are in peril. For her deception and ruse of acquiescence, we may have great charity.

Margaret of Anjou, restless shade of a dissonant and bloody past, remains a heroine. She alone, always and to his face withstands the powerful, dominant hunchback, "hell's black intelligencer." Even Richard must have admired her. " Bear with me," she cries not only to the Queen, but down the centuries it is her frank appeal to the judgment of history.

> Bear with me, I am hungry for revenge?
> And now I cloy me with beholding it.[1]

There are few instances of a passion more detestable in the heart of one more excusable for nursing it.

Great progress was making during the easy years of Edward, and the perturbed reign of Richard, in the development of literature. The Woodvilles, family of Edward's queen, encouraged learning and were patrons of Caxton, the first English printer, who, under an overruling Providence, did more by his art than kings by their swords, to make England great. After the preceding pages, it seems strange to connect the familiar names with peaceful arts. Yet the unfortunate Rivers was an accomplished author and translator, and the first English book printed was dedicated to "false fleeting perjured Clarence."

Even Richard has made letters his debtor, for in his reign was passed a tariff law expressly excepting from its provisions " any maner of bokes, written or imprynted."

With the spread of books, written or printed, went *pari passu* the intelligence of the commons. The people turned over the fluttering pages of Bible and Chronicle to learn many lessons for present and future. The minds of England's peasantry and minor gentry had been stagnant, until into the pools of standing water were poured the fresh streams of poet, prophet, chronicler.

[1] Act IV., Scene 4.

Henry Tudor looked out upon a new land as he lifted his eyes from Bosworth Field. The Baron was there, the Churchman was there, but there too was a swarming multitude who uttered the voice of a third power, more potent to influence kings than priest or noble, the power of the Common People, tilling the soil as of old, but reading their books as not of old, their Bible chief of all, and learning the lessons of self-government, self-restraint, and self-respect.

HENRY VIII.

There is no other known play with this reign as its theme from which Shakespeare seems to have borrowed. "The Life of Wolsey," by Cavendish (included in Holinshed), and Fox's "Book of Martyrs," were principal sources of information. Many passages are transcribed almost word for word from these originals.

CHRONOLOGY OF THE REIGN OF HENRY VII.

BEING THE INTERVAL BETWEEN SHAKESPEARE'S PLAY OF RICHARD
III. AND HENRY VIII.

1486. Henry VII. marries Elizabeth of York, daughter of
Edward IV., thus uniting the rival claims of the Yorkists and
Lancastrians.

1487. Lambert Simnel, pretending to be the young Earl of
Warwick, son of George, Duke of Clarence, invades the kingdom and is defeated.

1492. War with France.

1492–99. Perkin Warbeck, pretending to be the Duke of York,
who was believed to have been murdered in the Tower,
carried on a desultory warfare in support of his claims to the
throne. He is finally executed. Arthur, son of Henry and
Elizabeth, married to Katharine of Aragon.

1502. On the death of Arthur, a contract of marriage is made
between his widow and his brother, afterward Henry VIII.

1509. Death of Henry VII.

CHRONOLOGY OF HENRY VIII.

FROM HIS ACCESSION, 1509, UNTIL 1533.

1509. Henry ascends the throne. Marriage between the King, aged eighteen, and Katharine of Aragon, aged twenty-six.

1513. Henry defeats the French in the battle of the Spurs. English defeat the Scotch at Flodden Field.

1514. Peace with France.

1515. Wolsey created Cardinal and Lord Chancellor.

1517. Wolsey made Papal Legate.

1520. Charles V. of Spain, and Emperor, makes a visit of state to Henry. Henry makes a visit of state to Francis I. of France. The Field of the Cloth of Gold.

SHAKESPEARE'S PLAY BEGINS.

1521. Impeachment and execution of Buckingham. Henry writes a book against Luther and receives the title of "Defender of the Faith" from Pope Leo X.

1523. Disagreement between Wolsey and the Commons.

1525. Forced loans resented by the people, and the policy abandoned by Henry.

1527. First doubts raised as to the validity of Henry's marriage with Katharine. Henry submits the question of divorce to Pope Clement VII.

1528. Wolsey and Campeggio appointed commissioners by the Pope to try the cause of the divorce.

1529. Queen Katharine appeals to Rome. Wolsey deprived of his dignities by the King.

1530. Wolsey apprehended for treason. His death.

1531. Katharine withdraws from the court.

1532. Anne Boleyn made Marchioness of Pembroke and privately married to Henry. Act of Parliament forbidding appeals of any sort to be made to Rome.

1533. Cranmer made Archbishop of Canterbury. Cranmer declares the marriage with Katharine null, and that with Anne Boleyn legal. Birth of Elizabeth, afterwards Queen.

CHAPTER VIII.

HENRY VIII.—THE ENGLISH REFORMATION.

Position of this play as epilogue to the series.—Henry VIII. unites the houses of Lancaster and York.—In his reign, civil-political strife succeeded by civil-ecclesiastical strife.—The significant period covered by the play.—Three tragical events, elaborately interwoven, form the centres of dramatic treatment.—(I.) The execution of the Duke of Buckingham. — (II.) The divorce of Katharine of Aragon.—(III.) The disgrace and fall of Cardinal Wolsey.—The Reformation writ large over the whole play. — The Field of the Cloth of Gold. — Contempt for the French.—Growing hatred against Wolsey.—Buckingham the scapegoat of this feeling.— His apprehension.—His real offence.—His execution.—The people see in him a victim of Wolsey's ambition.—Origin of the divorce question still in a haze of historic doubt.—Partisans settle it off-hand.—Students do not.—Henry's three-cornered dilemma in his relations with the Pope, the Emperor (Katharine's nephew), and the King of France.—Interwoven with these Wolsey's ambitious designs on the papal tiara —Henry's alleged scruples as to validity of his marriage with Katharine.—His conscience and Anne Boleyn.—Wolsey at first in favor of, then opposed to, the divorce. —Shuffling of all parties in the matter of the divorce.—Henry cuts the knot by breaking with Rome.—Cranmer appears.—Marriage and coronation of Anne.—The poet's treatment of Henry and the divorce.— Wolsey's fate grows out of the divorce proceedings, and the shadow of this great man is over the whole play.—His autocratic sway.—His extortions.—Three strands in the cord of his fate.—The rising tide of the reformation had its effects also.—Wolsey and Katharine.—Henry disgraces the once powerful subject.—His submission, repentance, and death.—The dominant note of these stirring times, nationalism, not protestantism.—Cranmer and Gardiner.—Henry's break with Rome more political than religious.—End of the play with the baptism of Elizabeth and a prophecy of England's future glory.

THE last of the English historical plays, and in many respects the most complete and picturesque in its portrayal of the period it covers. It was without doubt the last of the chronicles in order of composition, as well as in historic sequence. Its probable date, from internal evidence, was about 1603, before the death of Elizabeth, which occurred in the last of March that year. Malone dates it in 1601, Skottowe in 1603. And although most modern commentators agree upon a later date, no two fix the same. The reasons for holding to an early date are enlarged upon in the Appendix.[1]

As already noted, after the exhausting struggle of York and Lancaster, ending with the battle of Bosworth Field, Henry VII. came to the throne of England and united the warring factions by his marriage with Elizabeth of York, daughter of Edward IV. In their son Henry VIII. the people saw the blood of York and Lancaster mingling for the first time. The long duel was over, and England became once more a homogeneous nation, under a king who could be claimed by no faction, the founder of what was practically a new epoch for the English race. As John is shown to have been the first of English rulers to separate the nation from continental entanglement (barring those after ephemeral conquests which gave only a titular sovereignty over France to English kings), so Henry was the first to unite the English people among themselves, to stop the bloody flux of civil wars, and to lay the foundation, albeit amidst confusion and sorrows, of a happier and more prosperous national life.

These were the bright dreams of nobles and commons when Henry came to the throne, a handsome,

[1] Appendix, p. 299.

gallant youth in 1509. But when the play of Shakespeare opens twelve years later, in 1521, we find these
hopes disappointed.

Times have changed. Henry is no longer a generous
lad looking for honest guidance and submitting to wise
counsellors, but a headstrong, arrogant man, now
swayed by the meanest favorites who would pander to
his tastes ; again refusing all interference in his plans
whatsoever ; cold-blooded toward his best friends, re-
lentless in dealing with his enemies. Such favorites
as he has are looked upon with suspicion by the lords
of his court, and the abuse of taxation has aroused the
masses to protest against exaction. We are introduced
at once to an *entourage* of jealousy, avarice, vaulting
ambition, and self-seeking. The air is impure; the
surroundings are tawdry ; the motives of most of the
dramatis personœ are for the great part sordid.

The prologue to the play deftly indicates this, and
is a keynote to the whole well worth study. It begins
with these lines :

> I come no more to make you laugh : things now
> That bear a weighty and a serious brow,
> Sad, high, and working, full of state and woe :
> Such noble scenes as draw the eye to flow
> We now present. . . .

It ends with these :

> Think ye see
> The very persons of our noble story,
> As they were living ; think you see them great
> And followed with the general throng and sweat
> Of thousand friends ; then in a moment, see
> How soon this mightiness meets misery.[1]

---

[1] Vide Prologue to Henry VIII.

This last line gives a key-note to the play. In the lives of many of the characters "mightiness met misery." So also with the nation at large. The poet has cleverly brought his drama to an end in the baptism of Elizabeth, as a prophecy of how in her reign might should conquer misery, and he breaks off not too soon in the march of events; for the succeeding years of his titular hero's reign would not have borne transference to the stage.

There are three events, all tragic in their nature, around which the action of the play revolves. All are historic, and there is but little deviation, even in details, from the actual history as recorded in Cavendish's "Life of Wolsey," from which the poet took not only his facts, but occasionally his language.

The Cranmer incident in Act V. will be found in Fox's "Book of Martyrs," and is an almost literal reproduction from its pages. These three historic occurrences which give vertebrate consistency to the play are (I.) The Execution of Buckingham. (II.) The Divorce of Katharine; and (III.) The Fall of Wolsey. In addition, although there is very little direct reference to the wide-spread prevalence of the new religious doctrines, we are carried by the action of the play over that important and troubled period which may be called the threshold of the English Reformation. It is a singular coincident fact, that the year 1521, in which the play opens, marked the publication of Henry's celebrated book against Luther and his heresy, which won for him from the Pope the title "Defender of the Faith;" and that in 1533, the year with whose happenings the play closes, were enacted those acts of

Parliament which cut off England forever as a. spiritual fief of the Roman See.

The dramatic use made of the accusation and arrest of Buckingham presents in strongly drawn outline the England of the pre-Reformation period.

We have first an indication of that semi-barbaric taste of even cultivated monarchs, for such displays as that of the Field of the Cloth of Gold, when

> To-day the French
> All clinquant, all in gold, like heathen gods,
> Shone down the English ; and, to-morrow they
> Made Britain India ; every man that stood
> Showed like a mine.[1]   .   .   .   .

So Norfolk describes this celebrated pageant, and in the conversation which ensues, creeps out the growing hatred of Cardinal Wolsey's despotic policy in state affairs, while it is more than hinted that the glittering display was managed by him to further selfish ends. The sober second sense of England is expressed to the effect that such stupendous shows, however gratifying to the national pride, were not in the end worth the price paid, but were " purchased at a superfluous rate." The treaty made with France at this time was soon broken, and there were not a few who made bold to charge the " o'er great Cardinal " with the rupture, again for selfish ends, even as the result of a bargain with Charles the Emperor.[2]   For purposes of the

[1] Act I., Scene 1.

[2] The introduction of Wolsey's name so early in the play, as influencing the course of events, is a happy dramatic foreshadowing of the influence which this single great character is to have on all the persons and incidents involved.   Wolsey is as essential a personalty to the drama of Henry VIII. as Hamlet to the tragedy which bears his name.

drama the strongest expressions of popular feeling are put in Buckingham's mouth, as "This top proud fellow . . . I do know to be corrupt and treasonous," and

> He (the emperor) privily
> Deals with our cardinal; and as I trow
> Which I do well; for I am sure the emperor
> Paid e'er he promised; whereby his suit was granted
> Ere it was asked.[1]

But this was the sentiment of the majority of the proud lords who clustered about Henry's throne, and Buckingham is the dramatic puppet to give it voice, because he was the one to suffer the vengeance of the Cardinal, as a sort of scapegoat to warn the rest that Wolsey was not to be trifled with.

Buckingham was arrested for treason, tried, and condemned to death. The main charge against him was a too free boasting of what he would do on coming to the throne in case of the failure of issue to Henry.[2] There were confused allegations of treasonable remarks concerning the King's own person also, based upon the confession of a discharged servant. It is probable that Buckingham was involved in some of the discontents of the period, and as the next male heir to the throne, his name would have probably been used in every Cave of Adullam gathering of those discontented times. This would account for much, but it is questionable whether he would ever have been executed, had it not been that he was head and front of the op-

---

[1] Act I., Scene 1.

[2] He was the next heir if Henry died without issue, being the lineal descendant of Thomas, Duke of Gloucester, seventh son of Edward III.

position to Wolsey. High born himself, of royal descent, with the possible contingency of the throne before him, he could ill brook the insolence and court influence of the " venom mouthed butcher's cur," who by his rise from lowly surroundings to the pitch of prime favorite, had made a " beggar's book outworth a noble's blood."

Shakespeare correctly represents the popular feeling to have been with Buckingham. Perhaps this was partly from the sentimental pity which always accompanies the sharp misfortunes of a gifted and gallant leader, and partly from the well-known fact that he was convicted on the testimony of his own household, who thus basely betrayed the indiscreet words and actions uttered and expressed in the assumed safety of domestic confidence, " a most unnatural and faithless service." But chiefly the people deplored the Duke's taking off because they saw in him a hapless victim of the great Cardinal, whom they were learning to hate and fear. The two gentlemen who meet and exchange opinions over the trial, express the common opinion.

2d Gent.   Certainly,
          The cardinal is the end of this.
1st Gent.   'Tis likely,
          By all conjectures ; first Kildare's attainder,
          Then deputy of Ireland ; who, removed,
          Earl Surrey was sent thither, and in haste too,
          Lest he should help his father.
                         . . .   This is noted,
          And generally, whoever the king favors
          The cardinal will instantly find employment
          And far enough from court too.

2d Gent.   All the commons
Hate him perniciously, and o' my conscience
Wish him ten fathoms deep.[1]

In Buckingham's farewell speech, a splendid and
pathetic outburst, the poet puts in the Duke's mouth
words which he would hardly under the circumstances
have used, but particularly prophetic of Wolsey's
downfall, and finely indicative of the truth. After saying he heartily forgives those who sought his death,
he continues :

> Yet let them look they glory not in mischief,
> Nor build their evils on the graves of great men ;
> For then my guiltless blood must cry against them.[2]

These incidents of the accusation and trial of the
Duke of Buckingham are made to foreshadow the course
of future events which held in their last analysis the
fate of both Katharine and Wolsey. As over the
whole play the latter may be seen to throw the sombre
shadow of his influence, so throughout the greater
part of it, Katharine is set forth as a sort of glowing
foil to his ambitious schemes.

Historically out of place as Katharine's plea[3] for
the heavily taxed people is, it was probably substanti-
ally true, and another evidence that the poet grasped
the truth of history while not always keeping to its
letter. Katharine's appearance as the accuser of Wolsey here, is evidently made for purposes dramatic. It
is a striking picture. The Queen secure yet in her
wifely dignity, pure and spotless in her matronly in-
tegrity, strong in her position as wife of a great prince

[1] Act II., Scene 1.   [2] Ibid.   [3] Act I., Scene 2.

who grants her request before it is uttered, making plea for the oppressed commons, and charging the iniquity of unfair and burdensome exactions upon the first subject of the realm, and most powerful minister of state. This is the first indication in the play, and perhaps in point of actual time, where Henry traverses the action of his trusted cardinal.

Knight infers that Henry knew of the exactions, but that, after the manner of kings, he threw the blame on his minister, who took it humbly to himself as became a faithful servant. Shakespeare would have us suppose that Wolsey was the real source of

> . . . The subject's grief
> . . . Which compels from each
> The sixth part of his substance to be levied
> Without delay." [1]

And in furtherance of this he conveys the reasonable idea that kings must be unknowing to a great deal of their minister's transactions. "By my life," exclaims Henry, "this is against our pleasure." [2] The truth probably lies between the two. When Henry wanted money for his wars or his pleasures, he notified Wolsey, and so long as no complaints reached his royal ears, was careless of how his purse was filled. We must, however, bear in mind that Shakespeare's delineation of Henry's character was softened down as to its worst side by the fact that it was probably written for Elizabeth's eye ; and Elizabeth had quite too much of her father's blood in her veins, to allow one of her Majesty's Players to make too free with the reputation of her Majesty's father.

[1] Act I., Scene 2.   [2] Ibid.

Henry VIII. was a great king and Wolsey a great minister, but of the two Wolsey was the better man even before his downfall. Shakespeare makes him the worse, although he redeems at once the Cardinal's character and the truth of history, in the scenes depicting the last days of Wolsey's life.

The central point of the play, and perhaps the *tour de force* of Shakespeare's genius, is his treatment of the divorce of Katharine of Aragon, for twenty years "true and loyal wife" of England's king. Let the historic setting of Shakespeare's time be recalled, the better to demonstrate this opinion. The reigning sovereign was Henry's daughter Elizabeth by Anne Boleyn, for whose sake he had divorced his first wife. Elizabeth Tudor was an object of popular love and admiration. Mary, her predecessor, daughter of Henry by the divorced Katharine, was as eagerly detested. The state of religious parties was by no means conducive to partisanship in a stage play performed upon the public boards. The old faith was still the fond memory and passionate belief of many. The Established Church was the bulwark of national defence against Spain and France, and the majority of Englishmen were as loyal to it as to the state, in many cases doubtless for the same reason. The Puritan movement was deepening and strengthening, frowning alike on missal and prayer-book.

For a public composed of these elements Shakespeare wrote on the most delicate of all subjects—the revolt of England from the papal supremacy, the occasion of which, although not the cause, was Henry's quarrel with the Pope in the matter of the divorce of

Katharine. To say that Shakespeare accomplished his task without giving offence in any quarter, is much. But he did more, in that, with one possible exception, he so used the materials at his hand as to depart in no essential point from the truth of history. The exception is in his treatment of the character of Henry. In spite of Mr. Froude's learned and brilliant special plea, the student of history, unbiassed by religious prejudice or national pride, can have but one judgment on the life of Henry VIII. That dastard domestic life beginning with the divorce of Katharine, is marked by the sad names of Anne Boleyn, beheaded; Jane Seymour, dying in child-birth; Anne of Cleves, divorced; Catharine Howard, beheaded; and Catharine Parr, who survived him. This is a heavy record. But added to it must be the cruelty of heart which suffered him to discard without remorse one by one his most trusted and faithful servants, and the savagery of disposition which made his last breath a death-warrant. By the farthest stretch of charity, we may only give Shakespeare the credit of trying to reflect the spirit of his age regarding Henry, and that the subversion of the papal power in England was considered by Englishmen sufficient to wipe away all scores against the moral abasement of the king who was instrumental, whatever his motives, in establishing the church and nation on the strong foundation of autonomous government.[1] Through the tortuous web of these delicate facts the

---

[1] It is only fair to the poet also, to observe that the course of his drama does not touch upon the period of Henry's most conspicuous villainy. There is room for the apologist of Henry up to the birth of Elizabeth. There is none after the beheading of Anne.

poet deftly picked his way. No resentment could rise in Elizabeth's heart against the treatment of Anne Boleyn or Katharine. They are not pitted against each other in the play. The one is a picture of joyous and happy youth, drinking the first drop of a delicious cup; the other is presented in the dignity of conscious innocence and nobly borne grief. Elizabeth's legitimacy remains unquestioned, while Katharine's request to be buried as a queen obtains.

> When I am dead, good wench,
> Let me be used with honor : strew me over
> With maiden flowers, that all the world may know
> I was a chaste wife to my grave : embalm me ;
> Then lay me forth, although unqueened, yet like
> A queen, and daughter to a king, inter me.
> I can no more.[1]

The great question of the divorce, although bruited in 1527, was not completed until after Wolsey's death. Yet it was so intertwined with his fall from power and the king's grace, that it must be considered next now in order of events. The origin of it is still, after three centuries and a half, wrapped in mystery.

The political situation, and Henry's relation with the pope, and Charles of Spain, also emperor, must first be noted, and underlying all these, the ambitious plans of Wolsey, which affected them all. The Pope Clement was bound to Henry for the latter's services as Defender of the Faith, and a strong arm to be relied upon to help put down the new doctrines, which were fast spreading over Europe. But Wolsey had been a candidate for the papal tiara, which Clement

[1] Act IV., Scene 2.

had secured, and his personal feelings were not friendly toward his successful rival.

Charles of Spain, who was the nephew of Henry's wife, had assisted Clement to the papal chair, and had failed to make some (perhaps promised) recompense to Wolsey for his disappointment. The first reference of the play to the matter is given in a conversation between two gentlemen anent the arrest of the Duke of Buckingham, referring to certain public rumors.

1st Gentleman. . . . Did you not of late days hear
    A buzzing of a separation between the king and Katharine ?
2d Gentleman. . . . Yes, but it held not :
    For when the king once heard it, out of anger
    He sent command to the Lord Mayor straight
    To stop the rumor.[1]

Wolsey is at once connected with the matter (which connection is given more prominence than it deserved because of Shakespeare's desire to shield Henry so far as possible).

          'Tis the cardinal,
    And merely to revenge him on the emperor
    For not bestowing on him at his asking
    The Archbishopric of Toledo.[2]

Now as an historical fact the first known suggestion of the divorce arose in the alleged conscientious scruples of Henry over the legitimacy of his marriage with Katharine, because she had been previously married to his brother Arthur, who died.

It was a point brought forth by the Bishop of

[1] Act II., Scene 1.   [2] Ibid.

Tarbes, early in 1527, in the course of negotiations touching the marriage of Mary (Henry's daughter by Katharine) to the son of the French king. This envoy " questioned the validity of the pope's dispensation, and therefore of the marriage, and consequently Mary's legitimacy." This may well have touched Henry's pride, and we are called upon to believe his statement that it also touched his conscience :

> My conscience first received a tenderness,
> Scruple and prick, on certain speeches uttered
> By the Bishop of Bayonne, then French ambassador,
> Who had been hither sent on the debating
> A marriage, twixt the Duke of Orleans and
> Our daughter Mary.[1]

This whole speech of Henry's, too long to be here quoted, is singularly true in detail of what actually happened. Illuminated by the genius of the dramatist the dry facts present a striking picture of what Henry may have passed through in what he claims to have been a mental struggle that gave to him " many a groaning throe." The popular judgment, however, as to the origin of Henry's " mazed considerings," which with a deference to the well-known facts Shakespeare has allowed himself to indicate here and there throughout the play, and which has been practically accepted as the judgment of history, barring Mr. Froude, is summed up as follows :

> *Lord Cham.* It seems the marriage with his brother's wife
> Has crept too near his conscience.
> *Suffolk.*   No, his conscience
> Has crept too near another lady.[2]

[1] Act II., Scene 4.   [2] Act II., Scene 2.

17

After Wolsey began to fight shy of bringing the divorce to a consummation, the cause of his zeal to prevent, and Henry's to proceed, was plain to all eyes.

> For if
> It [the divorce] does take place "I do," quoth he, "perceive
> My king is tangled in affections to
> A creature of the queen's, Anne Bullen." [1]

Among the throng who witness the coronation of Anne is one sturdy gentleman who declares:

> Sir, as I have a soul she is an angel;
> Our king has all the Indes in his arms,
> And more, and richer, when he strains that lady.
> I cannot blame his conscience. [2]

Mild, gentle, and womanly as Katharine is, in her interview with Wolsey and Campeius (Campeggio), when they endeavor to move her to consent to the divorce procedings, she exclaims:

> Can you think, lords,
> That any Englishman dare give me counsel,
> Or be a known friend 'gainst his highness' pleasure
> (Though he be grown so desperate to be honest)? [3]

The fine scorn of this thrust at the king's troubled conscience is a touch of genius. But in the light of the king's own action of marrying Anne before the decree of divorce was pronounced, what more can be said in support of the conscientious twinge. The marriage took place about St. Paul's day, January 25, 1533. The divorce was pronounced May 23d, four

---

[1] Act III., Scene 2.   [2] Act IV., Scene 1.   [3] Act III., Scene 1.

months later. Elizabeth was born September 7th.
These dates are the condemnation of Henry, and perhaps also the condemnation of Anne.

About the time of the first whispering of the divorce
Wolsey, as already noted, was the enemy of Katharine's nephew, Charles of Spain, and was seeking close
alliance with the King of France. Whatever his reason was—probably he had his eye upon the papal succession again—the humbling of Charles through Katharine was a sweet morsel to him, and his hoped-for
marriage of the divorced king to the Duchess of Alençon (Francis's sister) would strengthen his influence at
the French court.

Norfolk and the Lord Chamberlain sum up the
public estimate of Wolsey's activity in the matter of
the divorce as follows :

Nor. How holily he works in all this business,
And with what zeal ; for now he has cracked the league
Between us and the emperor, the queen's great nephew.
He dives into the king's soul, and there scatters
Dangers, doubts, wringing of the conscience,
Fears and despairs, and all these for his marriage.
. . . .
Cham.   'Tis most true.
These news are everywhere ; every tongue speaks them,
And every true heart weeps for't. All that dare
Look into this affair see this main end,
The French king's sister.[1]

There is no doubt that Wolsey knew of Henry's attachment for Anne Boleyn before the divorce was
spoken of. He gave many entertainments in honor of

[1] Act IL, Scene 2.

the pair, one of which is exploited in Act I., Scene 4, an anachronism here, but an actual occurrence so famous as to have been noted in the chronicles. It is not to be supposed, however, that Wolsey contemplated Anne as anything more than the temporary diversion of the king. There was no reason in Wolsey's schemes for divorcing Katharine to replace her with Anne. Anne was known to be infected with the Reformed doctrines. As a favorite wife of the King of England she would have been a power for that spreading infection of Lutheranism which Wolsey hated with his whole soul. Listen to his soliloquy when he realizes Henry's purpose to be marriage :

> It shall be the Duchess of Alençon,
> The French king's sister ; he shall marry her.
> Anne Bullen. No, I'll no Anne Bullens for him.
> There is more in it than fair visage. Bullen,
> No, we'll no Bullens.
>
> .   .   .   .
>
> The late queen's gentlewoman ; a knight's daughter,
> To be her mistress' mistress, the queen's queen.
>
> .   .   .   .
>
> What though I know her virtuous
> And well deserving. Yet I know her for
> A spleeny Lutheran, and not wholesome to
> Our cause, that she should lie i' the bosom of
> Our hard-ruled king.[1]

Now it is certain that when once Wolsey knew the mind of the king concerning Anne, he cooled visibly in the matter of the divorce. He dragged out the proceedings interminably, and was disgraced and died before they came to effect.

[1] Act III., Scene 2.

Shakespeare, for purposes of dramatic unity, groups these events without much regard to the actual sequence of their happenings, but by so doing focussed more accurately the reader's eyes upon the salient truth.

Schlegel says : " I undertake to prove that Shakespeare's anachronisms are for the most part committed purposely and after great consideration." This is surely a truism. A student of the Reformation in England will get more real light as to the moving occasion of that event from this play of Henry VIII. than from any history, whether ecclesiastical or secular. And this not only in spite of, but because of, the anachronisms which were the work of a master-painter, who knew by intuition the effect of foreground and perspective, and proceeded by no formal rules.

This may be illustrated by comparing the words of the Chronicle in this affair of Wolsey's delay of the divorce with what has been already quoted from the poet's pen :

While things were thus in hand, the Cardinal of York was advised that the king had set his affections upon a young gentlewoman named Anne . . . which did wait upon the queen. This was a great grief unto the cardinal, as he that perceived aforehand, that the king would marrie the said gentlewoman if the divorce took place. Wherefore he began with all diligence to disappoint that match, which by reason of the misliking which he had to the woman, he judged ought to be avoided more than present death. While the matter stood in this state, and the cause of the queen was to be heard and judged at Rome, by reason of the appeal which by her was put in; the cardinal required the pope by letter and secret messengers, that in any wise he should defer the judgment of the divorce, till he might frame the king's mind to his purpose.[1]

These are the bald facts. Compare them with the cardinal's formerly quoted words concerning Anne Boleyn, and with that other nobler and pathetic utterence to Cromwell, when the king discovers by an accident his minister's treacherous course. The long and difficult path through which Henry was obliged to travel for his cherished end is sufficiently indicated, but not too tediously dealt with, in the play. It was a series of moves on the political chess-board of Europe as well as within the palace of England's king, alike shuffling and disingenuous on the part of all concerned. No stone was left unturned by Henry. The appeal to the universities :

> All the clerks,
> I mean the learned ones in Christian kingdoms,
> Have their free voices.

The appeal to Rome :

> Rome, the nurse of judgment,
> Invited by your noble self, hath sent
> One general tongue unto us, this good man,
> This just and learned priest, Cardinal Campeius,
> Whom once more I present unto your highness.[2]

The final disgust of the king and his determination to go on with the business in spite of pope, legates, or emperor, the break with Rome, and the beginning of the new *régime* are set forth in a paragraph :

---

[1] Chronicle quoted in Hazlitt's *Shakespeare's Library*, Part I., Vol. IV., pp. 95, 96.
[2] Act II., Scene 2.

King Henry.   I may perceive
These cardinals will trifle with me. I abhor
This dilatory sloth, and tricks of Rome.
My learned and well-beloved servant Cranmer,
Prithee, return : with thy approach I know
My comfort comes along.[1]

Previous to being called into the king's service, where
he was rapidly advanced to the Archbishopric of Canterbury, Cranmer had expressed an opinion publicly
that the divorce might be legally and morally settled
by decisions of learned men and universities.[2] Henry
is said to have sent for Cranmer upon hearing that he
had made such a statement, and from that moment the
first Protestant archbishop's star was in ascendency.
The old *régime* headed by Gardiner began to weaken
in power, and the autonomy of the English Church began to rise from the wreck of the old feudal depend-
ence upon Rome.

Once the break with Rome is assured there is no
further obstacle in Henry's path. The highest authority of the national Church dissolves the marriage
with Katharine, who is given the title of Princess
Dowager, which she steadfastly refuses to accept.
Anne Boleyn is crowned in great state in Westminster
Abbey, and enters upon her few years of royal progress. A paragraph or two may be quoted here illus-
trating Shakespeare's inimitable manner of catching
the spirit of a scene and making it glow with life and

---

[1] Act II., Scene 4.
[2] Bishop Burnett makes this statement, *History of the Reformation*,
Vol. I., p. 128. Courtenay makes the strange mistake of quoting Cranmer's
opinion, "the question of the marriage might be decided by native authorities," referring to Burnett I., 144, where it does not appear.

color.   One gentleman describes the coronation ceremonies to another:

1st *Gent.*   God save you, sir, where have you been broiling?
3d *Gent.*   Among the crowd i' the Abbey, where a finger
   Could not be wedged in more.   I am stifled
   With the mere rankness of their joy.
    . . . . . .

          The rich stream
   Of lords and ladies, having brought the queen
   To a prepared place in the choir, fell off
   A distance from her; while her grace sat down
   To rest awhile, some half an hour or so,
   In a rich chair of state, opposing freely
   The beauty of her person to the people.
    . . . . . .

      Which when the people
   Had a full view of, such a noise arose
   As the shrouds make at sea in a stiff tempest,
   As loud and to as many tunes : hats, cloaks,
   Doublets, I think, flew up ; and had their faces
   Been loose, this day they had been lost.[1]

What was the real position of Anne now in the midst
of all these stirring events?   Shakespeare's portrait
of her in the two scenes (aside from the coronation) in
which she is introduced has all the delicacy of a rare
water-color, daintily washed in.   Before the subject of
Katharine's divorce is touched upon, the poet with his
dramatic instinct presents Anne to his audience at one
of the fashionable masques of the time, in Wolsey's
house, where she meets the king by poetic license for
the first time.   The meaning is to convey, subtly and
without offence to Henry's memory, the well-known

[1] Act IV., Scene 1.

fact that the king had long known and paid his royal attention to Anne. Perhaps there was here a delicate reference to the often-referred-to fact, that although Anne accepted favors from the royal hand in the shape of titles and estates, she bestowed none in return until as a lawful wife she could with honor. Such an inference could not fail to be gratefully received by Anne's daughter, and Shakespeare among his other talents possessed those of an accomplished courtier.

The masque party where we first meet with Anne was a type of the entertainment then most affected by the English nobility.[1] The appearance of the king and some of his nobles in the fanciful garb of foreign shepherds, who " because they speak no English " send in a request to Wolsey by the Lord Chamberlain that they may be permitted to " share an hour of revels with them," was one of those freaks permitted to royalty. It was one of the causes of muttered discontent in Henry's early and middle reign that he encouraged too much the importation of foreign fads and fashions. A fresh treaty with France, as that of the Field of the Cloth of Gold, was sure to be followed by a fresh outbreak.

> New customs,
> Though they be never so ridiculous,
> Nay, let them be unmanly, yet are followed,
> As far as I see, all the good our English
> Have got by the late voyage is but merely
> A fit or two of the face.
> Their clothes are after such a pagan cut, too,
> That sure they have worn out Christendom.[2]

[1] Act I., Scene 4.   [2] Act I., Scene 3.

That there were jealousies and discontent among the untravelled courtiers appears, also, as is most natural :

Sir T. Lovell.   Faith, my lord,
     I hear of none but the new proclamation
     That's clapped upon the court gate.
Cham. What is 't for ?
Lov.   The reformation of our travelled gallants
     That fill the court with quarrels, talk, and tailors.
Cham. I am glad 'tis there : now I would pray our *monsieurs*
     To think an English courtier may be wise
     And never see the Louvre.[1]

The picture of Anne at these revels is that of any fair and blithesome maiden of the court circles in those days. The favor of the king does not overwhelm her. She gives and takes her little share in the light talk and jesting of such a merrymaking with ease and quickness of tongue. If one is expected to find some special trait of character here it must be that of light-heartedness. The scene calls for no emotion, but such demands as it makes upon the social powers of a young girl among her equals of fortune and birth, in the bare dozen words she utters, Anne fully meets neither better nor worse than a thousand English girls would have done under like circumstances. The same must be said of that other scene, in her conversation with the old court lady, one of those charmingly carved Shakespearean pawns which he ever puts to such good use as material with which to work out his plans. Here Anne shows more of the woman's nature. But it is still on the surface. Mrs. Jameson remarks, as a

[1] Act I., Scene 3.

woman would, "How nobly has Shakespeare done justice to the two women, and heightened our interest in both by placing the praises of Katharine in the mouth of Anne Bullen. And how characteristic of the latter, that she should first express unbounded pity for her mistress, insisting chiefly, however, on her fall from her regal state and worldly pomps, thus betraying her own disposition. That she could call the loss of temporal pomp once enjoyed 'a sufferance equal to soul and body severing' . . . how natural." [1]

Shakespeare will allow himself to give us no unpleasant impressions of Anne, and I must say that a study of the whole story warrants the poet's lightness of touch. He was true to history in leaving his hearers with tender and gentle thoughts of the mother of Elizabeth, as he was true to his art in, as Mrs. Jameson points out, "constantly avoiding all personal collision between" her and Katharine.

Anne was sincere in her pity for Katharine's fate:

> Here's the pang that pinches:
> His highness having lived so long with her, and she
> So good a lady that no tongue could ever
> Pronounce dishonor of her . . .
>   It is a pity
> Would move a monster.

She was sincere in her own first feeling:

> I swear 'tis better to be lowly born,
> And range with humble livers in content,
> Than to be perked up in a glistering grief
> And wear a golden sorrow.

[1] Mrs. Jameson's *Characteristics of Women*, art. Katharine of Aragon.

She is sincere in her avowal that she " would not be
queen, no, not for all the world ; " and when almost immediately after, being informed that she is raised to the
dignity of Marchioness of Pembroke,

> To which title
> A thousand pound a year, annual support,
> Out of his grace he adds,

she is also sincere in her joyous thanks :

> Beseech your lordship,
> Vouchsafe to speak my thanks and my obedience,
> As from a blushing handmaid, to his highness,
> Whose health and royalty I pray for.[1]

In all these various stages of feeling Anne was equally
sincere, because she was, albeit at this time a sweet
woman, not a very deep-natured one. The impression
of the moment was vivid, but readily, if not effaced,
essentially dimmed by that of the next. Could Shakespeare's purpose have embraced the last years of Anne
Boleyn's life, he might have left on record a character
quite as touching and pathetic in its way as that of
Katharine. Anne's letter to Henry, when accused of
the crime for which she was condemned to die, is iden-
tical in spirit and dignity with the speech of Katharine before the divorce tribunal at Blackfriars.

Katharine's part in the tragedy of her divorce has
become a classic of grievous wrong and undeserved
sorrow nobly borne. Dr. Johnson declares that the
genius of Shakespeare goes in and out of the play
with this character. His admiration of her character

[1] Act II., Scene 3.

worked up Heine to the point of declaring that but for the Englishman's praise he would be tempted to give Katharine her just deserts.[1]

Johnson's remark is in support of the critical position that Shakespeare had very little to do with the composition of "Henry VIII." Hudson, following a number of the orthodox critics, takes the same view, and gives the Stratford poet credit for about one-half the play. For purposes of historical study, it makes no difference if Thomas Fletcher wrote the whole of it. But as Skottowe says, "While there may be truth in the supposition, it is impossible to assume it as a fact without better evidence than mere conjecture."

Certainly the genius of Shakespeare cannot be mistaken in the whole story of the play, the unity of its theme, and especially in its treatment of Wolsey as well as Katharine.

But Katharine is superbly drawn. From the moment of her introduction, pleading for the oppressed people of her husband's realm, until the last scene in which she dies unqueened, yet never more a queen, there is a sustained harmony in the delineation of her character which makes her one of the most perfectly chiselled cameos of the Shakespearean casket. Her voice is raised in behalf not only of the despised commons, but of the noble Buckingham. She links Wol-

---

[1] I cherish an insuperable prejudice against this queen, to whom, however, I must ascribe every virtue. As a wife she was a pattern of domestic fidelity. As a queen she bore her part with the highest dignity and majesty. As a Christian she was piety itself. . . .

Shakespeare has employed all the might of his genius to glorify her, but all this is in vain, when we see that Dr. Johnson, that great pot of porter, falls into sweet rapture at her sight, and foams with eulogy.—*Shakespeare's Maidens and Women.*

sey instinctively with both events, and when she finds that the web of casuistry he has wound about his affairs is too stout for her woman's lance to pierce, expresses the hope or hopelessness of the great mass of England's every-day people—confused by the jangling sophistries of the court circles whose centre was the cardinal, and utterly helpless to prove what was instinctively believed to be true—in the sad ejaculation which must have risen to the lips of many of England's noblest citizens, " God mend all."

When she is finally brought to face the stunning catastrophe of her own life, and pleads her queenly rights and dignity in that pathetic speech which Shakespeare has redeemed with the alchemy of his genius from the blunt chronicle of Holinshed, the unfortunate Katharine, again by instinct, lays the charge of her heavy sorrow at Wolsey's door, and rightly.

> I do believe,
> Induced by potent circumstances, that
> You are my enemy ; and make my challenge
> You shall not be my judge, for it is you
> Hath blown this coal betwixt my lord and me.[1]

Even Henry is touched by the nobility of her nature and the hot grief of her insulted soul.   He cries as she is led away :

> Go thy ways, Kate.
> The man i' the world who shall report he has
> A better wife, let him in naught be trusted,
> For speaking false in that.   Thou art alone
> .   .   .   .
> The queen of earthly queens.[2]

[1] Act II., Scene 4.   [2] Ibid.

We next meet Katharine in the scene where she is visited by Wolsey and Campeius, who endeavor to win her over to the king's wish that she renounce her wifely rights, and accept the title of Princess Dowager. Grief and misery have softened her proud temper, and as she sits sorrowful in the midst of her women, so she meets with more resignation the advances of the legates, although not to be stirred from her resolution to live and die a queen.

> Let me have time and counsel for my cause,
> Alas, I am a woman, friendless, hopeless.[1]

but her final decision is :

> My lord, I dare not make myself so guilty
> To give up willingly that noble title
> Your master wed me to ; nothing but death
> Shall e'er divorce my dignity.[2]

This was not a yearning desire to hold to the rank and honors of her queenship. These were little to her, divorced already from her husband's heart. But the honor of her wifehood, the stainless birth of her child were at stake. Perhaps, who will say, there was that yet left in her heart for the man who for twenty years she had called husband, which was not even a pardonable jealousy of one who had supplanted her in his affections, but a noble shame for him, her lord and king, to be so self-exposed a villain in the eyes of men.

But it is in the last scene of this pathetic tragedy, at Kimbolton, whence the queen had retired to die. where

[1] Act III., Scene 1.   [2] Ibid.

are shown the noblest traits of her fine character—forgiveness of Wolsey who had so wronged her, and an anxious care for the men and women servants who had clung to her through all her misfortunes, with a last appeal to Henry on behalf of their daughter Mary.

> Didst thou not tell me, Griffith, as thou led'st me,
> That the great child of honor, Cardinal Wolsey,
> Was dead?
>
> .   .   .   .
>
> So may he rest, his faults lie gently on him.
>
> .   .   .   .
>
> Peace be with him.[1]

To Capucius, the ambassador of the emperor, she gives a letter for the king:

> In which I have commended to his goodness
> The model of our chaste loves, his young daughter,
> The dews of heaven fall thick in blessings on her;
> Beseeching him to give her virtuous breeding
> (She is young and of a noble modest nature;
> I hope she will deserve well) and a little
> To love her for her mother's sake that loved him,
> Heaven knows how dearly.   My next poor petition
> Is that his noble grace would have some pity
> Upon my wretched women, that so long
> Have followed both my fortunes faithfully.
>
> .   .   .   .
>
> The last is for my men; they are the poorest;
> But poverty could never draw them from me,
> That they may have their wages duly paid them,
> And something over to remember me by.[2]

There are many affecting passages in the works of the great dramatist, but these last messages to Henry, es-

---

[1] Act IV., Scene 2.   [2] Ibid.

pecially the final words from the deserted and dying
wife to the husband who had already taken another in
her place, are perhaps the most touching :

> Remember me
> In all humility unto his highness.
> Say his long trouble now is passing
> Out of this world ; tell him in death I blessed him,
> For so I will. My eyes grow dim. Farewell.[1]

When we remember what was back of this—neglect,
suspicion, calumny, and finally an unjust divorce—and
contrast these with the pride of the queen, the dignity
of the wife, the love and honor of the woman : the poet
will be seen to have painted one of the most exquis-
ite portraits of his rare collection in the character of
Katharine of Aragon.[2]

The historic fidelity of Shakespeare's portrayals of
these two women can hardly be questioned. It must
be remembered of Anne that he leaves her at her
coronation before the faintest suspicion against her
purity had been whispered. What she became after
the birth of Elizabeth will always be a fiercely disputed
question. It is quite possible that her lightness of
mind, and shallowness of spiritual culture, acted upon
by what she too well knew to be the fickleness of the
king, developed into indiscretions, and hardened into
selfishness. Contemporary accounts are confusing,
and neutralize each other. If the burden of testimony
is, as Mr. Froude claims, against Anne, it must be remembered that contemporary testimony is apt to be

---

[1] Act IV., Scene 2.
[2] Katharine did not die, however, until 1536, three years after the birth
of Elizabeth.

18

swayed by undue influences. The politics of the English and continental powers in the middle of the sixteenth century were too tortuous, too honeycombed by the self-seeking and ambitious plots of individuals, to throw much real light upon the private indiscretions of the wife of Henry VIII. She might well have been the victim of circumstances over which she, no more than Buckingham or Katharine, had control. But as to Shakespeare's etching of her character there can be little criticism save that his lines are too few, and the general profile somewhat indistinct. He could not have done otherwise in a play to be witnessed perhaps by Anne's daughter. He could not have done otherwise, historically, up to the point of time where she disappears from the stage, the happy mother of that

"—royal infant (Heaven still move about her)
Though in her cradle, yet now promises
Upon this land a thousand, thousand blessings
Which time shall bring to ripeness.[1]

The affair of the divorce cannot be fully estimated without one or two words concerning him who was the virtual author of it, Henry himself. We have sufficiently indicated already what must be the judgment of posterity upon the whole career of this second, and, next to Elizabeth, greatest of Tudor sovereigns.

It will be noted by the careful reader of the play that Henry is not set forth as an object of condemnation. His character is very gently touched upon. We have already suggested how far this may have been the result of the poet's delicate situation, patronized

[1] Act V., Scene 4.

by the court of Elizabeth. But there is another reason also, and one which again makes clear the claim of Shakespeare's general fidelity to historic truth. There is an alternative view to the one most modern historians have taken, of Henry's motives both in seeking the divorce and in marrying again. If we shut out the after career of the king, as Shakespeare was bound to do by the limitations of his dramatic purpose, there is much to support a far more favorable view than that we have here taken. The poet gives Henry the benefit of this doubt, and allows himself no partisanship for one side or the other. He illuminates the facts, and allows each witness of his mask to go away with what picture he will in his mind. It is but fair to Henry, as it is necessary to an understanding of Shakespeare's neutrality, to state this other side. It is well known that at first Henry was opposed, as a youth, to his marriage with Katharine because she had been his brother's wife. The then pope, Julius, had granted a dispensation ; but it was the validity of this dispensation, and therefore the validity of the marriage itself, which was brought into question by Henry and his advisers. The question having been brought up once, whether instigated by Wolsey or Henry, forced the latter to face the prospect of a disputed succession to his throne, in case any party after his death should be interested to present the early marriage as null and void. All England was interested to prevent another devastating war of succession, like that of the Wars of the Roses, which brought Henry's father to the throne. Henry may have been troubled in conscience. His superstitious fears may have been aroused by the fate of Katharine's children dying one after another, leaving only Mary alive. He longed for a son to take up his work after him. All this is in extenuation. All this may have, and to an extent probably did have, an influence with the king at the time of the divorce. And all this is subtly indicated in Shakespeare's gentle treatment of the king's relations to Katharine and Anne, in that affair which became the tragedy of both their lives:

> Hence I took a thought,
> This was a judgment on me; that my kingdom
> Well worthy the best heir o' the world, should not
> Be gladdened in it by me; then follows that
> I weighed the danger which my realm stood in
> By this my issue's fail; and that gave to me
> Many a groaning throe. Thus hulling in
> The wild sea of my conscience, I did steer
> Toward this remedy, whereupon we are
> Now present here together.[1]

That the king's mind was afterward altered, perhaps by "many a groaning throe" of remorse, we have evidence, for by his will he left the throne, first, after his infant son Edward, to Mary the daughter of Katharine, before it should fall to Elizabeth, the daughter of Anne, and they succeeded in that order. Much as we find to despise in Henry VIII., we may be justified in thinking that he thus answered the prayer of a discrowned queen, in placing her daughter first in succession over the daughter of her immediate successor to the royal couch.

Out of the divorce in the drama, if not quite directly,

---

[1] Act II., Scene 4.

is evolved the fall of Cardinal Wolsey. The crafty and delaying policy of Rome became evident in the actions of the king's great minister, and without doubt the suspicions thus first aroused, aggravated by his opposition to the marriage with Anne Boleyn, caused Henry to open his eyes to the fact that Wolsey had grown too great a subject for a sovereign's entire safety.

Thomas Wolsey was of humble origin, but of sufficient family means to have been educated for the Church at one of the universities. Tradition called his father's trade that of butcher; an honest enough business, and no shame to Wolsey were it true. But the highborn nobles of Henry's court could not perceive with equanimity the rise of such an one to the place of Cardinal Archbishop of York, and first favorite of the king. Buckingham expresses the popular view of one who for fifteen years "outworthed a noble's blood:"

> This butcher's cur is venom-mouthed, and I
> Have not the power to muzzle him. Therefore best
> Not wake him in his slumber.

His abilities were admitted:

> There's in him stuff that puts him to these ends,
> For being not propped by ancestry,
> .   .   .   .
> The force of his own merit makes his way.[1]

But at the time the play opens this "butcher's cur" holds all the noble hounds of England in short leash. Shakespeare represents him truly as at this time generally unpopular with both nobles and commons. He

[1] Act I., Scene 1.

had taught Henry to govern with the least interference of Parliament, and carried matters of state with a
high hand. Burnett says "the king liked him well,
which he so managed that he quickly engrossed the
king's favor to himself, and for fifteen years together
was the most absolute favorite that has ever been seen
in England. All foreign treaties and places of trust at
home were at his ordering. He did what he pleased,
and his ascendant over the king was such that there
never appeared any party against him all that while."[1]
This Shakespeare puts into the mouth of Buckingham
anent the treaty of the Field of the Cloth of Gold:

> Why the devil
> Upon this French going-out took he upon him
> Without the privity o' the king to appoint
> Who should attend on him? He makes up the file
> Of all the gentry: for the most part such
> To whom as great a charge as little honor
> He meant to lay upon, and his own letter
> (The honorable board of council out)
> Must fetch him in, he papers.[2]

The nobles were thus touched in their vanity and
pride, but the people felt more heavily the power of
Wolsey's usurping hand. The well-filled treasury
which Henry VII. had bequeathed to his son was
soon exhausted, and Wolsey was expected to replenish
it. The exposure of some of his extortionate measures
made by Katharine to the king, already noted, received
the royal censure, but gave Wolsey a double opportunity to strengthen his position, first in that fine plea

[1] Burnett: History of the Reformation, vol. i., p. 11.
[2] Act I., Scene 1.

against public detraction which, as Courtenay observes, "is generally just, though not applicable to the particular case."

> If I am
> Traduced by ignorant tongues, which neither know
> My faculties nor person, yet will be
> The chroniclers of my doings, let me say
> 'Tis the fate of place, and the rough brake
> That virtue must go through.[1]

and so on in a passage bristling with acute philosophy.

The second point made by Wolsey out of his temporary discomfiture is indicated thus:

> (To the Secretary.)
>   A word with you.
> Let there be letters writ to every shire,
> Of the king's grace and pardon. The grieved commons
> Hardly conceive of me: let it be noised
> That through our intercession this revokement
> And pardon comes.[2]

So cunningly he endeavored to turn the king's mercy into his own, and to pose as the friend of the "grieved commons." But the commons of England, even in those days before the daily newspapers, were not easily hoodwinked, although mightily fickle with their favor. They cried aloud for Wolsey's fall and mourned at the touching spectacle of Wolsey fallen. The lighter side of Wolsey's character, brought out in the mask festival given at York Palace for the king's pleasure, is equally true with the stronger phases of his political and ecclesiastical ambition. That a cardinal arch-

---

[1] Act I., Scene 2.   [2] Ibid.

bishop should be, in a sense, the pander of the king's appetites, was one of the relics of a morally barbarous age, fast passing even in that time, and Katharine's characterization of it would be the estimate of people not over-pious in their own lives:

> His promises were, as he then was, mighty,
> But his performance, as he is now, nothing.
> Of his own body, he was ill, and gave
> The clergy ill example.[1]

The story of these times would scarce have been complete, however, without some such scene as that in which Anne is introduced to the king, and the connection of the cardinal with it. The setting of that feast has all the local color of the day. Gathered there were high birth, riches, fame, and pleasure. There was feasting and mirth and witty badinage; king, bishop, nobles, commons, and fair women; and jostling these were treasons, plottings, conspiracies, detractions. The palace was lighted for revelry, while great affairs of Church and State were seething to the boiling-point in the caldron of destiny.

Shakespeare causes Henry to disclaim Wolsey's primal influence in the affair of the divorce:

> My lord cardinal,
> I do excuse you: yea, upon mine honor,
> I free you from it.
> .   .   .   .
> —you ever
> Have wished the sleeping of this business, never
> Desired it to be stirred.[2]

---

[1] Act IV., Scene 2.   [2] Act II., Scene 4.

But Shakespeare indicates plainly enough, leaving the original stirring of the business an open question so far as Wolsey is concerned, that the cardinal eagerly seized and used it as an occasion to further his own ambitious designs, which had as their object the papal chair.

Wolsey's relations to Katharine are set forth as they really appeared to the actors in the tragedy. No human eye could pierce the motives of Wolsey in his treatment of Katharine, or estimate the actual truth of his opinion of the queen, who was his victim. His intercourse with her, even in the face of her sharp accusations of his treachery toward the king, the people, and herself, is marked by that suave courtesy and diplomatic reserve which characterized his public career. He does not retort. He knows his power and waits. In his schemes Katharine was a pawn only, to be used in a larger game than her domestic relations with the king. He was personally more bitter against Anne than against her. To him, as to the great ministers of state before and after him, a woman's happiness was nothing in the balance against the consummation of a statesman's purposes. After his fall from power he showed symptoms of a warmer humanity than his mightiness had allowed him to display. One may think that he had some pity for this woman who fathomed his designs, and fought desperately against his ambitious plots, because she had a brave heart and a high courage, two elements which he, who possessed them both, must have admired.

There were three strands twisted in the cord of fate that strangled Wolsey's life, for the failure of his schemes was the end of his life. One was his open opposition to Anne Boleyn, as the wife of his king, at a time when her influence was stronger than his own. The weak point in Wolsey's strategy was in not allowing for the obstinate nature of Henry in matters of love, as in matters of state. History is full of examples, which Wolsey must have known, where the silken thread held in a woman's hand is stronger than the stoutest cable held by another. The opposition of the man who had been his pander in all things else, irritated Henry. There were not lacking those who inflamed him by hinting that Wolsey treated him too much as a tool and too little as a master, and Anne's personal influence must surely have been used against him whom her woman's instinct would have taught was her enemy.

Another element in the downfall of the cardinal was the muttering of the storm which preceded the Reformation. Wolsey, as papal legate, had again and again broken the law of England in the matter of its relations with the papal see. So long as this was not counter to Henry's interest, Henry was undisturbed. But when he discovered that his divorce must be gained without the pope's bull, and probably against the papal decree, the political and ecclesiastical relations of England and Rome were violently ruptured. In this web Wolsey, a loyal churchman, was caught. The truth of history compels us to state that the list of charges preferred against Wolsey, and catalogued by Suffolk and Surrey in the play, while all true, were one and all accusations which came with ill grace from the king's majesty. Almost without exception he had the royal sanction for them. Well might he exclaim in hope of the king's interference :

> So much fairer
> And spotless shall mine innocence arise
> When the king knows my truth.

And again :

> Speak on, sir :
> I dare your worst objections. If I blush
> It is to see a nobleman want manners.[1]

Wolsey had sinned, but Henry was the craven, in that he punished what he permitted.

But the chief cause at the root of Wolsey's fall lay in himself, apart from king, nobles, and commons.

Shakespeare brings this fully out in the treatment of Wolsey's reception of the news that he is deposed and that the sun of the royal favor for him had passed behind a cloud. We would be glad to believe that the poet's portrait in its last touches is accurate. For the final view we have of Wolsey, both by means of his own words, and the spoken epitaph of Griffith to Katharine, is of a man who, once proud, arrogant, unscrupulous, false to his own vows of priesthood, over-ambitious in his loyalty to his prince, has become through misfortune, humble, gentle, single-minded, repentant, and restored to the simplicity of his youth, when, without thought of greatness, he studied to be a useful and unambitious priest.

We do not feel in this tremendous transition that Wolsey is anything else than sincere. It may be the poet's art, but the art must have been colored from the

[1] Act III., Scene 2.

life. In evidence of this is the eloquent speech which Shakespeare puts in his mouth, as addressed to Cromwell, ending with the famous words :

> O Cromwell, Cromwell,
> Had I but served my God with half the zeal
> I served my king, he would not in mine age
> Have left me naked to mine enemies.[1]

This speech is based upon an interview of the dying cardinal with one Master Kingston, who attended him in his last hours at Leicester Abbey, where he died, which interview and incident are faithfully transcribed by the dramatist from Holinshed's Chronicle :

> " Sir, quoth Maister Kingston, you be in much pensiveness, doubting that thing, that in good faith ye need not. Well, well, Maister Kingston, quoth the cardinal, I see the matter how it is framed, but if I had served God, as diligently as I have doone the king, he would not have given me over in my greie haires : but it is the just reward that I must receive for the diligent pains and study that I had to do him service, not regarding my service to God, but only to do his pleasure."

Ambition, the "vaulting ambition that o'erleaps itself and falls on the other side," was the great man's sin. When the king by accident discovers of what enormous wealth he is possessed Wolsey's horror lies not in the fear of losing money, but of losing the means to that end his very soul sighed for :

> This paper has undone me : 'Tis the account
> Of all that world of wealth I've drawn together
> With mine own hands ; indeed to gain the Popedom,
> And fee my friends in Rome.[2]

---

[1] Act III., Scene 2.   [2] Ibid.

Ambition of this same exaltation was it that caused his shuffling policy with Rome and Henry in the matter of the divorce. It was nothing to him whether Katharine, or Anne, or the Duchess of Alençon were queen. It was much to him that he should so shuffle the cards of state as that Henry should draw the one best fitted for the furtherance of his plans on the triple tiara of Rome, and Wolsey, once the scales had fallen from his eyes, and he saw clearly that the game was not his, perceived as clearly as any outsider wherein he had failed:

> Mark but my fall, and that that ruined me.
> Cromwell, I charge thee fling away ambition;
> By that sin fell the angels: how can man then,
> The image of his Maker, hope to win by it.
> Love thyself last, cherish those hearts that hate thee,
> Corruption wins not more than honesty.[1]

Shakespeare draws out the character of Wolsey at length in the interview between Katharine and Griffith. The man conveys to her the story of the cardinal's death, and in gentle language draws a picture of the scene in Leicester (historically accurate and taken from Holinshed almost word for word):

> Where the reverend abbot
> With all his convent honorably received him:
> To whom he gave these words: "O father abbot,
> An old man broken with the storms of state
> Is come to lay his weary bones among ye;
> Give him a little earth for charity."[2]

---

[1] Act III., Scene 2. We may compare this confession of Wolsey's with the warning of the king at the time of the cardinal's plea for consideration, in the matter of the oppression of the king's subjects, Act I., Scene 2.

[2] Act IV., Scene 2.

Alternately picturing the lights and shadows of his character in the dialogue of that scene, we have a fair and accurate *résumé* of his life and influence. And in spite of the detraction which gathered about him from the friends of the Reformation, which in his soul he hated, the truth of history is summed up in Griffith's words, concluding,

His overthrow heaped happiness upon him,
For then, and not till then, he felt himself,
And found the blessedness of being little.
And, to add greater honors to his age
Than man could give him, he died fearing God.[1]

As the influence of Wolsey is seen to be cast over the drama, "no man's pie being free from his ambitious finger," so the careful reader will perceive the dawn of the English Reformation slowly shining through its clouds of social, political, and religious confusion.

I have already noted how significantly begins and ends the play. It must be noted further that the change of national religious faith is so handled by the poet that no reproach is visited upon the central figures of one or other of the great ecclesiastical parties.

The dominant note of Shakespeare's England was not so much Protestantism as Nationalism. The people were slowly, very slowly, but surely, crystallizing their faith apart from the spiritual headship of the pope. It had been a good thing for England to have done, had she never gone farther in what her

[1] Act IV., Scene 2.

divines insisted was a real reformation of religious doctrine.

Henry was an uncouth instrument of Christian progress, and yet he was essentially the master-mind to guide the outward and necessarily political part of the English revolt from Rome. It must always be insisted by the fair historian that Henry VIII. and his domestic affairs were not the causes of the English Reformation, but the occasions. He himself, without doubt, died in the old faith. That was a part of his character. And it must be further noted by the historian and reader of histories, that not the moral leprosy of Henry, the feeble and inefficient energy of Edward, nor the nipping and eager frost of Mary's persecution, could prevent the religious movement, which, for good or ill, according to the personal bias of this or that critic, came to the full flower of its development under Elizabeth the superb.

This Reformation is writ large over the play. There are very few direct references to it, which makes the skill of the dramatist all the more pronounced. Here and there a sentence indicates the working of the leaven. That these are so few is a marvel indeed when we recall the popular feeling of the epoch when it was placed upon the stage.

A faint reference is made in Lord Sands's speech to the Chamberlain as they set forth to attend the masque at Wolsey's house. They are commending the cardinal for his bounteousness :

> In him
> Sparing would show a worse sin than ill doctrine.[1]

[1] Act I., Scene 3.

Wolsey knows Anne for a "spleeny Lutheran,"[1] and again :

> There is sprung up
> An heretic, an arch one, Cranmer ; one
> Hath crawled into the favor of the king,
> And is his oracle.[2]

The mob discuss the relations of Bishop Gardiner and Cranmer, at that time standing types of the old faith passing away and the new faith coming forward :

2d Gent.   He of Winchester
Is held no great good lover of the archbishop's,
The virtuous Cranmer.
3d Gent.   All the land knows that :
However, yet there's no great breach, when it comes
Cranmer will find a friend will not shrink from him.

The last act of the play is occupied almost wholly with such scenes as shall leave the impression that the Reformation is an accomplished fact. Cranmer, who, as has been said, may be taken as a sort of allegorical figure representing the English Church separated from Rome, is brought in direct conflict with Gardiner, who is the incarnation of the old faith, which in him dies hard. The stock from which the expected heir of Henry springs, Anne, he wishes it were "grubbed up now." Cranmer is "a most archheretic, a pestilence that doth infect the land." With a dramatic license allowable for the effect he desires to produce, the poet places Cranmer's arraignment before the Council for heresy, in the lifetime of Anne, while it did not occur until the time of Catherine Parr, Henry's sixth wife.

[1] Act III., Scene 2.   [2] Ibid.
[3] Act IV., Scene 1.

From this persecution, which Shakespeare transcribes
from Fox's "Book of Martyrs," wellnigh word for word,
the archbishop is rescued by the king's friendship.
That Cranmer is a "favorer of this new sect" weighs
not with the stubborn foe of Rome. In the face of the
accusing Council the king says:

> My lord of Canterbury,
> I have a suit which you must not deny me,
> That is a fair young maid, that yet wants baptism—
> You must be godfather and answer for her.[1]

And so ends the play with the baptism of Elizabeth,
in the dawn of a new epoch for England and the world.
Well might the Virgin Queen be flattered by the references to her royal person with which the last scenes
are strewn. At Anne's coronation one says:

> And who knows yet
> But from this lady may proceed a gem
> To lighten all this isle.

And Suffolk, courtier-like:

> She is a gallant creature and complete
> In mind and feature. I persuade me, from her
> Shall fall some blessing to this land, which shall
> In it be memoriz'd.[2]

The final speech of Cranmer, which some critics will
have is an interpolation, may be or not. It seems to
me to be in Shakespeare's vein, and the reference to
James to have been inserted after the death of Elizabeth. It does not go harshly, but rather supplements

[1] Act V., Scene 2.   [2] Act III., Scene 2.

19

smoothly what precedes. The student of history gains by it, whether Shakespeare or Fletcher wrote it; whether Elizabeth herself ever read it or not. It is a literal statement in poetical language of the splendid work the Virgin Princess had brought to such perfection and handed on to her successor James, whose praise is also prophetically sounded in it. And so the play ends fittingly, a glowing, seer-like vision of the glorious future of England.

It ends under the vaulted roof, in the soft dim light of the palace chapel; with high altar blazing from myriad twinkling points; the sound of rich harmonies rising and falling through its fretted arches and adown its majestic aisles. About the altar and font is clustered a striking group. Cranmer's is a typical voice, the richly dowered babe christened Elizabeth a congruous personage, with which to bring to an end that series of splendid chronicles which then stirred the English heart, and since has broadened the English mind. We may truly reflect that it was because Shakespeare was so essentially the prophet of his own, that he has become the poet of all ages.

CHAPTER IX.

SUMMARY.

In summing up the results of this study of English History in Shakespeare's plays the object must be to set forth not what Shakespeare may have intended to do, but what he actually accomplished, as a contribution to the understanding of English History.

With whatever intention and on whatever model constructed, the ten Chronicle plays tell a definite story from which may be drawn a clear moral.

The literal historical event which forms a framework for the series is, as has been already noted in the body of this work, the Decline and Fall of the House of Plantagenet. Working through this, and at times seen to be hastening its consummation, are discerned certain movements of English thought, and certain marked stages in the development of the English people, which were elements in the making of modern England.

From Richard II. to Richard III., inclusive, every reign is touched upon in the eight plays of Shakespeare. The story begins with a dramatic recital of the occasion of the usurpation of the Lancastrian family in the person of Henry Bolingbroke, son of John of Gaunt, "time-honored Lancaster," and cousin to the reigning monarch. Richard II. is the victim of his own weak unkingliness, as well as of the semi-bondage in which his youth was passed. He resigned his crown and sceptre to the man whom he had wronged and persecuted, and in so doing sowed the seeds of an internecine strife that blossomed finally in the Wars of the Roses. Henry IV. was not innocent of "devious ways" in forcing the abdication of his cousin. His punishment came swiftly upon him in the uprising and revolts among his nobles which made his reign a melancholy and barren bauble of royalty. His personal necessities, however, forced him to strike a deadly blow at the feudal power of the English nobility, and with the decay of that institution the commons began to assert themselves, blindly and feebly enough at first, but with an ever-growing self-knowledge, self-poise, and self-respect.

Henry V. was driven, by the uncertain tenure of his paternal heritage, to pursue once more those " foreign quarrels," which, while they have ever reflected glory on the English name, have never done aught to increase the domestic harmony and strength of the English people.

The brightness of great victories quickly paled; and the territories won were speedily lost. All that Henry V. had gained was dissipated in the time of his son and successor, Henry VI.; and the miseries of this reign, culminating in the tragedy of civil war, are directly traceable to the use and abuse of the French conquests of Henry V. They provoked rivalries among the barons, which took overt shape in the formation of parties at court, each intent upon controlling the policy of the king. The marriage of Henry VI. with Margaret of Anjou was brought about at the cost of many of the French provinces won in bloody wars. The contentions of the rival nobles penetrated to the commons. All England became an armed camp. The disinherited house of York craftily enough conspired to snatch back what Henry IV. had taken by an act of usurpation. Edward IV. seized the throne while Henry was yet alive, inheriting from his father the claim which had lain in the person of Edmund Mortimer, great grandson of Lionel, third son of Edward III., when Bolingbroke succeeded Richard II. Exhausted by war, and at the bottom. indifferent to the claims of the rival families, the nation, through its Parliament, settled down under Edward, and he reigned in undisputed security.

English historians count the thirteen troubled weeks between the death of Edward IV. and the accession of Richard III. as the " reign " of Edward V. The time was occupied by Richard Gloster in disposing of all obstacles in his own pathway to the throne. When Richard III. accomplished his ambition and became by parliamentary title King of England, the cup of the Plantagenets was full.

The usurping Duke of Gloster, confirmed though he was in his royal dignity by the obsequious voice of the commons, was not to reign unchallenged. The Duke of Richmond, last of the Lancastrians, was summoned by a handful of barons, who still hoped better things for England than that she should be the plaything of a bloody tyrant, and the final struggle of the Roses was made on Bosworth Field, where Richard III. died, and with him the dynasty which, for good and ill, had ruled England for many generations.

The manner of Henry VII.'s accession to the throne
marks the epoch toward which all previous reigns in
English history had been contributing, viz., the voice
of the people in the choice of a king. For Richmond
was seated upon the throne, and reigned, neither by
hereditary right, by right of conquest, nor by being
lifted on the shields of a few barons, but through the
voice of a free Parliament. In that act we perceive a
denial of the extreme doctrine of hereditary right, the
death of feudalism, and the voice of the commonalty.
The commons were often thereafter to be oppressed,
deluded, beaten back and silenced, but generation
after generation found them lifting their heads higher
and making their voices more distinctly heard. The
monarchy remained, and still remains, but so limited
and conditioned as to make England to-day one of the
most soundly democratic of all earthly governments.
The dull quiet of Henry VII. was succeeded by the
lusty vigor and revolutionary movements of Henry
VIII. Shakespeare ends his *Epopee* with the baptism
of Elizabeth, not merely as a compliment to that vain
but glorious virgin, but with dramatic point and historic truth. The whole movement of the Shakespearean epic, from the prologue of King John and Magna
Charta, to the epilogue of Henry VIII. and the Reformation, is toward that England which is best described
and illuminated by the adjective Elizabethan.

We trace the gradual separation of England from
the continental complications which were inevitable
with a family of half-foreign kings upon the throne;
the revolt of the barons against the tyranny and oppression of absolute kingcraft; the rejection of papal in-

terference with the autonomy of the English Church; and through these more conspicuous movements, the ever growing self-consciousness of the commons — until in the England of Elizabeth we find all these strands woven together in the imperishable fabric of a people fitted for, and destined to become the mother of new nations, to give law, language, and literature to a large part of the civilized world.

England thus had a destiny—and this is the moral we draw from Shakespeare's noble histories — with which was bound up the larger freedom, more liberal culture, more refined development of the human race. The Anglo-Saxon shut up in his " sea-girt isle," must first fight out the battle with himself before he could become a dominant force in the affairs of others. The feudal baron must become the loyal integer of the central government; the feudal serf must become the free man; the feudal state must become the government of, for, and by the people. All these changes would have been evils if suddenly grafted upon the stock of England's mediæval life. They had their reasons for existence *pro tempore.* They were not monuments, however, but stepping-stones. They marked not points of complete development, but were merely registers of local and temporary accomplishment. In few and admirable words the philosophic historian, John Henry Green, sums up the process, which Shakespeare in the ten Chronicle plays has so brilliantly set forth : " The structure of a feudal society fitted a feudal king with two great rival powers in the Baronage and the Church, . . . but at the close of the Wars of the Roses these checks no longer served as restraints upon the action of the crown. With the growth of the Parliament the might of the Baronage as a separate constitutional element of the realm, even the separate influence of the Church, had fallen more and more into decay."

The restraints upon the action of the crown were henceforth to be more powerful, more influential, more constitutional, because they lay not with this or that class, but deep rooted in the life of the people. Parliament was to be the reflection not only of the views of members but of constituencies. It was to be in touch with not only the political, but with the social, the religious—with all phases of the people's expanding consciousness. Modern England is among nations not what its hereditary rulers choose, but what its people declare it must be.

APPENDIX I.

BIBLIOGRAPHY.

SOURCES OF SHAKESPEARE'S HISTORY.

Edward Hall's *Chronicle*, 1577; reprinted 1809.

Raphael Holinshed's *Chronicle*, 1577; reprinted 1807.

  In Holinshed is included Sir Thomas More's *Life of Richard III.* (1557) and George Cavendish's *Life of Wolsey*, written between 1554–57.

Robert Fabyan's *Chronicle*, 1516; reprinted 1801.

John Foxe's *Acts and Monuments*, commonly called the "Book of Martyrs," 1563; reprinted frequently, in part.

E. de Monstrelet's *Chronicle*, about 1450; reprinted 1846.

The Paston Letters, 1422–1509; reprinted in Bohn Library.

MODERN HISTORIES REFERRED TO.

Bishop Burnett's *History of the Reformation.*

Hallam's *History of the Middle Ages.*

Hume's *History of England.*

Charles Knight's *Popular History of England.*

J. H. Green's *History of the English People.*

Lingard's *History of England.*

J. A. Froude's *History of England* (for Henry VIII.).

J. A. Froude's *Katharine of Aragon.*

SHAKESPEAREANA.

T. P. Courtenay's *Commentaries on the Historical Plays.* 2 vols. London, 1840.

Bishop Wordsworth's *Notes on the Historical Plays.* 3 vols.
London and Edinburgh, 1883. (These Notes are seldom ori-
ginal, but compiled from various sources.)
Professor Henry Reed's *Lectures on English History.* Philadel-
phia, 1856.
Wm. J. Rolfe's *Historical Plays.* 10 vols. New York, 1892.
Shakespeare's Library, six volumes, containing various plays,
romances, novels, poems, and histories employed by
Shakespeare. The second edition, edited by Wm. Carew
Hazlitt. London, 1875.
Augustine Skottowe's *Life and Enquiries* into the originality of
the dramatic plots. London, 1824.
Joseph Hunter's *New Illustrations of Shakespeare.* 2 vols. Lon-
don, 1845.
Mrs. Jameson's *Characteristics of Women.* Bohn Library.
Helen Faucit Martin's *Some of Shakespeare's Female Characters.*
London, 1888.
Ulrici's *Shakespeare's Dramatic Art.* Bohn Library.
Gervinus's *Commentaries on Shakespeare,* translated by F. Bun-
nett. New York, 1883.
A. W. Schlegel's *Dramatic Literature.* Bohn Library.
Coleridge's *Notes and Lectures on Shakespeare.* Bohn Library.
Wm. Hazlitt's *Characters of Shakespeare.* Bohn Library.
Hudson's *Life, Art, and Characters of Shakespeare.* 2 vols. New
York, 1888.
Richard Grant White's *Studies in Shakespeare.* Boston, 1886.
Charles Knight's *Shakespeare Studies.* London, 1851.
H. Heine's *Shakespeare's Maidens and Women,* translated by C.
G. Leland. New York, 1891.

SPECIAL HISTORIES.

Gairdner's *Life of Richard III.,* supports, in the main, Shakespeare's view of Richard's character, and Miss Caroline F.
Halstead's *Life of Richard III.* seeks to combat the tradi-
tional view.

APPENDIX II.

THE date of Shakespeare's workmanship on the "masque or show play," as Coleridge calls it, of Henry VIII., has an important influence on our reading of the play, and the period of history which it illuminates. And this date is in dispute. Charles Knight, who believes in the later authorship (1612 or 1613), frankly confesses that the majority of commentators hold to the earlier composition (1600–1603) during the reign of Elizabeth. Malone, one of the most accurate and painstaking of the earlier Shakespearean critics, followed by such authorities as Skottowe and Drake, place it no later than 1603. This is my opinion, and as it has something to do with our view of the play as a side-light on the Reformation, I shall take the reader over the path which leads to this conclusion.

Malone and those who think with him base their belief on the internal evidence offered in the play itself, together with what knowledge we possess of Shakespeare, his times, and his manner of composition.

The opposition, holding to a date after Elizabeth's death, as late even as 1613, justify their argument by one internal and one external bit of evidence. The internal evidence is that apostrophe to James I., which is put into the mouth of Cranmer at the baptism of Elizabeth:

> Nor shall this peace sleep with her: But as when
> The bird of wonder dies, the maiden phœnix,
> Her ashes new create another heir,
> As great in admiration as herself;
> So shall she leave her blessedness to one
> (When heaven shall call her from this cloud of darkness)
> Who from the sacred ashes of her honor
> Shall star-like rise as great in fame as she was,
> And so stand fixed: Peace, plenty, love, truth, terror,
> That were the servants to this chosen infant
> Shall then be his; and like a vine grow to him;
> Wherever the bright sun of heaven shall shine,
> His honor and the greatness of his name
> Shall be, and make new nations : He shall flourish,
> And, like a mountain cedar, reach his branches
> To all the plains about him—Our children's children
> Shall see this, and bless heaven.[1]

Now here is a very certain reference, not only to James, the successor of Elizabeth, but to those famous colonies to which he gave the impetus, and which in his time throve mightily. It was certainly not written before James came to the throne, for Elizabeth was the last of sovereigns to hear her successor greeted in such glowing terms. The passage is manifestly an interpolation. It was inserted in the speech of Cranmer when the play was first produced after James began to reign. It may have been the work of Shakespeare or of Fletcher, a question which may be left to the verbal critics, who trace the progress of Shakespeare's genius by "verse-tests," "stopped lines," "weak endings,"

---

[1] Act V., Scene 4.

etc. Neither are the advocates of an Elizabethan authorship alone in claiming this passage as a late emendation. Ulrici, one of the most earnest in behalf of the 1613 date, admits it, following Hertzberg, another competent German critic (see Ulrici's "Dramatic Art," vol. ii., book vi., ch. xi., note).

As opposed to this internal evidence adduced from one doubtful scene, we submit the internal evidence afforded by the whole play, and the external circumstances which must have had an important influence in shaping its construction.

There are a number of laudatory allusions to Elizabeth in the play, such as that of the Lord Chamberlain's apostrophe of Anne Boleyn:

> And who knows yet,
> But from this lady may proceed a gem
> To lighten all this isle.[1]

And Suffolk, again, speaking of Anne's approaching coronation, says:

> She is a gallant creature, and complete
> In mind and feature : I persuade me from her
> Will fall some blessing to his land, which shall
> In it be memoriz'd.[2]

The pleasant things said of Anne Bullen (as the play hath the name) are all indirect incense to the Virgin Queen. The speech of Cranmer, so well known and quoted in part above, is fulsome in its prophecies of the royal infant. Now I maintain that these allusions to his predecessor on the throne could not have been

---

[1] Act II., Scene 3. [2] Act III., Scene 2.

written for the ears of James, nor is it conceivable that they could have been written for public recitation after, and so near, the day of her death. Elizabeth had not only cut off the head of James's most unfortunate mother, but she had held himself in a sort of tutelage (*vide* their published correspondence) which must have been galling to a man so vain, irritable, weak, and conscious of the scorn in which he was held. She scolded him like a virago. A man may stand such things perforce, but he does not forget them. James was a friend of the players. One of his first royal acts was in their favor and for their benefit. He was glad enough to escape from the gloom of the Scottish court, with its environment of sad-faced Puritanism, into the warm life and brilliant color of London. He set up as a theologian and was the foe of tobacco, but he did encourage the drama. Shakespeare was too much of a courtier to make the mistake of courting a dead sovereign.

Ulrici fuddles over this difficulty of the later authorship as follows:

"However, the flattery to Elizabeth is also interwoven with compliments to James." Now there is but one allusion or "compliment" to James in the whole play (quoted above), and Ulrici himself admits this to be an interpolation.

So much for the internal evidence.

We have to deal now with a single fact of external evidence, which is the real ground of belief in a late origin of the play. The Globe Theatre was burned on June 29, 1613. Three references to the play being performed on that occasion lead critics to infer that it was Shakespeare's Henry VIII. Howes, the chronicler, describing the fire, says: "The house being filled with people to behold the play of Henry VIII." A letter of Sir Henry Wotton to his nephew also records the event and refers to what may have been the masque in Wolsey's house as the point at which the fire broke out: "The King's Players had a new play called 'All is True,' representing some principle pieces in the reign of Henry VIII., which was set forth," etc. In a letter from Thomas Lorkin to Sir Thomas Puckering we read: "While Burbage's company were acting at the Globe the play of Henry VIII. . . . the fire catched . . . consumed the whole house."

There is nothing in all this testimony to disprove the Elizabethan authorship, except the words "new play" in the Wotton letter. It is argued that this was a first production, and, therefore, that it was newly written. This seems a very slender basis as against the internal evidence already noted. Many of Shakespeare's works were written long before they were published. It is merely an assumption also that this burned-out play was Shakespeare's. There was another on the general theme of Henry VIII., well known at the time. Sir Henry Wotton's name for the play, "All is True," gives color to the suggestion that it was not the Shakespearean work at all. But the chief reliance of the late-date argument is on the alleged fact that this is the first mention of the play, and that it does not appear again until incorporated in the first folio. And yet we have the record (all thanks to the labors of Mr. Fleay, whose zealous and monumental toil is a fair set-off for some fantasticisms of criticism) of the

Stationer's Register, answering to our copyright entry, for, among other years, that of 1604–5, in which, under date of February 12th, is the record of "King Henry VIII., an interlude."

This seems to the ordinary reader, and even to a modest student of the times of Elizabeth, to offer at least a fair ground of presumption that Shakespeare's Henry VIII. is noted previous to the fire of 1613. The critics who are wedded to their idols of metrical tests, and will allow no facts to interfere with their theories, say practically, as Hudson says literally: "There is no good reason for ascribing this piece to Shakespeare: on the contrary, there is ample reason for supposing it to have been a play by Samuel Rowley, entitled, 'When you See Me You Know Me; or, The Famous Chronicle History of King Henry VIII.'"

On the contrary, there is ample reason—save the fact that the adjective "new" is used in familiar correspondence, as it might be nowadays concerning a revival of the same play, which would be new to this generation—why this entry should refer to Shakespeare's play.

On the whole, therefore, we must concede the earlier authorship, as admitted by the greater number of Shakespearean critics. My own theory of the history of this often-disputed play is as follows:

It was constructed, as Knight says, "an historical drama to complete his great series," in the last years, perhaps the last year, of Elizabeth's reign. At just this date (1603–4) broke out the Great Plague, whereof more than thirty thousand people died in London alone. The theatres were closed for a time, and when they reopened James was King of England. The play of Henry VIII. was therefore laid aside, or perhaps forgotten, save for its possible entry in the Stationer's Register. In the course of a few years it was revived (possibly, according to many writers, for the festival attendant upon the marriage of Elizabeth, daughter of James, to the Elector Palatine), and called a new play because it was practically new to the stage of that period. The passage concerning James was inserted to throw a sop to the vanity of the reigning monarch, and to temper the laudation of the Virgin Queen, his predecessor. The references to "new nations" were evidently to commend the play to the pit and galleries, crowded with people who were all more or less touched with an enthusiasm for colonization, and had ventures on the seas.

This seems to me, without unduly straining or overlooking any important point of the evidence, to include and account for all divergent views. If Elizabeth did not see the play acted, she heard it read, as I believe, and it was written for this destiny. Otherwise there would have been no such gentle handling of Henry VIII. and Anne Boleyn, and we should have missed the clever workmanship which places the divorced Katharine in such a tender and touching relief, without reflecting upon the legitimacy of England's Virgin Queen.

APPENDIX III.

TABLE OF SHAKESPEARE'S ENGLISH KINGS.

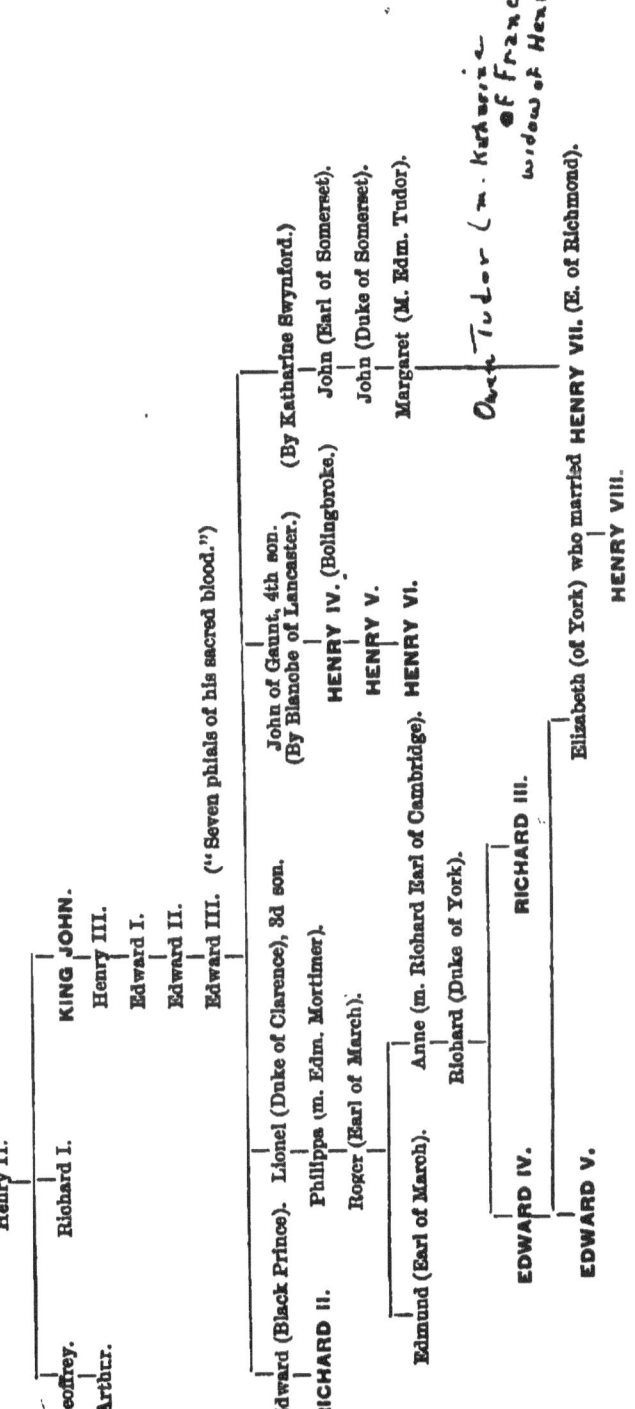

Henry II.

Geoffrey. Richard I. KING JOHN.

Arthur. Henry III.

Edward I.

Edward II.

Edward III. ("Seven phials of his sacred blood.")

Edward (Black Prince). Lionel (Duke of Clarence), 3d son. John of Gaunt, 4th son. (By Katharine Swynford.)

RICHARD II. Phillippa (m. Edm. Mortimer). (By Blanche of Lancaster.) John (Earl of Somerset).

Roger (Earl of March). HENRY IV. (Bolingbroke.) John (Duke of Somerset).

Edmund (Earl of March). Anne (m. Richard Earl of Cambridge). HENRY V. Margaret (M. Edm. Tudor).

Richard (Duke of York). HENRY VI.

EDWARD IV. RICHARD III. Owen Tudor (m. Katherine of France widow of Henry.)

EDWARD V. Elizabeth (of York) who married HENRY VII. (E. of Richmond).

HENRY VIII.

APPENDIX IV.

ON THE GENEALOGY AND CONNECTIONS OF THE HOUSES
OF YORK AND LANCASTER.

FOR the better guidance of the student I have appended a list of the kings of England whose reigns are touched upon in Shakespeare's play, together with their immediate ancestry.[1]   It has been convenient to condense this list somewhat, and I did not think it necessary to give the whole table of descendants from Edward III.   Only those sons' names are mentioned with whom Shakespeare directly or indirectly deals. The "seven phials of his sacred blood," in order of seniority, are as follow:

Edward the Black Prince, William of Hatfield (who died in childhood), Lionel, Duke of Clarence ; John of Gaunt, Duke of Lancaster ; Edward of Langley, William of Windsor, and Thomas of Gloucester.   From the last mentioned were descended the Dukes of Buckingham, who figure in " Henry VI.," " Richard III.," and " Henry VIII."

A complete and detailed list of all the kings, their ancestry and posterity, may be found in Professor Wm. Francis Allen's little *Reader's Guide to English History*, to which I acknowledge indebtedness.

The following extract from "Henry VI." is a verbal statement, with one or two inaccuracies only, of what

[1] Appendix III.

the above table contains. It is from a conversation between Richard (Earl of Cambridge and afterward Duke of York), Salisbury, and Warwick, in which the former sets forth his title, "which is infallible, to England's crown." [1]

York.   Edward the Third, my lord, had seven sons,
   The first, Edward the Black Prince, Prince of
    Wales.
   The second, William of Hatfield, and the third,
   Lionel, Duke of Clarence ; next to whom
   Was John of Gaunt, the Duke of Lancaster ;
   The fifth was Edward Langley, Duke of York ;
   The sixth was Thomas of Woodstock, Duke of
    Gloucester ; [2]
   William of Windsor was the seventh and last.
   Edward, the Black Prince, died before his father,
   And left behind him Richard, his only son,
   Who after Edward the Third's death reigned as king,
   Till Henry Bolingbroke, Duke of Lancaster,
   The eldest son and heir of John of Gaunt,
   Crowned by the name of Henry the Fourth,
   Seized on the realm, deposed the rightful king,
   Sent his poor queen to France, from whence she came,
   And him to Pomfret, where, as all you know,
   Harmless Richard was murdered traitorously.
Warwick. Father, the duke has told the truth ;
   Thus got the House of Lancaster the crown.
York.   Which now they hold by force and not by right ;
   For Richard the First's son's heir being dead
   The issue of the next son should have reigned.
Sal.   But William of Hatfield died without an heir.
York.   The third son, Duke of Clarence (from whose line
   I claim the crown), had issue, Philippe, a daughter,

---

[1] Henry VI., Part II., Act II., Scene 2.
[2] The poet reverses the actual order of the last two names.

	Who married Edmund Mortimer, Earl of March.
	Edmund had issue, Roger, Earl of March;
	Roger had issue, Edmund, Anne, and Eleanor.
Sal.	This Edmund in the reign of Bolingbroke,
	As I have read, laid claim unto the crown;
	And but for Owen Glendower had been king,[1]
	Who kept him in captivity till he died.[2]
	But to the rest.
York.	His eldest sister, Anne,

My mother, being heir unto the crown,
Married Richard, Earl of Cambridge, who was son
To Edmund Langley, Edward the Third's fifth
son.
By her I claim the kingdom. She was heir
To Roger, Earl of March, who was the son
Of Edmund Mortimer, who married Philippe
Sole daughter unto Lionel, Duke of Clarence;
So if the issue of the elder son
Succeed before the younger, I am king.

War. What plain proceeding is more plain than this?
Henry doth claim the crown from John of Gaunt,
The fourth son. York claims it from the third.
Till Lionel's issue fails, his should not reign.
It fails not yet, but flourishes in thee,
And in thy sons, fair slips of such a stock.

This passage sets forth the rival claims of the Yorkists and Lancastrians, in the settling of which the Wars of the Roses were invoked.

[1] As noted in the Chapter on Henry IV., the poet, misled by the chronicler, confuses Edmund Mortimer, who was a captive to Glendower, with his nephew (the heir), the young Earl of March, who does not appear in the play.

[2] Another error of the poet. It was not Mortimer who died a captive to Glendower, but another son-in-law of the Welsh chieftain, Lord Grey of Ruthven.

INDEX.